Reinventing Pedagogy of the Oppressed:
Contemporary Critical Perspectives

Also available from Bloomsbury

Education for Critical Consciousness, Paulo Freire
Pedagogy of the Oppressed, Paulo Freire
Pedagogy of Hope, Paulo Freire
Pedagogy in Process, Paulo Freire
Pedagogy of the Heart, Paulo Freire

Paulo Freire's Intellectual Roots, Edited by Robert Lake and Tricia Kress
The Student Guide to Freire's "Pedagogy of the Oppressed," Antonia Darder

Reinventing Pedagogy of the Oppressed: Contemporary Critical Perspectives

Edited by James D. Kirylo

BLOOMSBURY ACADEMIC

LONDON • NEW YORK • OXFORD • NEW DELHI • SYDNEY

BLOOMSBURY ACADEMIC
An imprint of Bloomsbury Publishing Plc
50 Bedford Square, London, WC1B 3DP, UK
1385 Broadway, New York, NY 10018, USA

BLOOMSBURY, BLOOMSBURY ACADEMIC and the Diana logo are trademarks
of Bloomsbury Publishing Plc

First published 2020

© James D. Kirylo and Bloomsbury, 2020

Cover design: Tjaša Krivec

A catalogue record for this book is available from the British Library.

A catalog record for this book is available from the Library of Congress.

ISBN: HB: 978-1-3501-1718-1
        PB: 978-1-3501-1717-4
        ePDF: 978-1-3501-1719-8
        ePUB: 978-1-3501-1720-4

Typeset by Integra Software Services Pvt. Ltd.
Printed and bound in Great Britain

To find out more about our authors and books visit www.bloomsbury.com
and sign up for our newsletters.

For
Ana Maria (Nita) Araújo Freire

Contents

Foreword

On the Road to Social Justice: Reinventing Paulo Freire

Ira Shor

Paulo Freire died unexpectedly May 2, 1997, at age seventy-five on an operating table in Brazil. The terrible news spread quickly around the globe, shocking and saddening many. For those who knew him or of him, a big hole suddenly opened in the world. When figures of Paulo's stature pass, the gap they leave behind can't be filled quickly or simply, though many have stepped up handsomely to the task. This book offers creative reports from some of the hands continuing the work Paulo Freire left behind.

Teacher, mentor, author, ally of the dispossessed and nurturer of opposition, Paulo spent his adult life walking the long road to social justice in Brazil and abroad. His passion for a just world inspired similar passion in those who met him, worked with him, or read his books. That passion was activist and insurgent, leading to his arrest and forced exile after the coup of 1964, then to a triumphant return in 1980 to his beloved Brazil and collaboration in founding the Workers Party, for whom he served as Secretary of Education for Sao Paulo, 1989–1991.

In life and after, Paulo became an icon of democratic opposition, so much so that in Brazil now he is once again targeted, this time by the right-wing regime of President Jair Bolsonaro. Freire's stand against autocrats and juntas derives from his faith that a better world is possible, one that enables us to become more fully human. That faith has appealed to several generations who informally comprise what I call a global party of hope and resistance. That party includes the authors in this current volume. Books like this continue the frankly Utopian project that Paulo embraced—to denounce dehumanizing schools and societies while announcing humane and democratic alternatives.

The 50th anniversary of Freire's most-influential work, *Pedagogy of the Oppressed*, in 2018, provoked books like this into print as well as memorial conferences like the gathering in Columbia, South Carolina, October 2018, convened by Prof. James D. Kirylo, editor of this volume. On his many travels, Paulo hoped to serve as a "magnet" or "pretense" (as he put it) for activist educators to gather and advance democratic opposition. Each book or gathering succeeds so far as it challenges an unequal status quo while also following Freire's advice not to copy him but rather to reinvent his work. "I always say," he wrote, "that the only way anyone has of applying in their situation any of the propositions I have made is precisely by redoing what I have done, that is, by not following me. In order to follow me it is essential not to follow me!" (Freire & Faundez, 1992, p. 30).

Freirean critical pedagogy is a situated politics, a dialogic process that "works" by being built from, for, and into the conditions of the students. Because conditions vary at differing sites of practice, educators adapt their practice to address the local situation. In this rich volume, readers will encounter a panorama of reinvention, not standardization, which is what Paulo called for, a praxis of adaptive local agency—action/reflection/action emerging for and from specific sites.

Educators who reinvent Paulo are also reinventing themselves as teachers and human subjects. Transforming self-in-society begins with *questioning the status quo and imagining interventions against the way things are.* From chapter to chapter herein, there is a shared political orientation: *questioning the status quo in the name of social justice,* which is a general foundation of Freirean pedagogy. The "status quo" or "society as we find it" defines the object of the questioning, interrogating in legible language everyday experience re-presented as problems. I called that disruptive questioning "extraordinarily re-experiencing the ordinary" in my first book, *Critical Teaching and Everyday Life* (1980).

"Questioning the status quo," the heart of Freire's original method, is simultaneously the goal and process of problem-posing. Freire conceived of dialogue as a horizontal process of mutual communication opposed to the authoritarian monologue of "banking pedagogy" (curriculum transferring pre-set knowledge from teacher to students). In other words, "Education must begin with the solution to the teacher-student contradiction, by reconciling the poles of the contradiction so that both are simultaneously teachers and students" (Freire, 2018, p. 72). The egalitarian process of learning (dialogue) and the democratic contents of learning (the cultural conditions, speech community, power relations, and ways of seeing of the students) make this a method for intellectual empowerment.

For Freire in his Brazilian time and place, empowerment was centered in the poor and working class. Freire called the largely illiterate multitude he worked among "the power not yet in power." This pedagogy for critical consciousness has evolved to address not only students from the bottom of the economic ladder but also students from diverse identities; inclusion now means not only representing lower class subjects but also engaging the profoundly unequal distinctions based on race, gender, sexual identity, ethnicity, national origin, immigration status, and physical abilities.

Such panoramic inclusion is a majoritarian road to social justice. On this road, social class differences are only one starting point for challenging the unequal status quo. While democracy is undermined in every society by oligarchy (rule of a wealthy elite minority), it is also negated by white supremacy, male supremacy, homophobia, nativism, and disfavored disabilities. The Freire studies in the coming pages show how Paulo's theory and practice have evolved inter-sectionally since his passing more than twenty years ago. They now comprise a big tent of inclusive locations and identities.

Outside the big tent, two ominous clocks are ticking. The first clock is July 2019, the warmest month ever recorded for planetary temperatures. Unaddressed global heating delivers historic warmth, catastrophic floods, prolonged droughts, calamitous forest fires, and ferocious hurricanes. Arctic regions are heating fastest, sending glacial melt into rising oceans. The second ticking clock is the rise of aggressive right-wing forces not only in Brazil but also in the United States and Europe. Liberal society is broadly under siege by misogynists, racists, homophobes, billionaires, and neoliberals; that siege narrows the political space for democratic opposition of all kinds, including critical pedagogy. The culture wars underway for four decades threaten civil society and the public sphere.

Culture wars require tools for resistance. This book is one such tool. It draws on Paulo Freire's defiant dreaming to resist dehumanizing rhetoric and government. When we dream like Paulo, we prepare ourselves to build a world less hateful and less violent, more just, more equal, and more humane. As Paulo proposed, "Liberatory education must be understood as a practice where we challenge the people to mobilize or organize themselves to get power." (*A Pedagogy for Liberation*, 1987, p. 34). The coming chapters challenge us to build the power needed by the party of hope.

Ira Shor
City University of New
York Graduate Center
August, 2019

References

Freire, P. (2018). *Pedagogy of the oppressed* (50th Anniversary Edition). New York: Bloomsbury Academic.

Freire, P., & Faundez, A. (1992). *Learning to question*. New York: Continuum.

Shor, I. (1987/1980). *Critical teaching and everyday life*. Chicago: University of Chicago Press.

Shor, I., & Freire, P. (1987). *A pedagogy for liberation: Dialogues on transforming education*. London: Bergin-Garvey, Greenwood.

Acknowledgments

Working on this text has been a powerful learning experience. My sincerest gratitude and respect for the chapter contributors who provide for us a wide array of themes in creative and thoughtful ways, emphasizing how Paulo Freire's thought continues to remain relevant in these contemporary times.

Thank you, Ira Shor, for beginning the text with your Foreword, reminding us that to follow Paulo is not to follow him, but rather to reinvent his work. Thank you, Antonia Darder, for your Afterword, closing this book with your beautiful words, exhorting the building of a more just and loving world. And with much gratitude, Henry Giroux and Peter Mayo, for supporting this important work.

Much appreciation, Mark Richardson at Bloomsbury who immediately saw the vision of this book, guiding me through the process to make it happen. Also, at Bloomsbury, thank you Kim Brown, Shanmathi Priya Sampath, and Zeba Talkhani for your great assistance in getting this book through production.

Thank you, Jon Pedersen, Dean of the College of Education, at the University of South Carolina. Your support for my work is something I do not take for granted. Not only my work, but also the support you provide for all faculty in our college who are doing justice work. Without justice, there is no liberation.

Most importantly, I am deeply grateful for my two sons, Antonio and Alexander, whose interests are always piqued with a proud smile when I tell them about a new book. May my efforts influence them to follow in the steps of being an instrument of peace, love, and justice.

Contributors

Ivor Baatjes is Director of the Centre for Integrated Post-School Education and Training, Nelson Mandela University, South Afraica, and a member of the *National Research Foundation's SarChi Chair: Community, Adult and Worker Education, South Africa*. His research interests include adult and community education and higher education, among other interests. His most recent work is *Learning for Living: Towards a New Vision for Post-School Learning in South Africa* (HSRC Press, Cape Town).

Alexandra Bethlenfalvy is PhD candidate in History at the University of South Carolina. Her dissertation, "We Shall Not Be Moved: Highlander Folk School's Citizenship Campaign from the Cultural Front to the Civil Rights Movement, 1932–67" draws a crucial connection in progressive activism from the New Deal through the Cold War.

Sascha Betts is an advanced doctoral student in the School Improvement program at Texas State University.

Nelio Bizzo is Senior Full Professor of Science Education at São Paulo University (USP) and Assistant Professor at São Paulo Federal University (UNIFESP). Nelio has served at the National Council of Education for the Brazilian Ministry of Education (2000–2004) and was Visiting Professor at Verona University (2011, Italy).

Drick Boyd is Professor Emeritus of Urban and Interdisciplinary Studies from Eastern University, Sat. Davids, PA. He is the author of *White Allies in the Struggle for Racial Justice* (Orbis, 2015) and *Paulo Freire: His Faith, Spirituality and Theology* (with James D. Kirylo; Sense, 2017).

Gregory Bruno is Assistant Professor in English at Kingsborough Community College in the City University of New York. He designs and teaches co-enrolled exchange program courses at correctional facilities in the greater New York City area. He earned his doctorate in English Education from Teachers College, Columbia University in 2019.

Nathaniel Bryan is Assistant Professor in the Department of Teacher Education at Miami University,Ohio. His research interests focus on the constructed identities and pedagogical styles of black male teachers in early childhood education, the schooling and childhood play experiences of black boys, and teacher preparation for urban education.

Antonia Darder holds the Leavey Presidential Endowed Chair of Ethics and Moral Leadership at Loyola Marymount University, Los Angeles, and a Distinguished Visiting Faculty at the University of Johannesburg, South Africa. She is the author of many books, including *Freire and Education* and *The Student Guide to Freire's Pedagogy of the Oppressed*.

Erin Rose Glass is the Digital Scholarship Librarian at UC San Diego, where she advises on participatory approaches to digital research and education. She received the 2018 Emerging Open Scholarship Award for #SocialDiss, a project that engaged public review of her dissertation drafts on a variety of digital platforms.

Deidre Geduld is the Head of Programme for the B Ed Foundation Programme (Gr R-3) at Nelson Mandela University, South Africa. Her research interests include teaching and learning in the early years, inclusive education, teacher education curriculum design, community schooling and engagement within communities of practice, and critical approach to research. Her latest work is titled *Towards Decolonising Teacher Education: Reimagining the Relationship between Theory and Praxis (SAJE)*.

Soumitree Gupta is Associate Professor of English at Carroll College in Helena, Montana. Her research and teaching interests include postcolonial studies, comparative race and ethnic studies, gender studies, transnational feminism, diaspora studies, and trauma and memory studies.

Jon Hale is Associate Professor of education at the University of South Carolina. His research focuses on the history of student and teacher activism during the civil rights movement. His book, *The Freedom Schools,* was awarded the AERA New Scholars Book Award and the AESA Critics Choice Award.

Petar Jandrić is Professor and Director of BSc (Informatics) program at the Zagreb University of Applied Sciences, Croatia. His previous academic affiliations include Croatian Academic and Research Network, University of Edinburgh, Glasgow School of Art, and University of East London. He is Editor-in-Chief of *Postdigital Science and Education*.

Débora Barbosa Agra Junker, a native of Brazil, is Assistant Professor of Christian Education at Garrett-Evangelical Theological Seminary. As founder and director of the Cátedra Paulo Freire since 2016, she is committed to furthering Paulo Freire's legacy in the field of religious studies and liberation theologies from the Global South.

James D. Kirylo is Professor of Education at the University of South Carolina. Kirylo has published works in a variety of educational journals, and among other books, he is the author of *Paulo Freire: The Man from Recife* (2011), *Teaching with Purpose: An Inquiry into the Who, Why, and How We Teach* (2016) and, co-author with Drick Boyd, of *Paulo Freire: His Faith, Spirituality, and Theology* (2017).

Tricia Kress is Associate Professor in the Educational Leadership for Diverse Learning Communities EdD program at Molloy College in Rockville Centre, NY, USA. Her research uses critical pedagogy, cultural sociology, and auto/ethnography to rethink teaching, learning, and research in urban schools in the United States.

Robert Lake is Professor at Georgia Southern University. He teaches undergraduate and graduate courses in curriculum studies and multicultural education. Robert is the author of (2012) *Vygotsky on Education* for Peter Lang and (2013) *A Curriculum of Imagination in an Era of Standardization: An Imaginative Dialogue with Maxine Greene and Paulo Freire* (Information Age).

Amy E. Laboe is a doctoral candidate in Social Foundations of Education at the University of Virginia. Previously, she was an ESOL teacher in Minnesota and Latin America. Her research interests focus on the field of anthropology of education on topics such as, teacher identity, transnational migration, and multiculturalism.

Dena Lagomarsino is a former high school educator and a doctoral candidate in the City, Culture, and Community program at Tulane University. Dena's chapter contribution is based on research from her Sociology of Education Master's program at New York University.

Jennifer Markides is a doctoral candidate in Educational Research at the Werklund School of Education, University of Calgary. She is Métis, and resides in High River, Alberta. Through her research, writing, teaching, and activism, she contributes to social justice discourses in education, Indigenous education, disaster recovery, and community-led research projects.

Shelley Martin-Young is a retired educator from Sand Springs schools in Oklahoma. She is currently finishing her PhD at Oklahoma State University, and also teaches Children's Literature and Language Arts at OSU. Her research focus is on using children's and young adult literature to disrupt the single story of the social studies textbook.

Peter McLaren is Distinguished Professor in Critical Studies at the Attallah College of Educational Studies, Chapman University, California, and Emeritus Professor at the University of California, Los Angeles. He is also Chair Professor at Northeast Normal University, Changchun. Professor McLaren writes from a Marxist humanist perspective influenced by liberation theology and is a political activist. Professor McLaren is the co-founder of Instituto McLaren de Pedagogia Critica in Mexico.

Meir Muller has earned rabbinical ordination as well as a doctorate in early childhood education. Meir serves as an assistant professor in the College of Education at the University of South Carolina. His research interests include cultural relevant pedagogy, anti-racist pedagogy, constructivist theory, and Jewish early childhood education.

Kaitlin Popielarz is a PhD candidate and instructor at Wayne State University's College of Education. Kaitlin's research and teaching interests include connecting teacher education programs to the grassroots community in order to provide future educators the opportunity to learn community-based and culturally sustaining pedagogy for education rooted in social justice.

Peter Roberts is Professor of Education and Director of the Educational Theory, Policy and Practice Research Hub at the University of Canterbury in New Zealand. His primary areas of scholarship are philosophy of education and educational policy studies.

Gerardo Rodríguez-Galarza is Assistant Professor of theology and religious studies. He holds a doctorate degree in historical theology from Saint Louis University. He currently teaches courses on the intersection of theology, history, and race at St. Norbert College.

Heloise Sathorar is the Head of Programme for the Bachelor of Education (High School Teacher Education Programme) at the Nelson Mandela University, South Africa. Her research interests include critical pedagogy, the democratization of knowledge, teacher education, higher education, and critical community engagement. Her most recent work is titled *Towards Decolonising Teacher Education: Reimagining the Relationship between Theory and Praxis (South African Journal of Education)*.

Ira Shor is Professor Emeritus at the City University of New York Graduate Center Programs in English and in Urban Education. He co-authored with Paulo Freire the first "talking book" Freire did with a collaborator, *A Pedagogy for Liberation* (1986), and published the first book-length volume on critical pedagogy in North America, *Critical Teaching and Everyday Life* (1980).

Rolf Straubhaar is Assistant Professor of Educational Leadership and School Improvement at Texas State University.

A. J. Tierney is Director of the Center for Student Advancement at the University of Oklahoma. She is also an educational psychology doctoral student at Oklahoma State University. She works to supporting students in finding their unique voice and sharing it with the world.

Sara Torres currently serves as an EPD Specialist at NASA Ames Research Center. She works with educators, families, and community members to support STEM efforts. Her research interests include STEM education. She holds degrees from TSU (MEd) and UTSA (BA). Sara is also pursuing a PhD at Texas State University.

Patricia Virella is Graduate Professor in the Art of Teaching Program at Sarah Lawrence College. Her scholarship focuses on education reform policy particularly in Puerto Rico. She also studies teacher education and principal preparation within the urban setting.

Jennie Weiner is Associate Professor of Educational Leadership at the University of Connecticut. Her scholarship focuses on leadership and organizational change particularly in under-performing schools and districts. She also studies gender and racial bias in educational leadership and building educational infrastructure at the local, district, and state level.

Introduction

The Enduring Legacy of Paulo Freire

James D. Kirylo

It has been over fifty years since the original release of Paulo Freire's landmark work, *Pedagogy of the Oppressed*.[1] Translated in over thirty different languages, with numerous printings, and over a million copies sold, one could argue that *Pedagogy of the Oppressed* is more popular and influential today than when it was first released, drawing in educators, academics, theologians, social justice workers, and many others from the world over. The circumstances and events that ultimately led to the publication of Freire's most famous text are worth a brief recounting.

In 1961, when the populist, João Goulart was elected president of Brazil, he had widespread support, and was particularly interested in having Freire implement his literacy program throughout the country. The implementation of the program was projected to reach 5 million adult learners who would be taught to read and write within a two-year period. The prompting of Goulart's interest was based on the success of Freire's earlier work in Angicos where 300 rural farm workers learned to read and write within forty-five days (Freire, 1996).

The implementation process was short-lived as Freire and his team were preparing for this massive literacy project the Goulart administration was overthrown by a military coup d'etat in 1964, resulting in Goulart fleeing the country to neighboring Uruguay, with another approximately 10,000 officials being dismissed of their duties, with many of them also going into exile

---

[1] The text was first published in Spanish in 1968, and later in English in 1970. The book was also early on translated into Italian, French, and German, with many of the foreign editions smuggled into Brazil. Because of the volatile political climate in Brazil, it wasn't until 1975 that *Pedagogy of the Oppressed* was published in Brazilian Portuguese (Freire, 1994; Kirylo, 2011).

(Barnard, 1981; Holst, 2006; Taylor, 1993). There was a combination of reasons that sparked the 1964 coup:

> First, President Goulart was not only supportive of left-leaning groups, but it was under his presidency that an exponential growth of radical and revolutionary groups emerged unlike the country of Brazil had ever witnessed (Elias, 1994). Second, along with the emergence of Marxist thought, Catholic progressives, agrarian reform groups, worker movements, and others became more intensely influential in mobilizing masses of people. Third, conservatives were rather nervous with the possibilities of those who would become literate as a result of Freire's literacy program …. It is worth reiterating that at the time of the coup, northeast Brazil had a population of some 25 to 30 million with approximately 15 million being illiterate. And, if Freire's literacy program had gone through on a national scale, the potential of new voters (more likely to support the populist regime) in the state of Sergipe would have numbered approximately 80,000, and in Pernambuco the number of new voters would have numbered approximately 500,000 (Torres, 1998). Freire was certainly not unaware of the percolation of discontenting voices and knew that his fate could land him in prison (Gadotti, 1994). (Kirylo, 2011, pp. 52–53)

Within the midst of the above-described events that triggered the coup, Freire, of course, was dismissed of his duties to conduct his literacy work. He was taken into police custody where he was interrogated, accused of being communist and a subversive. He spent the next two and a half months in jail, where he used his time "thinking things over" (Freire, 1985, p. 180), and began his first major work *Educação como Practica da Liberdade* (Education as the Practice of Freedom) (Collins, 1977). It is in this work that we see the emergence of Freire's philosophy, discussing the workings of cultural circles and how the making of generative words aids in literacy learning, while at the same time underscoring the harmful effects of colonial Brazil (Freire, 1994; Gadotti, 1994).[2]

[2] This text was later completed while in exile in Chile, where he also wrote "Extension or Communication" in which he examines the challenges of agrarian and education reform, underscoring that key to reform is dialogue as opposed to cultural invasion (Elias, 1994). *Education as the Practice of Freedom* combined with "Extension or Communication" was first released in Santiago, Chile, under the title as *Education for Critical Consciousness*, which was subsequently published in English in 1973 (Kirylo, 2011). Particularly for the English-speaking audience, this 1973 publication thusly appears as if that was Freire's second book, after *Pedagogy of the Oppressed*. Whereas *Education for Critical Consciousness* is practical and methodological in nature, *Pedagogy of the Oppressed* is more theoretical and revolutionary, suggesting as Elias (1994) asserts, that actually reading the former first is helpful in better understanding the latter.

Upon his release from jail, Freire was subject to more interrogation, with a major newspaper, *Globo*, calling for the military to throw him back in jail (Freire, 1985). Tired of the threats, the questioning, and not having the freedom to conduct his literacy work, Freire, along with his family, joined the thousands of others and went into exile. After a short stay in Bolivia, he spent five years in Chile, then in Harvard for a year, and then in Geneva, Switzerland, for ten years where he worked with the World Council of Churches, traveling around the world to share his ideas. Freire finally returned home in Brazil for good in 1980 under the umbrella of political amnesty climate (Kirylo, 2011).

It was while Freire was in Chile that he wrote *Pedagogy of the Oppressed* in which he drew from his experience in both Brazil and Chile. Whereas his first book, *Education as the Practice of Freedom*, is largely informed by a liberal developmentalist point of view, we see in *Pedagogy of the Oppressed* how Freire's thought has evolved, which is filtered through with Marxist humanism (Holst, 2006). Freire explores the exploitive nature of political and social systems, making the distinction between the notion of humanization and dehumanization, denouncing oppression of any kind and simultaneously announcing ways in which the oppressed can move to a critical consciousness space through the cultivation of a democratizing climate (Roberts, 2000).

To state differently regarding Freire's most well-known work, Macedo (2018) puts it this way:

> Thus, the central goal of Freire's *Pedagogy of the Oppressed* is to awaken in the oppressed the knowledge, creativity, and constant critical reflective capacities necessary to unveil, demystify and understand the power relations responsible for their oppressed marginalization and, through this recognition, begin a project of liberation through praxis which, invariably, requires consistent, never-ending critical reflection and action. (p. 2)

In the final analysis, "*Pedagogy of the Oppressed* … has transformed and deepened social justice educational discourses worldwide" (Darder, 2018, p. xxi), and "few books have been so widely debated, quoted, excerpted, and also used for teacher education, graduate and undergraduate courses, and in some high schools (as the banning of this book in Tucson in 2012 showed)" (Shor, 2018, p. 186).

A work of reinvention

As we consider this text, *Reinventing Pedagogy of the Oppressed: Contemporary Perspectives*, not only will it be evident that the chapter contributors are those who join the multitude of others from around the world who draw from Freire's classic work, but it will also be clear that a deep social justice thread is linked throughout the chapters. This social justice thread is not a formulaic endeavor, but rather a reinvention of Freire's thought that ultimately pulls from his entire body of work,[3] which "requires of me that I recognize that the historical, political, cultural, and economic conditions of each context present new methodological and tactical requirements, so that it is always necessary to search for the actualization of the substantivity of ideas with every new situation" (Freire, 1997, pp. 310, 326).

I am privileged to have assembled a cross-section of authors who have contributed to this important book, many of whom I met at conferences and other venues. One such place was the University of South Carolina in 2018, where a two-day conference was held, celebrating the fiftieth anniversary year of the original release of *Pedagogy of the Oppressed*. I have never met some of the other chapter contributors, but have been familiar with their scholarship for years. In fact, a notable aspect to this book is that there is a nice mix of both first- and second-generation Freirean-influenced scholars and emerging scholars who come from various geographic areas, with a cross-section of cultural, racial, and ethnic backgrounds and experiences.

We are entering into the third decade of the twenty-first century, and the reinvention of Paulo Freire in this book spreads through discussions related to theology, technology, ecology, school reform, pedagogy, curriculum, leadership, politics, gender, sexual orientation, race, culture, ethnicity, psychology, and

[3] Freire (1997) reaffirms the point, asserting, "This so-called Freirean educator, if he or she truly wants to understand me, must also go beyond *Pedagogy of the Oppressed*. He or she must continually be engaged in reading the works I have done since then..." (p. 310).

communication. It should be no surprise that the stretch of Freire's hand organically expands across disciplines, not only indicative of the power of his influence, but also a certain timeless nature of that influence. As long as there is injustice in the world, and that there continues to be those on the outside looking in, Paulo Freire's classic work, *Pedagogy of the Oppressed*, and, indeed, his entire body of work will always matter.

While the chapters themes are varied, they are loosely sectioned into topical thematic groups (see Table of Contents). Moreover, within the social justice thread that links all of the chapters, the notion of Freire's concept of conscientização (conscientization) also emerges, which stresses the importance of critical awareness, the understanding of self, reality, and its intersection with just action (Kirylo & Boyd, 2017). And within the dynamic of working toward just action, it must be infused through a process that simultaneously denounces injustice while announcing for a more just world. Freire (1985) further explains:

> Denunciation of a dehumanizing situation today increasingly demands precise scientific understanding of that situation. Similarly, the annunciation of its transformation increasingly requires a theory of transforming action. Yet, neither act by itself implies the transformation of the denounced reality or the establishment of that which is announced. Rather, as a moment in a historical process, the announced reality is already present in the act of denunciation and annunciation. (Freire, 1985, p. 57)

As one reads through *Reinventing Pedagogy of the Oppressed: Contemporary Perspectives*, it will be clear that chapter contributors not only "scientifically" write in their denunciation of unjust practices, policies, and ways of doing things relative to their chapter focus, but they also write in order to announce a way toward the door of transformation that leads to a more just and right world.

Overview of chapters

Chapter 1, "Preparing Foundational Phase Educators: Reading the Word and the World through Transect Walks," by Deidre Geduld, Ivor Baatjes, and Heloise Sathorar, discusses the development of critical pedagogical approaches in teacher preparation in the South African contexts, which is imperative, given the deepening crisis in the public schooling system of South Africa. Public discourse in education suggests that education for critical citizenship and substantive democracy is under threat and requires much greater critical engagement and scholarship that advance teaching practices of educators in support of citizen preparation in South Africa.

Titled "W. E. B. DuBois and Paulo Freire: Toward a 'Pedagogy of the Veil' to Counter Racism in Early Childhood Education," Chapter 2, by Meir Muller and Nathaniel Bryan, explores Du Bois's double consciousness and Freire's notion of conscientization in order to foster critical consciousness among early childhood educators and their students so that they become authentic vehicles to dismantle racism and inequality in their thought and practice.

In Chapter 3, "The Community as a Teacher Educator: Preparing Critically Conscious Teacher Candidates in Detroit," Kaitlin Popielarz argues that future educators must look to understand the meaning of critical pedagogy in order to facilitate its intent in practice, particularly how this practice unfolds within a teacher education methods course. Key to this unfolding is the development of critical consciousness among teacher candidates through connections with the school community and the community at large in which an education for liberation is fostered.

Chapter 4, "Making Meaning in the Carceral Space: Freirean Dialogue and Existential Becoming in the Jail or Prison Classroom" by Gregory Bruno, asserts that the notion of dialogue must be rooted in trust, hope, and meaning, as Freire often conveyed. And while the fostering of dialogical spaces can be challenging enough in a typical classroom setting, it is near impossible in a prison setting. In that light, therefore, this chapter examines how the Freirean notion of dialogue can be cultivated as a foundation for literacy and meaning-making among students who are incarcerated.

Titled "Critical Race Counterstories and Freire's Critical Pedagogy: Navigating Race in an Interdisciplinary Literature and Religious Studies Course," Chapter 5, by Soumitree Gupta and Gerardo Rodriguez-Galarza, argues that critical race counterstories need to be paired with a strategic problem-posing learning model to enable the work of conscientization. This chapter also examines the existing research on—and our experience as—educators of color teaching race in PWIs (predominantly white institutions), and reflect on how we navigate the fraught process of student conscientization at a university setting classroom.

Erin Rose Glass, in Chapter 6, "Toward a Software of the Oppressed: A Freirean Approach to Surveillance Capitalism," writes how Freire's critical pedagogy provides a helpful framework for theorizing, resisting, and transforming the oppressive digital technologies and practices of surveillance capitalism specifically from the position of the classroom and higher education. The chapter also sketches out a Freirean theory of digital liberation in and through the classroom and points to examples that show how students and educators might critically participate in the shaping of our digital world.

Shelley Martin Young explores in Chapter 7, "Freirean Cultural Circles in a Contemporary Social Studies Class," how Freire's notion of cultural circles created a participatory climate in which participants became subjects of their history. In that light, the chapter further examines the implications and possibilities of cultural circles in the twenty-first century, particularly in the study of social studies in a K-12 classroom.

In Chapter 8, "The Liberatory Potential for Teacher Mindfulness," Amy E. Laboe looks to add to the discourse on mindfulness by proposing that we look at mindfulness more from its contemplative tradition—as a practice that could engage a teacher in a process of coming to know and inhabit herself. Drawing from the mindfulness literature and Freire's praxis of liberation, this chapter describes how teacher as a subject and one as a liberated self can work in freer ways within a culture of performativity.

AJ Tierney in Chapter 9, "Who's in Charge? Teacher Authority and Navigating the Dialogical-Based Classroom," argues that K-12 students are far from empty vessels to be filled through a banking system of education. Rather, they are filled with languages, rituals, and cultural contexts, which are brought to the classroom setting. In this chapter, therefore, through a Freirean and critical pedagogy lens, teacher authoritarianism and directivity are challenged, while at the same time the notion of dialogical-based spaces is cultivated in order to better meet the needs and interests of students.

"'To Speak a Book': Lessons from Myles Horton and Paulo Freire's *We Make the Road by Walking*" is the title of Chapter 10 where Jon Hale and

Alexandra Bethlenfalvy utilize a historical and a biographical approach to examine the genesis of Paulo Freire and Myles Horton's working relationship and their resultant seminal text, *We Make the Road by Walking*. The chapter also illustrates how Highlander Folk School anticipated Freire's philosophy as a site of political incubation, and how the school provided a foundation for a regional network that cultivated activist ties, developed organizational strategies, and raised a collective consciousness.

Drick Boyd writes in Chapter 11, "The Beloved Community and Utopia: Hope in the Face of Struggle as Envisioned by Martin Luther King, Jr. and Paulo Freire," how both Paulo Freire and Martin Luther King, Jr. articulated visions of hope in the face of oppression and opposition. Thus, this chapter examines their respective visions of hope, which for Freire is captured in the concept of Utopia and for King in his image of the Beloved Community.

In Chapter 12, "Less Certain but no Less Committed: Paulo Freire and Simone de Beauvoir on Ethics and Education," Peter Roberts contends that we live an era of exaggerated certainties, erupting in education, politics, religion, and other aspects of society, all of which cultivates a climate of extremism, intolerance, oppression, and even violence. It is for this reason that both Paulo Freire and Simone de Beauvoir remind us to be critically aware of what it means to live in that certain-uncertainty place and why that is a valued space, all of which is discussed in this chapter.

Chapter 13, "*Ley de Reformativa de Educactiva de Puerto Rico*: A Freirean Perspective," by Patricia Virella and Jennie Weiner, examines the Post-Hurricane Maria school reform initiative being implemented in Puerto Rico. Within the policy, Paulo Freire is cited as an influence of the policy creation, however seemingly missing from the policy are central tenets of Freire's philosophy which would give power to the people of Puerto Rico. In that light, through a Freirean lens, this chapter examines *Ley de Reformativa de Educactiva de Puerto Rico*, evaluating its impact, implications, and future of education in Puerto Rico.

Jennifer Markides articulates in Chapter 14, "Overcoming (In)Difference: Emancipatory Pedagogy and Indigenous Worldviews toward Respectful Relationships with the More-Than-Human World," how Freire's anti-oppressive pedagogy has been taken up toward transformational praxis in emancipatory work with marginalized people; however, little attention has been given to the liberating possibilities Freirean projects could hold for animals and Mother Earth. To that end, this chapter looks to the perspectives and insights of Indigenous scholars for ways of living well with the more-than-human world, and applies concepts of radical listening and care ethics to re-envisioning Freire's *Pedagogy of the Oppressed,* anew.

In Chapter 15, "We Write on the Earth as the Earth Writes on Us: Paulo Freire the (Post)Humanist," Tricia Kress and Robert Lake discuss how in this post-truth era people can find a myriad of "facts" online supporting preexisting beliefs and values, basing political decision-making on emotion rather than fact-based reasoning. In particular, this stymies the ability of research to inform policy in the service of preserving our planet and the welfare of its inhabitants. Thus, by attending to Freire's notion of humility and the role of emotions and the body in conscientization, this chapter illustrates how critical pedagogy can be reinterpreted as (post)humanist conscientizing in post-truth times, particularly with respect to the ecological discourse.

"The Postdigital Challenge of Paulo Freire's Prophetic Church" is the title of Chapter 16 by Peter McLaren and Petar Jandrić where they share how Freire attacked the reactionary elements within the Catholic Church, making clear that the neutral political position of "the traditionalist church" and "the modernizing church" reinforces the position of the oppressor. This is contrasted with what Freire calls "the prophetic church," which actively struggles for emancipation and liberation of the oppressed. And while the ethos of Freire's prophetic church remains as valid as ever, human interactions have been radically transformed by digital technologies. This chapter, therefore, explores possible ways of reinventing Freire's prophetic church in and for our postdigital reality.

Chapter 17, "Pursuing Critical Consciousness on the Tenure Track: Toward a Humanizing Praxis within the Neoliberal University," by Rolf Straubhaar, Sara Torres, and Sascha Betts, asserts that the dominant paradigm governing many contemporary academia leans more toward what Freire calls a banking education, defining "good" students by their ability to receive and repeat what they are taught, and similarly defining "good" faculty by what they are able to produce through publications in high-impact journals, externally funded research projects, and positive course evaluations. In that light, this chapter explores how the performative nature of university work can be one that is embedded in a system that is dehumanizing, further examining how university-based academics can negotiate that dehumanizing tendency to one that is more humanizing and critical-consciousness raising.

Chapter 18 by Dena Lagomarsino, "Living in the Contradictions: LGBTQ Educators and Critical Pedagogy," considers the education-related experiences of eight educators who are "out" as LGBTQ in the classroom and self-identify as practitioners of socially just pedagogies. Against the backdrop of an increasingly privatized, neoliberal national education system, these educators discuss the intersectional marginalization they and their students experience, providing examples of co-creating democratizing climates and creative resistance in which the Freirean notion of "naming the word and the world" is paramount.

Nelio Bizzo shares in Chapter 19, "An Eye-Witness Account of Freire's Return Back to Brazil after the Exile: Personal Reflections on Fighting Oppression," a personal account meeting with Paulo Freire soon after he returned to Brazil from exile in 1980. Moreover, Bizzo recounts how he was on the advising team when Freire was appointed Secretary of Education of *São Paulo* in 1989. Finally, he reminds us how current-day Brazil is being challenged by a newly elected president who rejects the work and thought of Paulo Freire.

The final chapter, "Dare to Hope: The Art of Untying the Tongue and Awakening the Resilient Spirit" by Débora B. Agra Junker, draws from three of Freire's constructs: the culture of silence, the internalized image of the oppressor, and the need for education in hope—implying both a critique of injustice and a liberating social praxis. By weaving these three concepts under the artistic eye of Doris Salcedo, a Colombian visual artist, this chapter asserts that the emblematic dehumanization of our contexts is not a cause of hopelessness, but of hope, anchored in praxis, which seeks the transformation of social reality, and the humanization of us all.

In closing these introductory remarks, one saw that this volume began with a Foreword from Ira Shor who reiterated the richness of this text on how chapter contributors uniquely reinvented Paulo Freire in these contemporary times, a reinvention that is threaded with the task to build a more just, more equal, more humane, and more hopeful world. And as this book closes with a bow of love, one will read an Afterword by Antonia Darder who passionately charges us to move forward, deeply grounded in a pedagogy of love that collectively works to make a world that is more loving and more just. Indeed, the enduring legacy of Paulo Freire is ultimately a message of love.

References

Barnard, C. (1981). Imperialism, underdevelopment and education. In R. Mackie (Ed.), *Literacy and revolution: The pedagogy of Paulo Freire* (pp. 12–38). New York: Continuum.

Collins, D. E., S. J. (1977). *Paulo Freire: His life, works and thought.* New York: Paulist Press.

Darder, A. (2018). *The student's guide to Freire's pedagogy of the oppressed.* London: Bloomsbury.

Elias, J. L. (1994). *Paulo Freire: Pedagogue of liberation.* Malabar, FL: Kreiger Publishing Company.

Freire, P. (1985). *The politics of education: Culture, power, and liberation.* New York: Bergin & Garvey.

Freire, P. (1994). *Pedagogy of hope: Reliving pedagogy of the oppressed* (Robert R. Barr, Trans.). New York: Continuum.

Freire, P. (1996). *Letters to Cristina: Reflections on my life and work* (D. Macedo with Q. Macedo and A. Oliveira, Trans.). New York: Routledge.

Freire, P. (1997). A response. In P. Freire, J. W. Fraser, D. Macedo, T. McKinnon, & W. T. Stokes (Eds.), *Mentoring the mentor: A critical dialogue with Paulo Freire* (pp. 303–329). New York: Peter Lang.

Gadotti, M. (1994). *Reading Paulo Freire: His life and work* (John Milton, Trans.). Albany: State University of New York Press.

Holst, J. D. (Summer 2006). Paulo Freire in Chile, 1964–1969: Pedagogy of the oppressed in its sociopolitical economic context. *Harvard Educational Review, 76*(2), 243–270.

Kirylo, J. D. (2011). *Paulo Freire: The man from Recife.* New York: Peter Lang.

Kirylo, J. D., & Boyd, D. (2017). *Paulo Freire: His faith, spirituality, and theology.* Rotterdam, Netherlands: Sense.

Macedo, D. (2018). Introduction to the 50th anniversary edition. In P. Freire (Ed.), *Pedagogy of the oppressed* (pp. 1–33). London: Bloomsbury.

Roberts, P. (2000). *Education, literacy, and humanization: Exploring the work of Paulo Freire*. Westport, CT: Bergin & Garvey.

Shor, I. (2018). "*A luta continua*": Afterword to pedagogy of the oppressed. In P. Freire (Ed.), *Pedagogy of the oppressed* (pp. 185–188). London: Bloomsbury.

Taylor, P. V. (1993). *The texts of Paulo Freire*. Buckingham, England: Open University Press.

Torres, C. A. (1998). The political pedagogy of Paulo Freire. In P. Freire (Ed.), *Politics and education* (pp. 1–15). Los Angeles: UCLA Latin American Center Publications, University of California.

Part One

The Criticality of Teacher Preparation

1

Preparing Foundational Phase Educators: Reading the Word and World through Transect Walks

Deidre Geduld, Ivor Baatjes, and Heloise Sathorar

Introduction

Public schooling in post-apartheid South Africa is in perpetual and deepening crisis, characterized by poor throughput and high dropout rates; large student-to-teacher ratio; an increase in race and gender violence; a decline in teacher morale; weakened teacher unions; and conflict and protests.[1] In addition to the above, privatization of education is rising while our public schools are stripped of resources, aligning them to the whims of the market, which furthers inequality as reflected in a national quintile system.

The decline in public education challenges critical pedagogues inside and outside the academy to continuously pursue pedagogical approaches vital to building educated resistance and reflective praxis in concert with student-teachers, community activists, and social movements to the neoliberal attack on our public institutions. As university-based scholars, therefore, our intellectual project is the development of a cadre of critical foundation phase[2] pedagogues committed to education for liberation and the struggle for substantive democracy. That is, we believe in the necessity of

---

[1] Many public schools in South Africa have recently been the focus of protests. These protests ranged from issues related to poor and a lack of resources, acts of gender and racial violence, and teacher and student abuse. All of these occur in the context of a broader social-economic crisis as highlighted by the Job Summit which took place in Johannesburg, South Africa on October 4–5, 2018.

[2] Foundation Phase in the South African context refers to Grade R to Grade 3. The other two phases are the Intermediate Phase (Grades 4–6) and Senior Phase (Grades 7–12).

curricula toward shaping critical consciousness and transformative practices in public education.

This chapter argues for greater use of participatory teacher preparation practices drawn from the theory and practice of Community Participatory Action Research (CPAR). We propose the use of transect walks as an instrument within a larger philosophical and methodological repository that encourages critical consciousness and the enhancement of student-teachers' ability to "reading the word and the world" (Freire & Macedo, 1987). While more on transect walks will be discussed later, in brief, they are systematic walks along defined routes across a community together with the local people to explore socioeconomic conditions by observing, asking, listening, looking, and producing educational responses that could assist in responding to socioeconomic realities. We believe that such methodological approaches are important to foster awareness and liberating praxis.

Background to teacher preparation in South Africa

Teacher preparation (TP) in post-apartheid South Africa has been the focus of ongoing restructuring. It has been the subject of rationalization; improved resource utilization; ongoing efforts to upgrade teacher qualifications; quality assurance, and efforts toward addressing the vast discrepancies in "race"-based participation in education (Mncube & Madikizela-Madiya, 2013). Various initiatives to address the challenges facing teacher education (TE) include the introduction of norms and standards for TE, policies, qualifications frameworks, and curriculum review (DHET, 2011).

Universities in South Africa are compelled to engage with and respond to policy directives. The Nelson Mandela University—an institution borne out of a merger process of three historically advantaged and two disadvantaged institutions with different historical and cultural traditions—adopted humanizing pedagogy as its philosophical, methodological, and ethic orientation in TE (Geduld & Sathorar, 2016). A significant challenge for academics was the transition from modernist paradigms and fundamental pedagogics (Cullen & Hill, 2013; Morrow, 2007) to a humanizing pedagogical approach as a new framing philosophical paradigm that underpinned TP. It required an internal educative process that encouraged academic consciousness oriented toward educational practices for progressive outcomes in education. Embracing humanizing pedagogy requires critical examination and reflection on how academics consider the larger determinants of education, the purpose of education in the South African context, how we perceive our students, and how we teach and learn with them as collective agents of change.

Humanizing pedagogy demands from both the teacher-educator and student-teacher a commitment and dedication to contemplate larger meta and meso-theoretical frameworks, such as the political economy, political sociology, and eco-pedagogy, rather than a narrow focus on technocratic rationality. Therefore, pedagogy should translate into the re-thinking of TE—a process integral to building a new vision of democratic schooling and the development of critical citizenship. This requires the adoption of a critical approach to curriculum implementation (Sathorar, 2018) that encourages the development of self-empowerment and self-identity of students as active, responsible, and moral citizens of a community. To be sure, this approach to TP should involve teachers and students in a process of ongoing critical analysis in order for them to act collectively to change oppressive systems and structures in society, adopt methodologies that are participatory, and provide students with critical self-knowledge that allows them to "read the world" and to incorporate a greater variety of educational techniques into TP.

Challenging the dominant discourse

Critical pedagogical practices—"people's education for people's power"— in the South African context have their own historical roots born out of struggle during the apartheid era (Motala & Vally, 2002, p. 179). While critical pedagogics is practiced in South Africa, it hasn't gained the necessary traction as the desired philosophical, methodological, and ethical orientation in education. South Africa has been trapped in more than two decades of neoliberal development which undermines emancipatory education by harnessing education to the dictates of formal labor markets and by embracing human capital approaches into education. Neoliberalism further reinforces the university as the "ivory tower," thus making less relevant the addressing of pressing socioeconomic issues. Freire reminds us that "a university that is beyond and above the social and political system of the society where it exists is unfeasible" (Escobar, Fernandez, Guevara-Niebla & Freire, 1994, p. 136).

A number of scholars in South Africa have argued for new conceptions of the university as sites of advancing critical citizenship and the adoption of critical engaged forms of scholarship (Badat, 2007; Motala & Baatjes, 2013). Swartz (2006) suggests a conception of universities as institutions that are more firmly and deeply embedded within society and that universities *inter alia*, need to respond to societal demands; effectively engage within their immediate habitat; and reconfigure their curricula, research, internal organization, and ways of processing "the intermediations of knowledge and the social" (p. 141).

Fundamental to this conceptual argument is the need for universities to recognize how they are implicated in crises of the poor and working class and that "universities [do] not stand 'outside' of the social and, reflect the characteristics of their environment" (Swartz, p. 140). We argue that universities are indeed integral *parts* of the local, social, political, cultural, and economic life of the communities in which it is located. When critical engaged scholarship is responsive to pressing social issues such as the crisis in education, the possibilities for a genuinely democratic and caring society are enhanced.

Critical pedagogues involved in TE have an important role to play in advancing critically engaged scholarship in literacy education. There are three key aspects to highlight. First, central to our vocation is Freire's concept of conscientization which has been the theme of much scholarly work (Darder, 2017; Roberts, 2013). For Freire, conscientization is a requirement of our human condition and has ontological, epistemological, ethical, and educational dimensions.

The dialectical relationship between "reading the word" and "reading the world" and its relationship to conscientization are a nonlinear and ever-changing and continuous process of cognition, reflection, and actions. This takes place through critical dialogical education with teachers fostering a better understanding of the "self" in relation to "others" and "society," enhancing a deeper awareness of ourselves and the world as "unfinished." In a society of incessant change, conscientization demands of us to remain restless, probing and inquiring, open-minded, curious, and to know that there is always more to learn.

A second important role for critical pedagogues is the challenge to resist techno-bureaucratic techniques and the ideological demands of the cult of efficiency (Collins, 1991; Giroux, 2009). Collins (1991) offers a stern warning to educators about the "technicist obsession" in pedagogical practice which reduces learning to "situations managed by technical formulations, such as standardized pre-packaged curricula and preconceived needs assessment instruments" put together by experts (p. 5). Collins further warns that such deficit practices—the technical planning by competency-strategists and packaging of instruction based on simplistic behavioral objectives—get in the way of individual learners' ability to think critically, and to evaluate everyday experiences on their own account.

All of the latter aforementioned serve to usurp "independent, reflective thought on the part of the individual learner" and to "subvert critical powers of insight and imagination" (Giroux, 2013, p. 5). One of the main problems with the technicist approach is its portrayal of teaching as a value-free, objective activity whose problems are solvable through the application of the rigorous procedures of scientific methods. Thus, choices of method, curriculum, language of instruction, and the timing and the location of classes might appear on the surface to be purely technical, but are in fact profoundly influenced by the political and economic context in which they take place (Youngman, 1990).

Third, Giroux (2013) draws attention to the connection between technocratic rationality and the deskilling of teachers that accompanies the adoption of management-type pedagogies. This management-type paradigm, he argues, seeks to "improve" education by "teacher-proofing" it. Teachers are then relegated to semi-skilled, low-paid workers in the massification of education (Giroux, 2009, p. 442). Giroux (2013) additionally argues that neoconservatives "wants public schools and colleges to focus on 'practical' methods in order to prepare teachers for an 'outcome-based' education system, which is code for pedagogical methods that are as anti-intellectual as they are politically conservative" (p. 5). Reed and Anthony (1992) contribute to this point by indicating that "all too often, the educational community has retreated into a narrow vocationalism which crowds out any sustained concern with the social, moral, political and ideological ingredients of education work" (p. 601).

Pedagogy is therefore reduced to teaching of methods and data-driven performance indicators that allegedly measure scholastic ability and improve student achievement. The deskilling of teachers and the emphasis placed on instrumental rationality pose a serious threat to education as democratizing force, the advancement of critical and analytical thinking, and the development of critical inquiry and engaged citizenship.

The university as an institution occupies an elite position within society and has the power to guide public opinion. In their status, therefore, universities have both a responsibility and an obligation to provide insight and guidance on matters that pertain to public life. Student-teachers are part of this elite, and make up the few in society that are privileged enough to access this level of education. They are society's role models, by both the virtue of their societal position and their influence on the youth within schooling communities. Accepting this, Alexander (2008) argues that it is within the university that student-teachers need to reclaim the meaning and purpose of education. It is within universities that students should learn how to mediate critically between democratic values and the demands of a capitalist society. Thus, universities need to politicize TE within the broader relations of power to raise awareness and inform actions to address how such relations perpetuate inequalities.

Transect walks

Three areas of importance are applied to TP and their relationship with the use of participatory techniques. First, the preparation of student-teachers in relation to the theory and practice of literacy education; secondly, the connection between literacy and "reading the word"; and finally, building networks of solidarity in advancing the struggle for emancipatory practices against the interconnected forms of oppression in society.

Students in foundation phase education are encouraged to engage with epistemological curiosity of Freire's construct of "reading the word and the world." Returning to this Freirean construct has significance in a context of neoliberalism, the ever-increasing vocationalism of the curriculum, an obsession with technocratic rationality and the cult of efficiency, and an embrace of technical and mechanical approaches to the teaching and learning of literacy.

Freire (2001) insists that we resist neoliberal inevitability and argues that "teacher preparation should never be reduced to a form of training. Rather, teacher preparation should go beyond the technical preparation of teachers and be rooted in the ethical formation both of selves and of history" (p. 23). He further stressed the important relationship between literacy and politics and argues that (critical) literacy involves critical perception, interpretation, and reflection. Freire's critical literacy is committed to a vocation of all human beings to become humanized (Roberts, 2013).

The second key theme is the development of "reading the world" which is dialectically related to "reading the word." Freire suggests that student-teachers should be encouraged to develop a critical analysis of their historical and contemporary experiences. Freire's emphasis in "reading the world" involves stimulating critical learning approaches that foster students' interest, curiosity, and appreciation of the contextual antecedent causes of their personal circumstances in the world as well as those of others.

Freirean pedagogy encourages an exploration of the broader context in which schooling takes place together with an investigation of the immediate environment in which education of students is provided. For many student-teachers who are placed within schools in working-class communities in South Africa, a critical examination of the historical and socioeconomic or cultural context becomes an important discussion and how they relate to the political economy of education and society.

The third important theme is the need to link TP to action to transform their contexts. "Reading the word and the world" combines textual and contextual knowledge that creates the potential for student-teachers to develop a "disposition to question a constructed reality and subsequently promote a democratic world through praxis" (Dale & Hyslop-Margison, 2010, p. 99).

In Freire's view, the critical consciousness that develops through "reading the word and the world" exposes unjust political and social structures that can be changed. It is therefore important for critical pedagogy to use educated "hope as an ontological requirement" (Freire, 1997, p. 44) to change the world through praxis. As part of their praxis, critical pedagogues should explore a variety of alternatives in relationship with scholars, activists, and social movements engaged in community struggles for social justice.

Community mapping, as an alternative educative tool, is a participatory approach that provides effective ways of collectively eliciting and examining peoples' experiences toward producing new knowledge and understandings. It further presents dialogical participant engagement in generating empirical material about the contextual realities and lived experiences within a defined location.

Community mapping through transect walks assists students in the collective organizing, refining, and summarizing of spatial information. This collective experience positions students as "co-constructors" of knowledge in dialogical relationship with others in a community of practice. Transect walks provide students with analytical tools that enable critical insight about the context of schooling, the development of teaching practices applied in diverse settings, and building solidarity in struggles to transform public schooling.

Experiences drawn on transect walks performed in three sites[3] demonstrate the contribution of transect walks as tools for building critical consciousness as part of TP. The Roots Driven Rural Development Programme in the Bojanala Region of the North West Province unlocked assets in communities and identified opportunities that could lead to sustainable social and economic projects (Nicolau & Delport, 2015). Winterveldt was one of the nine sites included in a national study to determine the livelihood strategies of youth with disabilities in South Africa (Lorenzo & Motau, 2014).

In the case of the Community Education Programme, community educators identified and gained critical insights into the socioeconomic issues prevalent in communities of the Nelson Mandela municipality in Port Elizabeth, Eastern

---

[3]   The experiments include the Roots Driven Rural Development Project; the Winterveldt Project and the Community Education Programme.

Cape (CIPSET, 2018). The co-constructed knowledge was then translated into popular texts for use in a community education program.

The findings from these case studies highlight a number of benefits to the participants, including the value of co-construction of knowledge, the production of radically different worldviews resultant from critical reflections, the conscious formulation of new ways of defining one's world, and the production of meaningful curricula and pedagogical techniques applicable to context. All three projects show that communities construct and possess knowledge that has transformative possibilities.

These case studies suggest that exposure to engage the context within which schools are located create opportunities for student-teachers to think more deeply about their practice; for instance, to problematize and reflect on social justice issues, to develop a critique of policy in education, and to learn to act in solidarity with others to bring about change. It is also through transect walks that student-teachers are encouraged to analyze the many contradictions in the curriculum and pedagogical practices of schooling.

Conclusion

This chapter argues for rethinking teacher preparation of foundation phase educators based on Freire's critical literacy of reading the word and the world. This, we believe, is fundamental for critical pedagogues committed to the struggle to reclaiming public education for critical citizenship in the South African context. Based on Freire's theory of consciousness, we argue for greater use and exploration of participatory approaches such as transect walks in TP. We believe that transect walks offer student-teachers a variety of benefits essential to building transformative practices in education. Embedding transect walks in the curricula for TE could further nurture critically engaged forms of scholarship among student-teachers and the production of knowledge that address more directly pertinent issues in public schooling. Finally, we believe that the use of participatory approaches could contribute to the development of solidarity and praxis that confront the oppressive forces that reproduce marginalization and exclusion in our society.

References

Alexander, R. (2008). Pedagogy, culture and curriculum. In K. Hall, P. Murphy, & J. Soler (Eds.), *Pedagogy and practice: Culture and identities* (pp. 3–27). London: Sage.

Badat, S. (2007). Higher education transformation in South Africa post-1994: Towards a critical assessment. Solomon Mahlangu Education Lecture, June 12, 2007, Constitution Hill.

CIPSET. (2018). *Curriculum for below*. Port Elizabeth: CIPSET, Nelson Mandela University.

Collins, M. (1991). *Adult education as vocation*. London: Routledge.

Cullen, R., & Hill, R. (2013). Curriculum designed for an equitable pedagogy. *Education Science*, 3(1), 17–29.

Dale, J., & Hyslop-Margison, E. (2010). *Paulo Freire: Teaching for freedom and transformation: The philosophical influences of the work of Paulo Freire*. London: Springer.

Darder, A. (2017). *The student guide to Freire's pedagogy of the oppressed*. London: Bloomsbury.

Department of Higher Education and Training (DHET). (2011). *Minimum requirements for teacher education qualifications*, Vol. 553, No. 34467. Pretoria: Government Gazette Printers.

Escobar, M., Fernandez, A., & Guevara-Niebla, G., with Freire, P. (1994). *Paulo Freire on higher education: A dialogue at the National University of Mexico*. Albany: SUNY.

Freire, P. (1997). *Pedagogy of the heart*. New York: Continuum.

Freire, P. (2001). *Pedagogy of freedom: Ethics, democracy and civic courage*. London: Rowman & Littlefield Publishers.

Freire, P., & Macedo, D. (1987). *Literacy: Reading the word and the world*. Westport, CT: Bergin & Garvey.

Geduld, D., & Sathorar, H. (2016). Leading curriculum change: Reflections on how Abakhwezeli stoked the fire. *South African Journal of Education*, 36(4), 1–13.

Giroux, H. (2013). Teachers as transformative intellectuals. In A. S. Canestrari & B. A. Marlow (Eds.), *Educational foundations: An anthology of critical readings* (pp. 189–197). Los Angeles: Sage.

Giroux, H. A. (2009). Teacher education and democratic schooling. In A. Darder, M. P. Baltodano, & R. D. Torres (Eds.), *The critical pedagogy reader* (pp. 438–459). New York: Routledge Taylor and Francis Group.

Lorenzo, T., & Motau, J. (2014). A transect walk to establish opportunities and challenges for youth with disabilities in Winterveldt, South Africa. *South African Medical Journal, 25*(3), 45–63.

Mncube, V. S., & Madikizela-Madiya, N. (2013). South Africa: Educational reform—curriculum, governance and teacher education. In C. Harber (Ed.), *Education in Southern Africa* (p. 165). London: Bloomsbury.

Morrow, W. E. (2007). *Learning to teach in South Africa.* Pretoria: HSRC.

Motala, E., & Baatjes, I. (2013). *A note on socially engaged scholarship.* Port Elizabeth: CIPSET, NMMU.

Motala, S., & Vally, S. (2002). From people's power to Tirisano. In P. Kallaway (Ed.), *The history of education under Apartheid (1948–1994)* (pp. 174–194). Cape Town: Pearson South Africa.

Nicolau, M., & Delport, C. (2015) Community Asset Mapping Progamme for roots-driven sustainable socio-economic change in rural South Africa. *International Journal of Social Sustainability in Economic, Social, Cultural Context, 10*(1), 1–12.

Reed, M., & Anthony, P. (1992). *Professionalizing leadership. Debating, education, certification and practice.* London: Palgrave Macmillan.

Roberts, P. (2013). *Paulo Freire in the 21st century.* Boulder, CO: Paradigm.

Sathorar, H. (2018). Exploring lecturer preparedness on applying a critical approach to curriculum implementation: A case study. Thesis. Nelson Mandela University.

Swartz, D. (2006). New pathways to sustainability: African universities in a globalizing world. In M. Nkomo, D. Swartz, & B. Maja (Eds.), *Within the realm of possibility: From disadvantaged to development at the University of Fort Hare and the University of the North* (pp. 127–166). Pretoria: HSRC.

Youngman, F. (1990). The political economy of literacy in the third world. *Convergence, Toronto, 23*(4), 5–13.

2

W. E. B. DuBois and Paulo Freire: Toward a "Pedagogy of the Veil" to Counter Racism in Early Childhood Education

Meir Muller and Nathaniel Bryan

Many critical scholars contend that racialization and racism are endemic to US society in general and education in particular (Dixson, Rousseau Anderson, & Donner, 2017; King & Swartz, 2016). Given the permanence of these social constructions in education and society writ large, early childhood education (ECE) is not immune (Baines, Tisdale, & Long, 2018; Milner, 2015; Muller & Boutte, 2019). Clearly, issues of race permeate early childhood (EC) pedagogies, curricula, and schooling practices.

Racism frequently persists in schools because often preservice teachers, 85 percent White middle class, are not well prepared to work against it (Wynter-Hoyte, Muller, Bryan, Boutte, & Long, 2019), lack critical consciousness, and a habit of mind to see how racism permeates schools and society (Boutte, 2016; King, 1991). Racism is perpetuated as new teachers join colleagues not focused on equity in curriculum and instruction (Asante, 2017; Sleeter 2016), and not taught to interrupt racist trends and therefore pass racist ideologies to children in EC classrooms.

Lortie (1975/2002) posited that PreK-12 children are apprentices of observation—observing, internalizing, and enacting the pedagogical practices of their teachers. However, Lortie undertheorized racial discrimination that can creep into teaching. Therefore, we need to interrupt such apprenticeship of observation to grow a new population who develops critical consciousness and appreciates the mosaic of racialized and other differences among us.

Drawing on Du Bois's *double consciousness* and Freire's *conscientization,* we introduce *pedagogy of the veil* as a pedagogical framework to support EC educators in deepening the critical awareness of young learners and in facilitating teachers' self-reflection and pedagogical, curricular, and schooling practices to address racial inequity in and beyond EC classrooms. This work is significant for several reasons. ECE is foundational to all educational experiences (Souto-Manning & Martell, 2016) and can be a space where children early on develop critical consciousness to become critically conscious adults. Children learn to engage in racist acts at extremely young ages (Derman-Sparks & Edwards, 2010; Miller, 2015). They can also learn to become aware of and undo their own racial microaggressions early on.

Second, schools are becoming more diverse (Boutte, 2016). Thus, teachers need to "check themselves before they wreck themselves and our children" (Matias, 2013, p. 69) and prepare to address diversity issues with young learners. Teachers should engage in ongoing self-reflection and reflection of their pedagogies so that they can help young learners develop critical consciousness to be change agents in the world (Souto-Manning, 2013).

Third, in critical pedagogical work, we need to recenter the notion of critical consciousness, whose meaning, over time, has been diluted. It is important to note that Freire's *conscientization* considers critical consciousness as a state of being that develops over time. Du Bois and later critical race educators not only agree with this stance but also operationalize critical consciousness as a tool for learners to use to question texts, pedagogies, and curricula in order to unveil bias, oppression, or marginalization. Ladson-Billings's culturally relevant pedagogy (CRP) and other theories stress using a critical consciousness lens but this does not often occur in practice (Ladson-Billings, 2017). Such omission occurs from teachers' consciousness gap (Carter, 2008). If teachers have consciousness gaps, can we expect them to deepen young children's critical consciousness?

Similar challenges persist in ECE where underutilizing critical consciousness is the norm, thus maintaining the status quo of children who are not taught to use a critical consciousness lens and therefore ignore the negative impact of race and racism. Hence, we find utility in Du Bois's double consciousness and Freire's notion of conscientization to explicate the teaching of critical consciousness and to develop critically conscious learners in EC classrooms who become what Love (2016) calls co-conspirators in the dismantling of race, racism, and White supremacy. For teachers and young learners, the pedagogy of the veil can unveil racialized realities in and beyond EC classrooms.

We begin by sharing our positionalities. The first author, Meir, is Jewish; the second author, Nathaniel, self-identifies as Black. The collective struggle for justice has created a unique relationship between the Black and Jewish communities (Dollinger, 2018). We then address how race and racism are standardized in teacher preparation and ECE. Subsequently, we introduce Du Bois's double consciousness and Freire's notion of conscientization. We argue their utility to introduce the pedagogy of the veil, a pedagogical framework preservice and inservice teachers, can infuse into their self-reflection, pedagogical, curricular, and schooling practices to deepen the critical consciousness of children in EC classrooms. Finally, we provide recommendations for EC teachers to better support children to grow into critically conscious beings who work to dismantle race, racism, and White supremacy in their everyday lives.

Autobiographical recognition

Milner (2009) recommended that critical scholars position themselves to consider how their social position may inform their critical work. Thus, as early childhood scholars, we keep who we are at the center of our research and decisions regarding why we address ECE from critical perspectives.

Meir is a Jewish American assistant professor who focuses on equity in race, ethnicity, and religion. His education in public schools and predominantly White private schools kept him oblivious to issues of race. Even post university, he was still grounded in the epistemology of ignorance (Mills, 2017)—oblivious to how racism and White supremacy informed his life and the lives of people of Color. Inspired by colleagues such as Nathaniel, he uses teaching methods that uncover educational inequities and shares strategies with students to dismantle issues of racism.

Nathaniel is a Black male assistant professor at a predominantly White institution (PWI). Previously, he worked at a southern PWI where Meir and he taught. He is a critical race scholar and is intentional about addressing issues of race, racism, and White supremacy in his teaching, research, and service. Colleagues including Meir have deepened his understanding of the global nature and standardization of race, racism, anti-Blackness, and anti-Semitism in and beyond schools.

The standardization of racism in teacher preparation and early childhood education

Preservice teachers enter inservice teaching unprepared or underprepared to address race and racism because schooling in the United States has a history galvanized by racialization and racism (Kohli, Pizarro, & Nevarez, 2017). Eurocentric practices drive curricular and pedagogical practices emphasizing developmentally appropriate practices (DAP) which are often unresponsive to the needs of students of Color (Boutte, 2016), who need pedagogies relevant to their academic, cultural, and sociopolitical needs.

Racism becomes standardized in EC classrooms replete with instructional practices and curricular resources that promulgate that everything great, good, efficient, fair, and honorable is white; everything mean, bad, blundering, and dishonorable is "yellow"; bad taste is "brown"; and the devil is "black" (Du Bois, 1920, p. 22). Consequently, children of Color find their lived experiences, cultural identity, and history ignored or mistreated (Bryan, 2017; Emdin, 2016), an erasure of children's culture referred to as "spirit murdering," which Love (2016) describes as slow death built on racism. Slow death is enacted not only through a Eurocentric school curriculum but also through disciplinary practices.

Children of Color are consistently over-referred to special education (Codrington & Fairchild, 2013), under-referred to gifted programs (Ford, 2013), and inequitably disciplined (US Department of Education Office of Civil Rights, 2014)—all components of the preschool-to-prison pipeline (Bryan, 2017). Unfortunately, EC teachers are enculturated to consider these practices as acceptable instead of being encouraged to use a critical consciousness lens to challenge systemic injustices. Therefore, we contend that conjoining Du Bois's notion of double consciousness and Freire's conception of conscientization can foster teachers' critical consciousness to teach young children who become co-conspirators to dismantle race, racism, and White supremacy.

The foundation of the pedagogy of the veil

Here, we discuss Du Bois's notion of double consciousness and Freire's conscientization to establish a foundation for the pedagogy of the veil. Readers may visit the following works to deepen their understanding of double consciousness (*The Souls of Black Folk*) and conscientization (*Pedagogy of the Oppressed*).

Du Bois's double consciousness

Du Bois's (1903) first experience with the slow death and erasure of self occurred in school. As a child, he presented a visiting card to a White girl in his class who "peremptorily" rejected this gift. At that moment it dawned upon him "with a certain suddenness that [he] was different from the others ... [and] shut out from their world by a vast veil" (p. 2), a metaphor of the obstruction created by the racial divide. Within the concept of the veil, Du Bois introduced one of his most famous ideas—double consciousness, which describes an individual whose identity is fractured by society. Du Bois (1903) wrote:

> It is a peculiar sensation, this double-consciousness, this sense of always looking at one's self through the eyes of others, of measuring one's soul by the tape of a world that looks on in amused contempt and pity. One ever feels his twoness, an American, a Negro; two souls, two thoughts, two unreconciled strivings; two warring ideals in one dark body, whose dogged strength alone keeps it from being torn asunder. (p. 2)

The concept of the veil can also be applied on a societal or institutional level. Winant (2004) wrote that the veil "signifies a profound social structure that has been built up for centuries, accumulating among the infinite contradictions of race and racism as they have shaped our identities and social organization" (p. 5). This veil has become part and parcel of our institutions, including those of learning. Just as the veil became evident to Du Bois in a school setting, many children of Color experience the veil as their teachers make them invisible through curriculum, pedagogy, and school practices.

Freire's conscientization

Paulo Freire (2014) introduced conscientization or critical consciousness, which is essentially the practice that enables "action and reflection of men and women upon their world in order to transform it" (p. 56). Burch (2016) described conscientization as "the process of learning to read powers and relation in society and in learning to grasp how our own subjectivities are in large part products of these selfsame relations" (p. 41). Du Bois's notion of double consciousness "as a transcendent position allowing one to see and understand positions of inclusion and exclusion—margins and mainstreams" (Ladson-Billings, 2000, p. 403) intersects with critical consciousness. Thus, the pedagogy of the veil is definitively informed by Freirean "action and reflection" in changing the understanding of the oppressor and oppressed.

Toward a pedagogy of the veil

Drawing on Du Bois and Freire, we propose the pedagogy of the veil as a pedagogical (and curricular) framework to facilitate EC teachers' self-reflection and to teach children how to combat racism. As shown in Figure 1, we contend that double consciousness and conscientization (center of the framework) can serve as foundation for every aspect of EC classrooms by driving teachers' ongoing self-reflection and micro/macro-level pedagogical, curricular, and schooling practices.

Like many frameworks (see Ladson-Billings, 2011; Souto-Manning, 2013), the pedagogy of the veil helps teachers examine their own White privileges, stereotypes, and ways they are anti-Black, anti-Brown, anti-Semitic, and

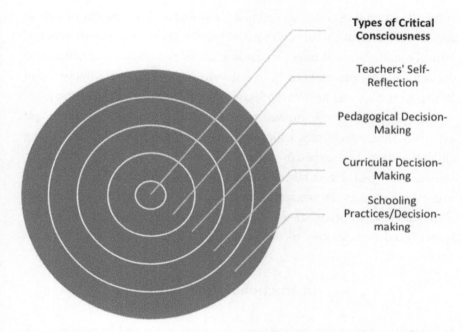

Figure 1 Conceptual framework for a pedagogy of the veil

other forms of "anti-" + marginalized populations. The pedagogy of the veil helps teachers select appropriate pedagogical tools to deepen the critical consciousness of children. Given the overemphasis of DAP (Boutte, 2016), the pedagogy of the veil helps teachers select culturally relevant resources across the ECE curriculum, for example, moving from culturally unresponsive books such as Dr. Seuss's *Green Eggs and Ham* to culturally responsive books such as *Flossie and the Fox*, which celebrates African American Language.

Finally, the pedagogy of the veil requires teachers to examine practices that may contribute to inequities in EC classrooms, for example, the preschool-to-prison pipeline, which documents the number of children, particularly Black children, disproportionately suspended and expelled from schools (Wright & Ford, 2016). The pedagogy of the veil positions teachers to unveil the ways they may contribute to the preschool-to-prison pipeline and other inequitable practices.

The pedagogy of the veil is important because while most critical frameworks (i.e., culturally relevant pedagogy, critical race pedagogy, culturally sustaining pedagogy) emphasize students' development of critical consciousness through curricular activities, few frameworks apply types of critical consciousness as tools that guide teachers' pedagogical, curricular, and decision-making processes in EC classrooms to dismantle race, racism, and White supremacy and help young learners develop critical consciousness.

Du Bois indicated that the veil can only be lifted through education and activism. Thus, specifically, educators must educate themselves and young children—daily and explicitly addressing injustice, analyzing underlying causes, and engaging in activism alongside their students. Teachers successfully using this pedagogy discuss racism candidly, develop reciprocal relationships with students, embrace standing against discrimination, and work with students and communities to create change.

Instructional strategies

ECE teachers and students can enact a pedagogy of the veil by adeptly using a critical consciousness lens to recognize inequities in all aspects of EC classrooms and society. Teachers must be self-aware, read books on confronting racism, and constantly examine their pedagogical practices and curricular selections. Wooldridge (2001) suggested critical learners' questions for readers to connect the personal and political in power imbalances, which can be used by both teachers *and* students: "Whose voices are excluded?" and "Whose power, ideas, and values are reinforced?" (p. 261). These critical questions can be used to inspect texts, curricula materials, and school structure in order to examine inequities. Baines, Tisdale, and Long (2018), Boutte (2016), Muller (2018) provided examples of this type of teaching throughout curriculum domains and grade levels.

Conclusion

Freire (1973) described the educational system in industrialized countries as a means of social control. He warned:

Most frightening of all is the level of alienation in which we become robots without even knowing it, marching to unspoken orders and failing to challenge the reason why. We are dehumanized, unable to express our feelings or even our fears. (p. 18)

In that light, we hope that this chapter prompts educators to use and foster their students' critical consciousness to unveil the unspoken orders that cause our schools to be places of inequity.

References

Asante, M. K. (2017). *Revolutionary pedagogy: Primer for teachers of Black children.* New York: Universal Write Publications.

Baines, J., Tisdale, C., & Long, S. (2018). *"We've been doing it your way long enough": Choosing the culturally relevant classroom.* New York: Teachers College Press.

Boutte, G. (2016). *Educating African American students: And how are the children?* New York: Routledge.

Bryan, N. (2017). White teachers' role in sustaining the school-to-prison pipeline: Recommendations for teacher education. *The Urban Review, 49*(3), 326–345.

Burch, K. (2016). Platonic & Freirean interpretations of W. E. B. DuBois's, "Of the Coming of John." *Educational Studies, 52*(1), 38–50.

Carter, D. J. (2008). Cultivating a critical race consciousness for African American school success. *Educational Foundations, 22*(1/2), 11–28.

Codrington, J., & Fairchild, H. H. (2013). *Special education and the mis-education of African American children: A call to action.* Washington, DC: The Association of Black Psychologists.

Derman-Sparks, L., & Edwards, J. O. (2010). *Anti-bias education for young children and ourselves.* Portland, ME: Stenhouse.

Dixson, A. D., Rousseau Anderson, C., & Donnor, J. (2017). *Critical race theory in education: All God's children got a song.* New York: Routledge.

Dollinger, M. (2018). *Black power, Jewish politics: Reinventing the alliance in the 1960s.* Waltham, MA: Brandeis University Press.

DuBois, W. E. B. (1903). *The souls of black folk.* Chicago, IL: A. C. McClurg & Co.

DuBois, W. E. B. (1920). *Darkwater: Voices from within the veil.* New York: Harcourt, Brace and Company.

Emdin, C. (2016). *For White folks who teach in the hood .... and the rest of ya'll too: Reality pedagogy and urban education*. Boston, MA: Beacon Press.

Ford, D. (2013). *Recruiting and retaining culturally different students in gifted education*. Waco, TX: Prufock Press, Inc.

Freire, P. (1973). *Education for liberation*. Melbourne: Australian Council of Churches Commission on Christian Education.

Freire, P. (2014). *Pedagogy of the oppressed: 30th anniversary edition*. London: Bloomsbury Publishing.

King, J. E. (1991). Dysconscious racism: Ideology, identity, and the miseducation of teachers. *The Journal of Negro Education, 60*(2), 133–146.

King, J. E., & Swartz, E. E. (2016). *The Afrocentric praxis of teaching for freedom: Connecting culture to learning*. New York: Routledge.

Kohli, R., Pizarro, M., & Nevarez, A. (2017). The "New Racism" of K-12 Schools: Centering critical research on racism. *Review of Research in Education, 41*, 182–202.

Ladson-Billings, G. (2000). Racialized discourses and ethnic epistemologies. In N. K. Denzin & Y. S. Lincoln (Eds.), *Handbook of qualitative research* (pp. 257–277). Thousand Oaks, CA: Sage.

Ladson-Billings, G. (2011). "Yes, but how do we do it?": Practicing culturally relevant pedagogy. In J. G. Landsman & C. W. Lewis (Eds.), *White teachers/diverse classrooms: Creating inclusive schools, building on students' diversity, and providing true educational equity* (2nd ed., pp. 33–46). Sterling, VA: Stylus Publishing.

Ladson-Billings, G. (2017). The (R)evolution will not be standardized: Teacher education, hip hop pedagogy, and culturally relevant pedagogy 2.0. In D. Paris & S. Alim (Eds.), *Culturally sustaining pedagogies: Teaching and learning for justice in a changing world* (pp. 141–156). New York: Teachers College Press.

Lortie, D. (1975/2002). *Schoolteacher: A sociological study*. Chicago, IL: University of Chicago Press.

Love, B. (2016). Anti-Black state violence, classroom edition: The spirit murdering of Black children. *Journal of Curriculum and Pedagogy, 13*(1), 22–25.

Matias, C. E. (2013). Check yo'self before yo' wreck yo'self and our kids: From culturally responsive white teachers? To culturally responsive white teachers! *Interdisciplinary Journal of Teaching and Learning, 3*(2), 68–81.

Miller, E. (2015). Race as the Benu: A reborn consciousness for teachers of our youngest children. *Journal of Curriculum Theorizing, 30*(30), 28–44.

Milner, H. R. (2009). *Diversity and education: Teachers, teaching, and teacher education*. Springfield, IL: Charles C. Thomas, Pub.

Milner, H. R. (2015). *Rac(e)ing to class: Confronting poverty and race in schools and classrooms.* Cambridge, MA: Harvard Education Press.

Mills, C. W. (2017). *Black rights/White wrongs.* New York: Oxford University Press.

Muller, M. (2018). Justice pedagogy: Elementary students challenge racist statues. *Social Studies and the Young Learner, 31*(2), 17–23.

Muller, M., & Boutte, G. (2019). A framework for helping teachers interrupt oppression in their classrooms. *Journal for Multicultural Education, 13*(1), 3.

Sleeter, C. (2016). Critical race theory and the whiteness of teacher education. *Urban Education, 52*(2), 155–169.

Souto-Manning, M. (2013). *Multicultural teaching in the early childhood classroom: Strategies, tools, and approaches, Preschool-2nd grade.* Washington, DC: Association for Childhood Education International and New York: Teachers College Press.

Souto-Manning, M., & Martell, J. (2016). *Reading, writing, and talk: Inclusive teaching strategies for diverse learners, K-2.* New York: Teachers College Press.

US Department of Education Office for Civil Rights. (2014). Dear Colleague Letter: Preventing Racial Discrimination in Special Education. Retrieved from https://www2.ed.gov/policy/gen/guid/school-discipline/index.html.

Winant, H. (2004). *The new politics of race: Globalism, difference, justice.* Minneapolis: University of Minnesota Press.

Wooldridge, N. (2001). Tensions and ambiguities in critical literacy. In B. Comber & A. Simpson (Eds.), *Negotiating critical literacies in classrooms* (pp. 259–270). Mahwah, NJ: Lawrence Erlbaum Associates.

Wright, B., & Ford, D. (2016). "This Little Light of Mine": Creating early childhood education classroom experiences for African American boys preK-3. *Journal of African America Males in Education, 7*(1), 5–19.

Wynter-Hoyte, K., Muller, M., Bryan, N., Boutte, G., & Long, S. (2019). Dismantling Eurocratic practices in teacher education: A pre-service program focused on culturally relevant, humanizing, and decolonizing pedagogies. In T. Hodges & A. Baum (Eds.), *A handbook of research on field-based teacher education* (pp. 300–320). Pennsylvania, PA: IGI Global.

3

The Community as a Teacher Educator: Preparing Critically Conscious Teacher Candidates in Detroit

Kaitlin Popielarz

Introduction

Paulo Freire's critical pedagogy may be engaged to center the life experiences of students and their communities to work toward purposeful learning opportunities. We must ask how future educators develop an understanding of critical pedagogy within the context of the local community in order to implement such a sustaining praxis into their own classrooms. In turn, teacher education programs may reimagine methods courses and field placements to model transformative critical pedagogy for education rooted in social justice. As such, this chapter will discuss the use of place-conscious and student-centered critical pedagogy within a social studies methods course for teacher candidates (TCs).

This chapter is significant because it will consider the possibilities and limitations of critical pedagogy within a community-based social studies methods course (Freire, 1974). I will discuss the importance of conscientização and praxis as fundamental components of community-based pedagogy within teacher education (Freire, 2000). I will share how community-based teacher education may be used to develop the critical consciousness of TCs by connecting a particular social studies methods course to the communities of their students. Finally, I will consider the nuanced community-engaged learning experiences of two specific TCs in order to suggest implications for teacher education programs.

Critical pedagogy

Freire's (2000) critical pedagogy encourages educators to utilize the ongoing process of *praxis*—reflection, dialogue, and action—within learning communities as a method for social justice. Within the classroom, critical pedagogy centers the life experiences of students and their communities in order to work toward purposeful learning opportunities (Freire, 1974). Critical pedagogy is dynamic and it responds to the strengths and/or needs of students within a particular place and time. As such, critical pedagogy may embolden educators to connect the curriculum to the very identity of students in order to foster empowering learning environments (Freire, 1992).

Freire's critical pedagogy is rooted in *conscientização*, or the praxis of social awareness and critical consciousness, which sees the classroom and local community as sites to either resist or reproduce systems of oppression through education. Conscientização—which "refers to learning to perceive social, political, and economic contradictions, and to take action against the oppressive elements of reality" (Freire, 2000, p. 35)—reminds us that education is never neutral and it holds the power to either suppress or liberate teachers, learners, and communities.

As a teacher educator, I ground the blossoming critical consciousness of TCs within the lived reality of the students they will teach (Freire, 1974). Through community-engaged learning experiences, I develop what Gruenewald (2003) calls a "critical pedagogy of place" in order to encourage TCs becoming active members of schools and communities. TCs begin to develop a sense of belonging and accountability through community-based learning opportunities (Gruenewald, 2003), which nurtures the transformative process of conscientização. In turn, TCs are encouraged to foster a justice-oriented social studies teaching praxis that is centered upon the everyday lives of their students and communities.

Community-based teacher education

Many teacher education programs are implementing community-based practices that provide TCs the opportunity to learn from and with the local community (Guillen & Zeichner, 2018). Through collaborative partnerships with community organizations and citizens, TCs gain a perspective otherwise limited within traditional teacher education courses (Lowenstein et al., 2018). This transformative practice encourages TCs to see both learners and the local community as assets, which fosters inclusive and affirming learning environments (Seidl & Friend, 2002). Thus, teacher education programs become a tool to dismantle and transform an education system that often perpetuates oppressive and exclusionary practices.

Community-based teacher education challenges traditional academic hierarchies of knowledge in order to include and place value upon the local community. Such a practice centers the holistic identity of young people, which supports TCs in their understanding of culturally relevant (Ladson-Billings, 2017) and culturally sustaining pedagogies (Paris, 2012). By amplifying the community cultural wealth of students, TCs begin to understand critical pedagogy as student-centered and place-conscious (Yosso, 2005). Thus, TCs develop the capacity to be critically conscious educators whose pedagogy is grounded in the people, places, and environment of their students (Zygmunt et al., 2018).

Critiques of community-based teacher education have encouraged reciprocal partnerships between local community organizations and universities (Lowenstein & Erkaeva, 2016). Intentional relationships between community members and educators are vital in order to foster place-conscious and justice-oriented learning environments (Wade, 2000). In turn, the dynamic knowledge, cultural heritage, and inherent strengths of students and their communities will be (re)centered in the classroom (Tuck, McKenzie, & McCoy, 2014). Within my own praxis, I am transparent about the critiques of community-based pedagogy with TCs in order to model purposeful strategies for collaborative community-engaged learning experiences.

Description of the course

I am an instructor for a particular social studies methods course in my college of education (COE). My access to this course provides an opportunity to analyze the development and implementation of community-based teacher education through a critical pedagogical lens. By connecting the social studies methods course to the local community in order to experience community-based pedagogies, TCs have the opportunity to meet graduation and certification requirements through meaningful and relevant practices. The foundation of the syllabus for this course has been designed through collaborative planning with colleagues in my COE.

The course encourages TCs to see the possibilities of how the community can be an equal teacher and partner in the cultivation of place-conscious learning experiences. This is particularly important in Southeast Michigan where an overwhelming majority of the teaching force is white, while schools in Detroit and some in the surrounding suburbs are composed of predominantly African American, Latinx, and Arab American students (Stackhouse, 2018). Given this context, sharing in community-based pedagogy with TCs becomes an opportunity for them to enter a space in which they may begin to see the importance of intimately knowing their students and the communities in which they teach.

During the course, TCs learn more about the students within their classrooms through community-engaged learning experiences (Hallman, 2012). The community-engaged learning experiences aim to bring TCs into the neighborhoods of their students, which connects to the culture, geography, history, anthropology, and sociology components of the social studies methods course. The structure of course assignments and collaborative inquiry within weekly seminar challenges TCs to grow in critical consciousness as they engage in learning through a critical pedagogical framework (Lee, 2018). Consistent steps are taken to name and discuss implicit/explicit bias and deficit mindsets in order to minimize the co-opting of community voices and experiences. TCs are encouraged to understand the importance of reciprocal partnerships between the classroom and local community.

Community-engaged learning experiences

During a recent semester of the social studies methods course, TCs engaged in two community-engaged learning experiences. As the instructor of the course,

I applied the relationships I have with community partners in the design of the course syllabus. Through this process, the work of the community partners inspired the development of assignments, readings, and learning experiences of the course. During the semester itself, all students in the course collaborated with community partners through site visits, which contributed to their understandings of community-based pedagogy and the process of consciousness-raising.

The first community-engaged learning experience was to the Black Bottom/Lafayette Park neighborhood of Detroit, which was once an epicenter for African American culture, community, and business before it was demolished by urban renewal projects (Black Bottom Street View, 2019). Following in-class preparation, TCs visited the Lafayette Park neighborhood of Detroit through a historical walking tour in order to uncover the history of Black Bottom. A multimedia project of Black Bottom primary sources through the Detroit Public Library was connected to the walking tour.

The community-engaged learning experience with Black Bottom/Lafayette Park was incorporated to the "Historical Perspectives and Inquiry" content of the course and analyzed the use of digital media to enhance learning experiences. Ahead of the visit to Black Bottom and Lafayette Park, TCs read select chapters from *Powerful Social Studies for Elementary Students* (Brophy et al., 2013) and *The Origins of the Urban Crisis: Race and Inequality in Postwar Detroit* (Sugrue, 2005). TCs viewed videos on Black Bottom and Lafayette Park before engaging in critical inquiry. Following the site visit, TCs reflected on the community-engaged learning experience in journal writings and collaborative dialogue.

The second community-engaged learning experience was to the Brightmoor Makerspace, which is a workshop that supports and encourages community sustaining projects developed by Detroit youth. This site visit allowed TCs to visualize cross-curricular learning experiences within the cultural and socioeconomic contexts of a Detroit neighborhood. The community-engaged learning experience with the Brightmoor Makerspace connected to the "Civics, Economics, Psychological, and Sociological Perspectives & Civics" content of the course. The Brightmoor Makerspace demonstrated the generative and meaningful relationship between classrooms and local communities for purposeful learning opportunities.

Before the visit to the Brightmoor Makerspace, TCs read select chapters from *Powerful Social Studies for Elementary Students* (Brophy et al., 2013) and practitioner-friendly articles on community-based social studies from the *Social Studies and the Young Learner* journal. TCs also viewed a video on the Brightmoor Makerspace and engaged in critical inquiry before the upcoming visit. Following the community-engaged learning experience to the Brightmoor Makerspace, TCs reflected through written journal responses and collaborative discussion.

In connection to the community-engaged learning experiences, TCs developed a place-conscious lesson plan for a semester-long course assignment. The assignment encouraged TCs to design a PK-8 social studies lesson plan that would incorporate the local community of Detroit. TCs were asked to visit and utilize a specific Detroit neighborhood or community site within their student-centered and community-based learning activity. TCs designed a social studies lesson plan that would encourage PK-8 students to make meaning of the subject matter through direct connections to the knowledge, cultural heritage, and assets of their own community. TCs reflected upon their interaction(s) within a Detroit neighborhood and/or community site in order to evidence how their own place-conscious learning experience impacted the intentional design of their lesson plan.

Through individual check-ins, peer-to-peer support, and direct connections to course experiences, TCs were able to use the lesson plan assignment as a tool to develop their student-centered and place-conscious social studies teaching practice. Assessment of the lesson plan assignment demonstrated that TCs were able to connect Michigan's PK-8 social studies standards to the socio-cultural capital of a local community for purposeful learning opportunities. Many of the reflections from the lesson plan assignment referenced the impact of the community-engaged learning experiences in TCs' understandings of community-based pedagogy in the social studies. Through the process of praxis, TCs engaged their emerging conscientização for meaningful and empowering learning opportunities in the social studies classroom.

For example, having experienced the impact of traditional and standardized social studies as a student, one particular TC expressed her desire to cultivate relevant learning opportunities by connecting the subject matter to the sociopolitical context of students' lives. This was evident in her lesson plan assignment in which she created an eighth-grade social studies lesson plan on the various perspectives of the 1967 Detroit Uprising. In her reflections, the TC shared the following:

> I saw the beginning stages of this exhibit for the 50-year anniversary of the Detroit Uprising in 1967, and I thought that it was so relevant to the protests and the events still happening in America. I chose this because it has multiple perspectives to examine as well as being able to connect these past events with current events.

Another TC demonstrated the importance of community-based pedagogy for place-conscious and student-centered social studies. Through the lesson plan assignment, this TC created a cross-curricular activity where her second-grade students engaged in project-based learning with peer mentors from the Brightmoor Makerspace. The TC explained the role of community in her reflection:

> We are surrounded by a community who literally creates solutions and has so much passion. That is the kind of teaching I want. When we talk about community I want to immerse my children into their own communities but also the community of Detroit and how it is changing because of the people around the city who believe in it.

Reflective dialogue with these two particular TCs indicated the impact of the community-engaged learning experiences to Black Bottom/Lafayette Park and the Brightmoor Makerspace. Both TCs conveyed they underwent a (re)learning of Detroit as the inherent assets of local neighborhoods were centered in the social studies methods course. By connecting the community-engaged learning experiences to their developing understandings of student-centered and place-conscious pedagogy, both TCs model the awakening that is necessary for a socially aware and critically conscious teaching practice.

Reflections

The community-engaged learning experiences of the social studies methods course have evolved with each passing semester, which speaks to my own critical and reflective teaching praxis. I have learned that TCs need tangible examples of community-based pedagogy in action within the PK-8 classroom. I now connect the social studies methods course to a middle school teacher in Detroit in order to provide TCs the opportunity to learn about community-based pedagogy from a classroom teacher and his students. In turn, TCs are able to witness, reflect upon, and discuss the possibilities and limitations of a community-based practice in the social studies classroom.

I now implement more opportunities for TCs to engage in critical reflection and dialogue throughout the social studies methods course. This is a vital component of fostering the critical consciousness of TCs within a community-based critical pedagogy. Course assignments and learning opportunities entail a variety of ongoing, multimodal reflective and dialogic opportunities that intimately support TCs in the development of conscientização. I also maintain open communication access with TCs after they have completed the social studies methods course, which supports the ongoing praxis of cultivating education for social justice.

I am currently developing more reciprocal and purposeful community partnerships for the social studies methods course. I now meet with community partners before, during, and after the design of the course syllabus in order to gain insight and feedback on their collaboration with the community-engaged learning experiences. This has encouraged community partnerships to be more sustainable and beneficial, which works to maintain consistent and genuine relationships through each passing semester. I am very transparent with TCs in the development of such community partnerships in order to demonstrate the flexibility and intention that are necessary for community-based pedagogies to flourish. In turn, TCs gain valuable insight as how to nurture community partnerships for their own classrooms.

Implications

The classroom experiences of the two TCs mentioned in this chapter provide implications for advancing community-based teacher education. Through the social studies methods course, the two TCs gained a great deal of understanding for community-based pedagogy in the context of the local community. However, it is challenging for TCs to implement student-centered and place-conscious practices within the realities of the classroom (Aronson, 2016). Teacher educators must be cognizant about the mentorship TCs need to enact critical pedagogies of place during field placements and in their own future classrooms.

To further our understanding of community-based teacher education, longitudinal research projects must share the outcomes of designing and implementing student-centered and place-conscious pedagogy in methods courses and field placements. Further research projects must aim to understand how TCs envision and apply a community-based pedagogy as they transition into the classroom. Such research projects would embolden the use of *conscientização* in teacher education programs for more loving futures. These contributions to the literature should not romanticize community-based pedagogy and instead further strengthen the role of teacher education programs in teaching and learning for social justice.

Conclusion

As we are now past the fifty-year mark of the original release of *Pedagogy of the Oppressed*, we must expand upon loving and courageous education for social justice. Freire's critical pedagogy centers the life experiences of students and their communities in order to foster meaningful learning opportunities. This chapter heightens Freire's critical pedagogy by discussing the use of community-based teacher education for cultivating the critical consciousness of future educators. In turn, TCs may engage in conscientização in order to reimagine student-centered and place-conscious classrooms. This will aim to transform the education system as the environmental, cultural, and socioeconomic contexts of the community are (re)centered in the classroom. In this way, we may collectively revitalize and sustain education as the practice of freedom.

References

Aronson, B. A. (2016). From teacher education to practicing teacher: What does culturally relevant praxis look like? *Urban Education*, 1–27. Retrieved from https://doi.org/10.1177/0042085916672288 (Visited February 2017).

Black Bottom Street View. (2019). "Black Bottom Street View: About." Retrieved from https://www.blackbottomstreetview.com (Visited January 2019).

Brophy, J., Alleman, J., & Halvorsen, A. (2013). *Powerful social studies for elementary students* (3rd ed.). Belmont, CA: Wadsworth.

Freire, P. (1974). *Education for critical consciousness.* New York: Bloomsbury Academic.

Freire, P. (1992). *Pedagogy of hope: Reliving pedagogy of the oppressed.* New York: Bloomsbury Academic.

Freire, P. (2000). *Pedagogy of the oppressed.* New York: Continuum.

Gruenewald, D. (Fall 2003). Foundations of place: A multidisciplinary framework for place-conscious education. *American Educational Research Journal, 40*(3), 619–654.

Gruenewald, D. (May 2003). The best of both worlds: A critical pedagogy of place. *Educational Researcher, 32*(4), 3–12.

Guillen, L., & Zeichner, K. (2018). A university-community partnership in teacher education from the perspectives of community-based teacher educators. *Journal of Teacher Education, 69*(2), 140–153.

Hallman, H. (2012). Community-based field experiences in teacher education: Possibilities for a pedagogical third space. *Teaching Education, 23*(3), 241–263.

Ladson-Billings, G. (2017). The (R)evolution will not be standardized: Teacher education, hip hop pedagogy, and culturally relevant pedagogy 2.0. In D. Paris & H. Samy Alim (Eds.), *Culturally sustaining pedagogies: Teaching and learning for justice in a changing world* (pp. 141–156). New York: Teachers College Record.

Lee, R. (2018). Breaking down barriers and building bridges: Transformative practices in community-and school-based urban teacher preparation. *Journal of Teacher Education, 69*(2), 118–126.

Lowenstein, E., & Erkaeva, N. (2016). Developing a language to support healthy partnerships in powerful place-based education: The experience of the Southeast Michigan Stewardship Coalition. In C. Bowers (Ed.), *Eco-Justice: Essays on theory and practice in 2016* (pp. 1–22). Eugene, OR: Eco-Justice Press.

Lowenstein, E., Grewal, I. K., Erkaeva, N., Nielsan, R., & Voelker, L. (2018). Place-based teacher education: A model whose time has come. *Issues in Teacher Education, 27*(2), 36–52.

Paris, D. (2012). Culturally sustaining pedagogy: A needed change in stance, terminology, and practice. *Educational Researcher, 41*(3), 93–97.

Seidl, B., & Friend, G. (2002). Leaving authority at the door: Equal-status community-based experiences and the preparation of teachers for diverse classrooms. *Teaching and Teacher Education, 18*(4), 421–433.

Stackhouse, S. (2018). Racial characteristics of the Michigan teacher workforce. *State of Michigan Department of Education*. Retrieved from https://www.michigan.gov/documents/mde/Racial_characteristics_of_the_Michigan_Teacher_Workforce_-_to_ADA_619243_7.pdf (Visited April 2018).

Sugrue, T. (2005). *The origins of the urban crisis: Race and inequality in postwar Detroit*. Princeton, NJ: Princeton University Press.

Tuck, E., McKenzie, M., & McCoy, K. (2014). Land education: Indigenous, post-colonial, and decolonizing perspectives on place and environmental education research. *Environmental Education Research, 20*(1), 1–23.

Wade, R. (2000). Service-learning for multicultural teaching competency: Insights from the literature for teacher educators. *Equity & Excellence in Education, 33*(3), 21–29.

Yosso, T. (2005). Whose culture has capital? A critical race theory discussion of community cultural wealth. *Race, Ethnicity and Education, 8*(1), 69–91.

Zygmunt, E. et al. (2018). Loving out loud: Community mentors, teacher candidates, and transformational learning through a pedagogy of care and connection. *Journal of Teacher Education, 69*(2), 127–139.

Part Two

Pedagogy and Practice

4

Making Meaning in the Carceral Space: Freirean Dialogue and Existential Becoming in the Jail or Prison Classroom

Gregory Bruno

Paulo Freire described dialogue as an "existential necessity" (1993, p. 69) and understood "mutual trust" and "hope" as integral to its purpose. Dialogue, which is "the encounter between men [and women] mediated by the world" (Freire, 1993, p. 69), is a critical vehicle to help students create meaningful relationships between texts, the world, and the various elements of their dialogical selves (Hermans & Hermans-Konopka, 2010). Yet, nurturing substantive discussions and creating an environment built on trust and hope can be challenging in any classroom setting and near impossible in a jail or prison setting.

This chapter, therefore, aims to explore how, by promoting an environment of "hope," "love," and "mutual trust" (Freire, 1993), instructors tasked with teaching in the context of prisons work to create a "dialogical space." In such spaces, "existing [identity] positions are further developed and new and commonly constructed [identity] positions have a chance to emerge" (Hermans & Hermans-Konopka, 2010, p. 6). These dialogical spaces create an opportunity for students in jails and prisons to experiment in processes of "ideological becoming" (Fecho & Clifton, 2017), which Bakhtin (1981a) described as "an intense struggle within us among various verbal and ideological points of view, approaches, directions, and values" (p. 342). As students in jails and prisons work toward the process of ideological becoming, they may embrace Freire's vision of "the dialogic man" as they work to derive meaning from both the world within themselves and the world around them.

A brief history of higher education in prisons

The first course taught in an American correctional facility was an "instruction in morals and religion through Bible reading" at the Walnut Street Jail in Philadelphia in 1790 (Lagemann, 2017). This trend of teaching morals and religion to the prison population became the norm and quickly spread across the country. In 1965, however, when President Lyndon B. Johnson signed the Higher Education Act into law, individuals incarcerated in state and federal correctional facilities became eligible for Pell Grant awards for higher education. Within the next few years, programs offering college in jails and prisons spread across the country, and by the early 1990s, funded by the Pell Grant program, nearly every jail and prison in the United States was offering some form of higher educational coursework (Agrawal, 2018).

Yet, when President Bill Clinton signed the Violent Crime Control and Law Enforcement Act in 1994, federal aid awards for students in jails and prisons were quickly withdrawn, thrusting prison education programs into hotly contested political issue, with arguments often anchored to the perception of the fundamental humanity, or lack thereof, of students in jails and prisons (Agrawal, 2018). To be sure, small and local initiatives have sought to restore funding for these programs, but when New York State Governor Andrew Cuomo proposed funding four-year degrees for students in jails and prisons, state conservatives strongly resisted. Consider the position of New York State Senator Greg Ball who launched an online petition titled, "Hell No to Attica University," arguing "in a world of finite resources, where we are struggling to find funding for education for our kids, the last thing New York State should be funding is college tuition for convicts" (Lennon, 2015, p. 9).

Ball's retort is a coded argument that "convicts" are not "our kids" and are thus unworthy of the same funding opportunities as what he later called "our hardworking New Yorkers" (Lennon, 2015, p. 9), but this ideological debate is inseparable from the prison-classroom, and the frank reality is that college classes are not always welcome in jails and prisons. From the perspective of the correctional facility administration, education programs might be viewed as liabilities. Teachers, and sometimes college students, have to go through background checks and screenings before being permitted on the grounds at a correctional facility, and classrooms need to be staffed with extra officers. Rooms and passage need to be secured. Bags and persons need to be scanned and searched for contraband. All of this could amount to, in the eyes of an administrator, unnecessary risk and extra work.

The classroom as a political space

Whenever teachers enter classrooms, they enter a dialogical space that is inherently political. Educators who have a grasp of the meaning of that space, more often than not, look to push the boundaries of the status quo and advocate for a dialogical exchange among their students (Shor & Freire, 1987); but these stances take on different meanings in the context of a prison. Enabling Freire's vision of a problem-posing pedagogy often means tasking students with the responsibility of challenging hierarchical structures, a practice which, in the context of prisons, might result in harm. For students in jails and prisons, the stakes are simply higher. Most facilities have a strict ban on any material tagged with the potential to incite a riot. In the words of Dylan Rodriguez (2006), "the student in prison is never really free to learn" (p. 104), and thus the prison-educator is beholden to a unique set of constraints.

The simple presence of teachers in a correctional facility can change the dynamic between people who are incarcerated and correctional officers as well as resonate beyond the classroom and into the cellblock, influencing the relationships between students and non-students. If we confront the fact that teaching in prison means teaching *with* the prison, it becomes clear that these governing constraints, while typically something we might address out loud and in the open in the context of school, have a palpable but silent influence on the prison-classroom. While critical pedagogies might seem like the most logical method for processing the realities of a prison-classroom, they may only exacerbate tensions. How then, after understanding that asking our students in a prison-classroom to think critically about the world, their contexts, and reading material, which could have a negative—even harmful—impact, can we ethically facilitate meaningful dialogue?

The dilemma with critical pedagogy

In the words of Henry Giroux (2011), "Critical pedagogy takes as one of its central projects an attempt to be discerning and attentive to those places and practices in which social agency has been denied" (p. 3). But, the prison may be the place where social agency is most clearly denied. Aleksandr Solzhenitsyn (2007) meditated on this when he described his arrest as "a breaking point in your life, a bolt of lightning which has scored a direct hit on you … an unassimilable spiritual earthquake not every person can cope with … [and] an instantaneous, shattering thrust, expulsion, somersault from one state into another" (pp. 4–5). The notion of a teacher attempting to be "discerning and attentive" in such a scenario quickly becomes both patronizing and absurd.

Critical pedagogy is rooted in an attention to the situations and circumstances relevant to students' lives. According to Freire, students learn to read the "world" before they can read the "word" (Freire & Macedo, 1987). And yet encouraging a student in the context of a jail or a prison to interrogate his or her world is charged with many ethical considerations. For example, what happens if a student questions the authority in the prison?

When Michel Foucault (1977) described the panoptic architecture of prisons, he seems to make the case for a critical education when he argues that the person who is incarcerated "is seen, but he does not see; he is the object of information, never a subject in communication" (p. 200). This language practically mirrors Freire's (1993) vision of the banking concept of education, wherein students are recognized as "empty vessels" waiting for instruction. When critical pedagogy seems the most appropriate liberatory strategy for empowering students, perhaps it is worth taking a moment to pause and consider the ethical implications of such methods in the context of the prison. In other words, "a pedagogy of liberation" (Shor & Freire, 1987) is one in which practitioners must ask themselves, *in what sense of the word are students being liberated, and what are the ethical implications of a pedagogy for liberation in a carceral state?*

Classrooms, chronotopes, and the dialogical self

The literature and language scholar, Mikhail Bakhtin (1981b) is notoriously difficult to pin down to definitions, but we can approximate his usage of the term "chronotope" to the representation of space and time in works of literature. The chronotope gives readers and researchers a framework through which they might organize space and time, but it "does not simply link particular times and spaces with specific cultural events. Instead, [chronotopes] delineate or construct sediments of concrete, motivated social situations of figured worlds ... [they] describe the lines of force that locate, distribute, and connect specific sets of practices, effects, goals, and groups of actors" (Kamberelis & Dimitriadis, 2004, p. 24). This means that identifying the prison-classroom as a chronotope implies recognizing not only the history of prisons, but also the history of prison education programs, the social and racial contexts of prisons, the economic incentives of an age of mass incarceration, the demographics most likely to live and work in prisons, and the political complexities of the prison-industrial complex.

Any and all of these aforementioned realities are present in the prison-classroom, and this could prove extraordinarily challenging to the prison-educator. In that light, more familiarity with the chronotope of the prison means that the educator may be more sensitive to the nuances of facilitating Freirean dialogue in the context of a prison.

Defining dialogue

As mentioned earlier, many of the core tenants of a critical pedagogy simply elude the prison-educator. For one reason or another, they are seemingly impractical, unethical, or simply impossible. This does not mean, however, that other elements of critical pedagogy are not applicable. Central to Freire's (1993) pedagogy is a complex and nuanced definition of dialogue, one from which the prison-educator might develop a classroom based on "mutual trust" and "hope." From this place of hope and trust emerges Freire's notion of problem-posing, wherein students come to the participatory center of conversation rather than receive the monologues of their instructors.

Like Freire, Bakhtin (1986) argues that dialogue is more than just talk, extending its definition to include a variety of nonverbal iterations. Certainly, this definition includes individuals in dialogue with other individuals, but also individuals in dialogue with a text, with themselves, even with history, etc. Implicit in such a description of dialogue is an understanding of *the dialogic*, which Bakhtin (1986) described in relation to meaning making when he argued:

> There cannot be a unified (single) contextual meaning. Therefore, there can be neither a first nor a last meaning; it always exists among other meanings as a link in the chain of meaning, which in its totality is the only thing that can be real. In historical life, this chain continues infinitely, and therefore each individual link in it is renewed again and again, as though it were being reborn. (p. 146)

These unending chains of meaning between the self and other, text, and a collective history speak to the larger capabilities of a dialogic pedagogy. While critical pedagogy often seeks to put students into conversation with the world around them, to ask key and critical questions about the systems of power represented in those worlds, dialogical methods honor and respect the ways in which individual students dialogue with text, with their instructors, and ultimately, with themselves.

The dialogical self

This notion of a dialogue with the self is representative of Hubert Hermans and Agniezka Hermans-Konopka's (2010) "Dialogical Self Theory," wherein they recognize that any given individual in any given social setting is not only engaged in dialogue with others in the room, but also they are simultaneously engaged in an internal dialogue with myriad and various iterations of their selves—what is theorized as the "I-position."

Our "I-positions" are often at odds with one another, though they almost always exist concurrently. As Hermans and Hermans-Konopka (2010) wrote:

> In the notion of *I-position*, multiplicity and unity are combined in one and the same composite term. Unity and continuity are expressed by attributing

an "I," "me," or "mine" imprint to different and even contradictory positions in the self, indicating that these positions are felt as belonging to the self in the extended sense of the term. (p. 9)

These positions might best be understood through example: "I as teacher," "I as student," "I as incarcerated," or "I as nervous." While these visions of the self might be positioned differentially, "the self functions as a multiplicity. However, as 'appropriated' to one and the same *I, me* or *mine,* unity and continuity are created in the midst of multiplicity" (Hermans & Hermans-Konopka, 2010, p. 9).

A dialogical approach to teaching

Given the peculiarities of teaching students in jails and prisons, critical pedagogy might present more problems than solutions. In practice, its application to social justice may have more influence outside of prison walls than it does inside of them, yet its (critical pedagogy) commitment to equity and resistance to pedagogical methods rooted in the "banking concept of education" *do* have unique application in the context of prisons.

Freire (1993) famously decried "the banking concept of education," instead promoting his vision of a problem-posing pedagogy. In the former, "the narrating Subject (the teacher)" assumes the center of the classroom, while the "patient listening objects (the students)" dutifully receive those instructions (p. 52). Freire imagines an empowering pedagogy rooted in dialogue and discussion. Such an approach has clear and obvious application in the prison-classroom.

While Bakhtin (1986) never directly intended for his philosophies to be applied to the prison, nor the classroom for that matter, his works have inspired countless thinkers from a variety of disciplines. Expanding on the theories of Bakhtin and the psychology of Hermans and Hermans-Konopka (2010), Fecho and Botzakis (2007) imagine a dialogical approach to teaching as one wherein:

The following practices occur with some regularity: (1) raising of questions and the authoring of response by and among all participants, (2) embracing the importance of context and the nonneutrality of language, (3) encouraging multiple perspectives, (4) flattening of or disturbance within existing hierarchies, and (5) agreeing that learning is under construction and evolving rather than being reified and static. (p. 550)

A pedagogical method as the one described above seems uniquely apt for the context of jails and prisons. Teaching in a correctional facility necessarily means entering into a dialogue with multiple perspectives, and while students in jails and prisons might be hesitant to overtly challenge hierarchical power structures—especially with a corrections officer in the classroom—the simple act of reading and writing in a college classroom subverts the prescriptive norms of these students as a mass of subjugated persons.

Freirean pedagogy and the dialogical self in the context of prisons

Freire (1993) understood critical pedagogy as rooted in dialogue between the self and society. Dialogical Self Theory, however, recognizes that there is a society within the self (Hermans & Hermans-Konopka, 2010). This society of the self, composed of various I-positions presents a new opportunity for critical pedagogy, one that might have unique application in the context of jails and prisons, as it enables meaningful dialogue without necessarily requiring students to emphasize their status in related fields of hegemonic power.

Like Freire, Hermans and Hermans-Konopka (2010) understood the significance of hegemonic power on dialogue, and it should be clear that hegemonic power is definitely—often physically—present in jails and prisons. A Freirean pedagogy anchored to Dialogical Self Theory recognizes the power dynamics between instructors, students, and even correctional officers, but it does not necessarily call them into question. From a dialogical stance, the tension between these relationships exists in the world as much as it does within the self, as each of these relationships not only positions students in a social structure, but it also prescribes related identity positions.

While calling the power structures of jails and prisons into question out loud might at first be cathartic, making such statements before the correctional officers, cameras, and correctional facility administration may put students in jails and prisons in an uncomfortable or perhaps even threatening position. It is possible instead to frame problem-posing dialogue among students who are incarcerated, around the dialogical self and as an act of making meaning between relevant identity positions.

When Freire talks about love as a precondition for dialogue, we might consider Hermans and Hermans-Konopka's Dialogical Self Theory and remember that dialogue can happen within the self, amongst our various I-positions (Hermans & Hermans-Konopka, 2010). There are certainly parts of us that are capable of love, parts of ourselves that we do—in fact—love, and maybe there are parts that we would even love to change or see grow. If we come to understand the dialogical classroom as existing beyond the physical context of the jail or prison and also in the dialogical selves of students and instructors, perhaps we can imagine a pedagogy close to what Freire intended, wherein all active participants are engaging not only with content and curricula but also with their lived experiences and respective contexts.

Freire, after all, was the first to remind us that fear is a natural response to critical and problem-posing pedagogies. In his dialogues with Ira Shor, Freire argued that when it comes to teaching with critical consciousness, "'fear' is *not* an abstraction ... we must know that we are speaking about something very normal" (Shor & Freire, 1987, p. 55). If we can infuse some of that comfort in our students who are incarcerated, we may find a way to approach some of the "love" Freire describes as necessary for forming meaningful dialogue and ultimately making meaning. Critical pedagogy in the context of prisons may not have to mean simply criticizing institutional power structures. It could be, as Nels Noddings (1984) argued, exercised with an ethic of care and pointed toward the student's dialogical self, rather than the incarcerated self.

References

Agrawal, K. (January 2018). Inside higher-ed: College-in-prison programs flourish, but for how long? Retrieved from https://www.historians.org/publications-and-directories/perspectives-on-history/january-2018/inside-higher-ed-college-in-prison-programs-flourish-but-for-how-long (Accessed September 21, 2018).

Bakhtin, M. M. (1981a). Discourse in the novel. (C. Emerson & M. Holquist, Trans.). In M. Holquist (Ed.), *The dialogic imagination: Four essays by M. M. Bakhtin* (pp. 259–422). Austin: University of Texas Press.

Bakhtin, M. M. (1981b). Forms of time and chronotope in the novel. (C. Emerson & M. Holquist, Trans.). In M. Holquist (Ed.), *The dialogic imagination: Four essays by M. M. Bakhtin* (pp. 84–259). Austin: University of Texas Press.

Bakhtin, M. M. (1986). From notes made in 1970–71. (V. McGee, Trans.). In C. Emerson & M. Holquist (Eds.), *Speech genres and other late essays* (pp. 132–158). Austin: University of Texas Press.

Fecho, B., & Botzakis, S. (2007). Feasts of becoming: Imagining a literacy classroom based on dialogic beliefs. *Journal of Adolescent & Adult Literacy, 50*(7), 548–558.

Fecho, B., & Clifton, J. (2017). *Dialoguing across cultures, identities, and learning: Crosscurrents and complexities in literacy classrooms.* New York: Routledge.

Foucault, M. (1977). *Discipline and punish: The birth of the prison.* New York: Vintage Books.

Freire, P. (1993). *Pedagogy of the oppressed.* London: Penguin Books.

Freire, P., & Macedo, D. (1987). *Literacy: Reading the word and the world.* Westport, CT: Bergin & Garvey.

Giroux, H. (2011). *On critical pedagogy.* New York: Bloomsbury.

Hermans, H., & Hermans-Konopka, A. (2010). *Dialogical self theory: Positioning and counter-positioning in a globalizing society.* Cambridge: Cambridge University Press.

Kamberelis, G., & Dimitriadis, G. (2004). *On qualitative inquiry: Approaches to language and literacy research.* New York: Teachers College Press.

Lagemann, E. (2017). *Liberating minds: The case for college in prison.* New York: The New Press.

Lennon, J. (April 2015). Let prisoners take college courses. *New York Times*, p. 9. Retrieved from http://nytimes.com (Accessed September 21, 2018).

Nodding, N. (1984). *Caring: A relational approach to ethics & moral education.* Berkeley: University of California Press.

Rodriguez, D. (2006). *Forced passages: Imprisoned radical intellectuals and the U.S. prison regime.* Minneapolis: University of Minnesota Press.

Shor, I., & Freire, P. (1987). *Pedagogy of liberation: Dialogues on transforming education.* Westport, CT: Bergen & Garvey Publishers.

Solzhenitsyn, A. (2007). *The gulag archipelago: An experiment in literary investigation.* New York: Harper Perennial Modern Classics.

5

Critical Race Counterstories and Freire's Critical Pedagogy: Navigating Race in an Interdisciplinary Literature and Religious Studies Course

Soumitree Gupta and Gerardo Rodríguez-Galarza

Introduction

In the current times, developing an effective union between critical pedagogy and race-focused courses remains as urgent as it has ever been. This urgency had led us to co-develop a survey course independently within each of our disciplinary home departments (Department of English and Department of Theology and Religious Studies) in our predominantly white, small, private, liberal arts institutions.[1] We have mobilized—and found especially valuable—Freire's notion of conscientization in critical pedagogy. Specifically, we contend that conscientization of students in our course happens at the intersection of strategically chosen critical race counterstories and implementation of a problem-posing education model.

Given the challenges of "White Fragility"[2] that students in PWIs (predominantly white institutions) often wrestle with *and* our locations as

---

[1] The National Endowment for the Humanities awarded us a grant at Carroll College to develop and teach separately a shared course syllabus on race in literary and theological narratives in 2017 and 2018. In 2017, Soumitree and Gerardo taught the course at Carroll College. In 2018, Soumitree taught the course at Carroll College while Gerardo taught the shared syllabus at St. Norbert College.

[2] DiAngelo (2011) defines White Fragility as "a state in which even a minimum amount of racial stress becomes intolerable, triggering a range of defensive moves. These moves include the outward display of emotions such as anger, fear, and guilt, and behaviors such as argumentation, silence, and leaving the stress-inducing situation. These behaviors, in turn, function to reinstate white racial equilibrium" (p. 57).

educators of color teaching race in higher education, we argue that Freire's discussion of conscientization needs to be further developed to address the teaching of race in PWIs in the current times. Specifically, we propose that conscientization is enabled through a critical awareness of racism as a multidimensional, non-binary process that is pervasive and enduring in our society in overt and covert forms.

To this end, our goals within our introductory course on race and identity, which fulfills an elective requirement in a PWI, are twofold: (1) to lead students into a deeper awareness of their identities as members and beneficiaries of the historically oppressive and dominant sectors of US society; (2) to engage students so that they begin developing a robust and intersectional commitment in allyship with marginalized communities. In this chapter, we outline the specific pedagogical strategies that supported our goals toward conscientization in our integrative course on race and identity in literary and theological narratives.

PWIs, conscientização, and critical race counterstories

Freire's concept of conscientização or conscientization does not inherently exclude the oppressor, but it is based on the experience of the oppressed who have been denied access and input in the structuring of their communities, and shaping of their future (Freire, 1970). While Freire worked with the disenfranchised, US educators in PWIs experience the challenge of working with student populations that are members, through inheritance, of the dominant group that has benefited from the oppression of racially minoritized communities. This challenge is amplified by the positionality of educators of color in the classroom, as documented in existing research (Pittman, 2012).

Multiethnic literature and theology disciplines are invested in the discussion of race and racism within social justice frameworks. As a first step toward conscientization, our interdisciplinary course centers "critical race counterstories" or narratives of lived experience by communities of color in the United States alongside theological readings on racism and justice. In particular, we focus on authors from four communities—African American, Latinx, Native American, and Muslim American.

Our selective focus on these communities is shaped by current issues of police brutality and other forms of systemic injustice against African Americans, debates around the building of the wall along the US southwest border, land justice issues among Native Americans, and the Islamophobia and Arabphobia in current US society. The selected critical race counterstories in our course play an important role in unveiling what Freire labels the "oppressor consciousness" (Freire, 1970, p. 55), which many students have internalized unconsciously throughout their education.

Critical race counterstories are oppositional narratives that center the lived experiences of "racism, classism, sexism, and other forms of subordination experienced by People of Color" (Huber, 2008, p. 167), and in the process, they challenge or disrupt the "majoritarian narratives" of race.[3] However, counterstories are not created solely as a response to majoritarian narratives (Solórzano & Yosso, 2002). Critical race counterstories also serve the crucial function of humanizing racially marginalized communities by bearing witness to their lived experiences, and, in turn, highlighting the pervasive, material, and psychological effects of different forms of racism on these communities.

In effect, these counterstories play a potentially powerful role in raising students' critical awareness of the different forms of racism—as structural oppression, as unconscious bias, as microaggression, etc.—which racially marginalized communities routinely experience and resist. This critical awareness is crucial for members of dominant communities to engage in the fraught questions of racism, justice, allyship, and solidarity. In order for members of dominant communities to engage constructively and empathically with critical race counterstories, these counterstories need to be strategically embedded within a problem-posing education model.

---

[3] Delgado and Stefancic (1993) define majoritarian stories as a "bundle of presuppositions, perceived wisdoms, and shared cultural understandings persons in the dominant race bring to the discussion of race" (462). These majoritarian narratives "are rooted in a dominant Eurocentric perspective[s] that justify social inequities and normalize white superiority (and thus, white supremacy)" (Huber, 2008, p. 167).

Problem-posing education

Within Freire's problem-posing model, both the educator and the student are actively engaged—through critical reflections and dialogue—in a process of recognizing the "problem." According to Freire (1970), recognizing and naming oppression or the "problem" is the first step to "action-reflection" or praxis that will result in transformative change and liberation of the oppressed (pp. 65–67).

In our experience, the work of conscientization in our pedagogy is most impactful when our students recognize the invisible power dynamics of race and racism in their everyday lives and critically think about their role in both perpetuating and resisting existing structures of racism. To this end, we propose a variety of problem-posing strategies. These strategies include providing the historical context of the idea of "race" in the West and the different institutions of racism that have systematically disenfranchised particular communities in the United States during the nineteenth and twentieth centuries so that students are able to analyze the critical race counterstories within these contexts.

We combine this important work of contextualizing critical race counterstories with creating a decentered classroom and assignments, such as media analysis and weekly critical reflections, which encourage students to freely think, dialogue, nurture, and critically apply their knowledge and analytical skills gained in the course to the lived realities of racism in the contemporary US society.

Contextualizing critical race counterstories

The work of problem-posing in our course begins with our course structure and context-building to facilitate self-education and mutual enrichment. Our primary goal in shaping our survey course is to foster a historical and structural understanding of (a) race as a social construct; (b) racism as systemic oppression that manifests itself in the form of institutional racism, unconscious biases, and microaggressions; (c) racial justice struggles within decolonial frameworks; and (d) students' own positionalities as perpetrators/

oppressors or allies within this struggle. In that light, our course is structured around five units.

Unit 1, which includes readings on Eurocentric genealogies of race and racism and educational videos such as *Race: The Power of an Illusion* and Chimamanda Ngozi Adichie's TedTalk "The Danger of a Single Story," serves as the conceptual and historical framework for the rest of the course. Our discussion of the readings and the videos in this unit allows us to engage our students with the foundational concepts of race and identity as well as historical developments that led to specific issues linked to the history of the United States within the framework of critical race theory.[4] In particular, the course texts in this unit lay down the framework for thinking about the origins of race (including Whiteness) as a social construct and racism as structural oppression in the founding of the nation and the ramifications for racially marginalized communities in the United States during the nineteenth and twentieth centuries to the present.

Another focus of this unit is to get students think critically about the often-invisible relationships between power, representation, knowledge-production, and identity—e.g., through our discussion of Adichie's TedTalk—from the very beginning of the course. In our experience, this foundational unit is valuable to the work of conscientization in our course because it provides students both historical knowledge and analytical tools to recognize and analyze both hegemonic and counter-hegemonic representations of race in the course texts as well as their everyday lives.

---

[4] Critical race as a theoretical paradigm was first developed by legal scholars of color, such as Mari Matsuda, Kimberle Crenshaw, Richard Delgado, and others, with the goal of decolonizing critical theory in legal studies (or critical legal studies in the United States) during the 1980s. This group of scholars argued that critical legal studies failed to acknowledge the "role of [race and] racism in American law" (Matsuda, 1991: cited by Yosso et al., 2004, p. 2), and the "lived experiences and histories of those oppressed by institutional racism" (Yosso et al., 2004, p. 2). Since its inception in legal studies, critical race theory has been embraced by various disciplines such as education, sociology, history, ethnic studies, women's and gender studies, and has branched out into multiple areas of specialization such as FemCrit, LatCrit, AsianCrit, and WhiteCrit (Huber, 2008, p. 160). Some of the basic tenets of CRT across these various disciplines and areas of specialization have included an examination of race as a social construction and an understanding of racism as structural and institutional. In these interdisciplinary scholarly conversations, CRT has emerged as a social justice project that *centers* the lived experiences of communities of color within the intersecting ideologies and structures of racism, sexism, and classism (Huber, 2008).

A common challenge in PWIs is that students typically react in ways that personalize the course subject matter and center the topic of racism as a question of personal character. Our emphasis in the first unit is to deconstruct the unconscious conditioning students have undergone in their social, intellectual, and emotional formation of personal identities. Thus, in our course, we accentuate the way socially agreed norms were codified to advantage certain members of a social group, while disadvantaging other members outside of the agreed upon group. Students explore early on the evolution of the understanding of race in the West to reflect on power as a significant factor for the consideration of race relations.

Integrating the concept of power into the discussion of race equips participants to question the power dynamics of any given situation. Thus, we emphasize that racism is not individual prejudice alone, but structural oppression. We invite students to question the common sense understanding of racism as singular racist acts, in order to see racism as a participatory reality where all members of the society are implicated within the structures of the community; the course question does challenge whether we are personally racist, but more importantly, how do we participate in the dynamics and manifestations of racism in US society.

We deepen this context-building work from Unit 1 in each of the remaining four units by situating—and encouraging our students to read—the critical race counterstories and theological reflections of each community within their specific historical contexts. It is precisely in the process of linking the complex past and multilayered present in each unit that we initiate the problem-posing dynamic of our course: "In problem-posing education, people develop their power to perceive critically *the way they exist* in the world *with which* and *in which* they find themselves; they come to see the world not as a static reality, but as a reality in process, in transformation" (Freire, 1970, p. 83). Our approach insists that the racial conflicts that students encounter in the present are the consequences of a long, dynamic history of racism and anti-racist struggles.

For example, in the unit entitled "African American Voices," students read a wide variety of texts that bear witness to the lived experiences—material and spiritual—of oppression and resistance within African American communities since colonization and slavery. For example, students read about the lived experiences of slavery in Frederick Douglass's autobiography and Sojourner Truth's speech "Ain't I a Woman?" to interrogate the Christianity of the slaveholder and the Christianity of the enslaved. The contextualization of the critical race counterstories in Douglass's narrative and Truth's speech within these historical contexts enables students to recognize how Douglass and Truth respond to and subvert racist and/or patriarchal interpretations of the Bible to reclaim their humanity and their agency from the dehumanizing institutions of slavery and/or patriarchy during the nineteenth century.

Juxtaposing Douglass and Truth allows students to wrestle with the intra-communal diversity of thought and blind spots. For example, Douglass's cooptation of White masculinity, while understandable given the circumstances (Carter, 2008, p. 302), stands in stark contrast to Truth's call for recognition of her humanity at the intersections of anti-slavery and feminist discourses. By juxtaposing Douglass with Truth, we intentionally highlight diversity within our chosen counterstories precisely to avoid facile generalizations and highlight the inherent multiplicity of perspectives within the communities we explore.

Our discussion of these nineteenth-century texts and contexts provides a segueway to anti-racist conversations in theology and literature during the Civil Rights era. Specifically, James Cone's Black theology of liberation during this era provides the historical context for reading influential texts by Martin Luther King Jr., Malcolm X, and Toni Morrison. Students read Martin Luther King Jr's "Letter from Birmingham Jail" in which he critiques police brutality against African Americans as well as the reluctance of the White Church and White moderate allies in Alabama to support nonviolent movements against Jim Crow laws. Alongside MLK's text, students analyze Malcolm X's speech on African Americans' right to self-defense to the larger structural violence of racism.

In addition, students read Toni Morrison's 1970 novel, *The Bluest Eye*. *The Bluest Eye* is a portrait of the multiple manifestations of racism—as a systemic process perpetuated by social institutions (children's literacy books, family, school, and mass media, Jim Crow laws), as unconscious bias, and as internalized oppression in 1930s' US society—as well as the struggle for reclamation of racial pride within African American communities, which was an important theme during the Civil Rights era.

A recurring theme of the critical race counterstories in Morrison's novel, MLK's letter, and Malcolm X's speech as well as Douglass's autobiography and Truth's speech is the question: Do Black lives matter? Do female Black lives matter? We conclude this unit with contemporary theological and feminist readings on the contemporary Black Lives Matter and Say Her Name movements. Our goal is to enable students to critically reflect on the fraught issues of police brutality and other forms of systemic racism against African Americans as well as this community's struggle for justice in this current moment within a continuing historical context of racism and anti-racist resistance.

Active learning through critical thinking, dialogue, and application

In alignment with Freire's problem-posing model, we implement practices that assist students in their personal growth as free and questioning agents within and beyond the classroom through dialogue and creative inquiry. As Freire (1970) states, "Problem-posing education bases itself on creativity and stimulates true reflection and action upon reality, thereby responding to the vocation of persons as beings who are authentic only when engaged in inquiry and creative transformation" (p. 84). Furthermore, our experience in this course confirms DiAngelo's (2011) assessment that race-critical dialogue requires practice. That is, DiAngelo's understanding of "White Fragility" reframes the question of critical dialogue on racism as one of habitus, which requires the instructor to guide the students to unveil and nurture the necessary predispositions and skills for meaningful dialogue and personal transformation.

To this end, we organize our classes with a deep commitment to integrate our counterstories with active learning strategies such as weekly critical reflections, think-pair-share activities, and student-led discussions, which creatively extend opportunities for in-class dialogue and creative synthesizing of students' knowledge to reflect and respond to the realities of our times.

A sustained critical analysis assignment implemented in our course is a media analysis project intended to develop students' skills to creatively reflect and act based on the output of different news media outlets. For this assignment, students develop as a group a portfolio of representations of their chosen community in mainstream, non-mainstream, and religious news media. At the end of the semester, each student writes a reflective essay and presents with their group a summative analysis of majoritarian and counter-narratives that they found in media coverage of their chosen community.

The assignment leads students to examine the representation of the community and voices included in the articles in relation to the history of the news organizations, the reporters assigned to cover the different ethnic communities, and the relationships of the reporters to the communities they cover. This assignment precisely directs students to perceive critically "the way they exist" in a world that is a "reality in process," and in effect, enables students to become active knowledge-producers.

By the end of this assignment and the course, students learn to be attentive to the representation of minoritized members of our communities as well as their own methods of knowledge-consumption. In effect, students become more discerning and self-reflective about their own perceptions and how those perceptions might humanize, or more often than not, dehumanize members from marginalized communities.

Conclusion

In all aspects of our course development and problem-posing pedagogy, we implement strategies to integrate critical pedagogy in race-focused courses—from the selection of critical race counterstories to course structure and active learning strategies. In doing so, we believe that our course serves as a model for preparing students from dominant communities to identify and respond to the complex dynamics of race and racism in the current times. Students work on their skills at decoding and developing effective counterstories to recognize and address diverse contemporary issues of racism and anti-racist struggles for justice that surface on a daily basis. Our approach integrates critical race theory and problem-posing pedagogy through historical contextualization of racism as structural oppression *and* through engagement with intra-communal diverse voices within minoritized communities.

Our course delivery introduces and deepens students' self-awareness of their positionalities as beneficiaries of historic racism and potentially as allies in the struggles of racially minoritized communities. This self-awareness and the analytical skills nurtured throughout the course are liberatory life-skills that are relevant to students' everyday lives outside of the classroom. In particular, these skills are valuable for empowering members of dominant communities to recognize and resist majoritarian narratives and institutions that marginalize and dehumanize the "other."

References

Carter, J. C. (2008). *Race: A theological account.* Oxford: Oxford University Press.

Delgado, R., & Stefancic, J. (1993). Critical race theory: An annotated bibliography. *Virginia Law Review, 79,* 461–516.

DiAngelo, R. (2011). White fragility. *International Journal of Critical Pedagogy, 3,* 54–70.

Freire, P. (1970, 2000). *Pedagogy of the oppressed.* New York: Bloomsbury.

Huber, L. P. (2008). Building critical race methodologies in educational research: A research note on critical race testimonio. *FIU Law Review, 4,* 159–173.

Matsuda, M. (1991). Voices of America: Accent, antidiscrimination law, and a jurisprudence for the last reconstruction. *Yale Law Journal, 100,* 1329–1407.

Pittman, C. T. (2012). Racial microaggressions: The narratives of African American faculty at a predominantly white university. *The Journal of Negro Education, 81,* 82–92.

Solórzano, D. G., & Yosso, T. J. (2002). Critical race methodology: Counter-storytelling as an analytical framework for education research. *Qualitative Inquiry, 8,* 23–44.

Yosso, T. J., Parker, L., Solórzano, D. G., & Lynn, M. (2004). From Jim Crow to affirmative action and back again: A critical race discussion of racialized rationales and access to higher education. *Review of Research in Education, 28,* 1–25.

6

Toward a Software of the Oppressed: A Freirean Approach to Surveillance Capitalism

Erin Rose Glass

Digital technology, to sum up Shoshana Zuboff's (2019) recent groundbreaking work, is being increasingly weaponized as an instrument of global surveillance and control for the benefit of an elite group of hyper-capitalists. In her book, *The Age of Surveillance Capitalism: The Fight for a Human Future at the New Frontier of Power*, Zuboff describes this weaponization as indicative of a new economic stage of technological development that she calls "surveillance capitalism," where predicting and modifying human behavior via digital technologies are key strategies for producing revenue and market control.

While computational forms of surveillance and manipulation of human behavior are certainly not new phenomena, the architecture for carrying out these activities has never been so widespread, powerful, and ingrained in daily life, mediating nearly all of our activities through phones, appliances, shopping platforms, communication systems, search engines, and other everyday digital technologies.

Many scholars have demonstrated how the business interests of digital companies often stand in direct opposition to the users or the public good (such as Tufekci [2017], Vaidhyanathan [2018], and Eubanks [2018]), but Zuboff takes this criticism one step further by showing how the broader economic logic of technological innovation itself represents an overstepping of democracy in the surveillance capitalist's aspirations to mass engineer human society for the sake of profit.

Under such conditions, the prospects of liberation seem bleaker than ever before. Zuboff herself, while advocating for the overthrow of surveillance capitalism for the sake of democracy, offers very little concrete advice about how we, as citizens and technology users, might begin to do so. As it happens, however, the methods used to cultivate and sustain surveillance capitalism follow an almost textbook application of Freire's identified techniques of oppression, which, as I aim to show by the end of this chapter, shine a light on what specific steps we can take as educators to fight this form of digital oppression.

As we recall, for Freire (1997), oppression is a systematic suppression of a people's right (or their "ontological vocation") to critically understand and transform the world as a means of turning subjects into objects that can be manipulated and controlled by a dominant class (pp. 44–45). Accordingly, this suppression is carried out by "precluding any presentation of the world as a problem and showing it rather as a fixed entity, as something given—something to which people, as mere spectators, must adapt" (Freire, 1997, p. 120).

Freire (1997) famously demonstrated how traditional forms of education often play a key role in this dehumanizing process by leveraging what he called the "banking method of education," where students learn to passively accept the knowledge of their oppressors rather than to critically engage the world on their own terms. What I'd like to offer here is that digital technology, like Freire's conception of education, is never neutral, and likewise, despite its reputation for extending opportunities for intellectual development, can also work in discreet but powerful ways to foreclose critical thinking. In its current, surveillance capitalist form, many of our everyday digital technologies share features with the "banking method of education," in that they are designed to make users passively accept their exploitative influence in their lives as an unchangeable given.

Strategies of digital oppression

Broadly speaking, digital companies apply a variety of interlocking technical, cultural, and political strategies to suppress users from collectively understanding and transforming their digital world, many of which have been so thoroughly normalized that they can be difficult to identify by most digital technology users. That is, these companies benefit from making their domination through digital technology appear natural, neutral, and inevitable, obscuring other possible social configurations for developing and using software that puts user understanding and control at the forefront.

At the level of code, many digital technology companies, despite their support and use of open source software in some areas, also implement closed source software code that prohibits users from collectively inspecting, modifying, and distributing code in ways that align with their own needs and interests. While the closed nature of code is often taken for granted as a necessary means of protecting digital companies' intellectual property, important arguments have been made regarding the political importance and economic viability of protecting users' rights to study and modify all software code that they encounter. The Free Software Foundation, for example, has been advocating for these rights and supporting software projects that abide by these principles since the 1980s ("What Is Free Software?", n.d).

While the value of such rights may seem meaningless to those who don't personally have the technical skills to inspect and modify code, their denial prohibits user communities as a whole from collectively carrying out these activities in ways that would likely benefit non-coders. For example, access to code would enable user communities to better understand and govern the types of algorithms that mediate search results or social media news feeds, and work against filter bubbles (Pariser, 2011), racism (Noble, 2018), and other unjust or undesirable features of our algorithmic environments.

Access to code would also allow user communities to better determine the extent of data collection practices software imposed on users, such as whether or not smartphones are "listening" to users—a question that is frequently brought up by reporters and which is impossible to technically determine without ability to access code (Nichols, 2018). Prohibiting access to code also actively reinforces the cultural divide between "coders" and "non-coders" by making it impossible for non-coders to casually explore and experiment with code in their everyday settings.

Prescribing user behavior via code

The closed nature of code also offers surveillance capitalists a powerful mechanism for carrying out what Freire describes as "prescription." Freire (1997) writes, "Every prescription represents the imposition of one individual's choice upon another, transforming consciousness of the person prescribed to into one that conforms with the prescriber's consciousness" (p. 29). Secret and unmodifiable code enacts prescription by enabling and disabling different user behaviors that reflect the worldview and interests of the developer.

Even when code is written to give choice in some aspects of the software's use, the choices themselves and the order in which they are presented represent a "choice architecture" that encourages certain types of user behavior. As Siva Vaidhyanathan (2012) argues, "the structure and order of the choices offered to us profoundly influence the decisions we make ... If a system is designed to privilege a particular choice ... people will tend to choose that option more than the alternatives, even though they have an entirely free choice" (p. 88).

Default privacy settings are one example of the way choice architecture has been used by companies like Facebook and Google to encourage users to be more permissive with what they share. However, software's prescriptive influence can be found wherever we use it, shaping even our intellectual and communicative behaviors. For example, Carolyn Handa (1990) argues that word processing software underscores an individualist idea of writing and intellectual processes, asserting, "We work with a concept of writing procedures arising from the programmer's view of the writing process and the way in which the particular programmer understands that we improve writing and gain knowledge" (p. 175). Prescription in our software, however, can be difficult to detect, given the power and immediacy in which it shapes our behavior and makes that behavior appear as if it was chosen freely by ourselves.

Secrecy of data use

Users are also prevented from critically understanding and transforming their digital world by being kept in the dark or outright lied to about the invasive and exploitative practices they are subjected to by surveillance capitalists. As already described, this secrecy is enabled at the level of code, but it is also characteristic of the broader business culture of surveillance capitalists. Zuboff (2019) recounts in her book that Google adopted a "hiding strategy" to keep users in the dark about the extent of their data collection practices.

Surveillance capitalists like Google and Facebook deter user understanding of these activities in multiple ways: they write license agreements that are too long, obscure, and rapidly changing to be sufficiently comprehended by users; they make no genuine effort to educate users on the types, uses, and value of data extraction; and as has often been discovered they secretly carry out data collection and user manipulation practices that are in direct violation of the law. This secrecy contributes to what Zuboff (2019) calls an "asymmetry of knowledge," where surveillance capitalists are able to learn more about user populations (and how to manipulate them) while keeping that knowledge from the users themselves (p. 81).

False generosity

Freire (1997) identifies "false generosity" as another tactic oppressors employ as a means to reinforce the dependence, loyalty, and self-perceived servility of the oppressed, thus inhibiting them from recognizing their oppression. In Freire's view, oppressors are only able to be generous because their oppression has enabled them to monopolize resources. Similarly, we may view surveillance capitalists enabling "free" access to their digital tools (such as email, search engines, and social media) as a technique of domination funded by wealth produced through the exploitation of user data. This form of false generosity is used to produce feelings of gratitude and dependence in the user as well as propel the illusion of free choice in the use of these tools. However, as many scholars and journalists have pointed out, the alleged "freeness" of these tools disguises their exploitative practices and imperialist ambitions, enabling surveillance capitalists to embed their tools and impose exploitative terms far and wide as part of what Dal Yong Jin (2015) calls "platform imperialism," or "the increasing role of U.S.-based platforms in capital accumulation and culture" in global internet use (p. 153). Although these tools are rarely overtly forced on users, their adoption is hardly based on independent choice. As Bruce Schneier (2015) observes, "These are the tools of modern life. They're necessary to a career and a social life. Opting out just isn't a viable choice for most of us, most of the time; it violates what have become very real norms of contemporary life" (pp. 60–61). For surveillance capitalists, false generosity is a powerful business strategy for capturing user populations.

The reproduction of digital oppression through education

The strategies highlighted above are only some of the oppressive techniques that surveillance capitalists use to reproduce passive users, or users who neither expect nor are able to critically understand how digital technology mediates their everyday activities nor participate in shaping that mediation according to their own interests. What I'd like to argue here is that the power of these strategies is doubly amplified by their normalization within institutions of schooling. By passively accepting digital tools that deny users the right to study and modify code, exploit user data, and impose surveillance and control on users, we are teaching students that these technological qualities are natural, neutral, and inevitable.

Our passive acceptance of these tools also forecloses important opportunities to redirect the investment of resources and technological practice of schools into forms of software use and development that prioritize the rights of users, such as that powerfully modeled by the Free Software Foundation. This missed opportunity is hardly the fault of educators, who likely received similar technological conditioning in their own education, but rather reflects a longer history of private exploitation of schools for capturing and training consumer markets, particularly by the information technology sector.

Today, the importance of the educational market for digital technology companies remains strong as ever including for new companies such as Google and Amazon, and new products like e-textbooks, email services, and cloud storage. As Google enterprise specialist Jeff Keltner (2007) states, "We think students are going to take these tools out to their personal lives, their professional lives" (para. 12). Tech writer Brian Heater (2017) observes that digital technology companies' intense interest in education "isn't entirely altruistic" (para. 54). He further writes, "Fostering an entire generation of first-time computer users with your software and device ecosystem could mean developing lifelong loyalties, which is precisely why all this knock-down, drag-out fight won't be drawing to a close any time soon" (para. 54). Surveillance capitalists know that the tools we adopt in education will have strong influence on the tools we adopt as a society.

Dialogic approaches to surveillance capitalism in education

What then is to be done? As journalists Daniel Oberhaus (2018) and Kashmir Hill (2019) independently demonstrated, it is nearly impossible to avoid big tech companies like Amazon, Facebook, Google, Microsoft, and Apple, even if you make it your full-time job as part of a paid reporting experiment. Rejecting these technologies outright from within institutions of education, which already struggle with so many other challenges, would be even more difficult. However, I'd like to suggest that we might fruitfully adopt Freire's emancipatory method of dialogue to develop a "software of the oppressed," or a mode of critiquing and transforming software and its role in our lives from the site of education.

For Freire (1997), dialogue is an activity foundational to freedom in that it represents a human being's active striving toward becoming a self-directed subject rather than a passive object. It consists of a dialectical and unending process of action and reflection as it conceives of humans and the reality they make as in the "process of becoming" rather than static and fixed. Freire (1997) asserts, "To exist, humanly, is to name the world, to change it. Once named, the world in its turn reappears to the namers as a problem that requires of them a new naming" (pp. 65, 69). This process of naming, as part of the activity of reflection, plays an important role in making aspects of the world available for transformation. It allows individuals to see what seemed to exist before "objectively" as now "assuming the character of a problem and therefore of challenge" (p. 64).

To that end, this practice of dialogue can be fruitfully put to use in resisting the oppressive impositions of software in the classroom. As many have pointed out, one of the biggest challenges of responding to the vast power wrought by our digital companies is our inability to effectively describe their presence in our lives, leaving us vulnerable to inheriting the uncritical language of surveillance capitalist boosters. Ellen P. Goodman and Julia Powles (2016) observe, "We call them platforms, networks or gatekeepers. But these labels hardly fit. The appropriate metaphor eludes us; even if we describe them as vast empires, they are unlike any we've ever known" (para. 2) Developing new concepts that challenge the uncritical representation of digital technologies from the point of view of users is an important first step toward transforming these technologies in ways that better suit the needs and values of users.

While schools have long considered the adoption of new technologies as a type of challenge requiring experts and research, they have rarely extended this challenge to students. Instead, technological adoption is typically considered a problem to be solved by IT specialists whose solutions are imposed on students without their understanding or participation. This de-politicization of digital technology in learning environments conditions students to passively accept digital technology in their broader lives. What we need to do instead is provide students and the broader academic community opportunities to see their digital environment as a problem available for transformation rather than as objective and fixed reality.

Although pedagogies focused on critical information literacy would be of profound importance to this venture, I am arguing here for their extension into genuine opportunities for mass student participation in shaping, governing, and critiquing the very digital technology that is sponsored or endorsed by their institutions of education in order to prepare them to carry the same critical digital consciousness out into their everyday lives.

Institutions could do this critiquing by incentivizing student advisory committees on academic technology (as I have done with UC San Diego's digital commons KNIT), hosting town halls to discuss academic technology contracts and privacy agreements, and supporting more forms of libre software that protects user rights and academic digital tools and services with strong ethical values, such as the Modern Language Humanities Commons, Commons in a Box, and Domain of One's Own.

Such large-scale efforts, however, as I have found in my own initiatives, often require an alignment of will, interest, and resources among institutional actors that can take a great deal of time to develop. Although these goals are still worth working toward, there are also a variety of smaller steps we can take to help cultivate dialogic technical consciousness in students who need not rely on massive forms of institutional support or collaboration.

For example, educators can experiment with replacing surveillance capitalist technologies with alternatives that more forcefully protect user privacy and freedom (Glass, 2018). My colleague, Nathan Schneider, and I are currently working on an Ethical Edtech wiki project that aims to help educators find these alternatives and use them in meaningful ways in their classroom. Educators can also develop ways to bring up the non-neutrality of tools in their teaching, such as by providing notices on syllabi about the potentially surveillant and exploitative nature of digital tools used for learning or developing assignments that interrogate oppressive features of digital technology like user terms and conditions agreements.

In the end, however, educators should work toward developing their own methods for lifting digital technology out of "background awareness" of their classrooms and into the realm of dialogue and transformation that work best with their students, curriculum, and institutional environments. As our world becomes ever more prescribed by the conventions of surveillance capitalism, educators should consider how Freire's dialogical method may be our most promising tool for liberating ourselves from it.

References

Eubanks, V. (2018). *Automating inequality: How high-tech tools profile, police, and punish the poor*. New York. St. Martin's Press.

Freire, P. (1997). *Pedagogy of the oppressed*, revised ed. New York: Continuum.

Glass, E. (2018). Ten weird tricks for resisting surveillance capitalism in and through the classroom. *HASTAC*. Retrieved from https://www.hastac.org/blogs/

(Accessed April 1, 2019). erin-glass/2018/12/27/ten-weird-tricks-resisting-surveillance-capitalism-and-through-classroom.

Goodman, E. P., & Powles, J. (2016). Facebook and Google: Most powerful and secretive empires we've ever known. *The Guardian*. Retrieved from https://www.theguardian.com/technology/2016/sep/28/google-facebook-powerful-secretive-empire-transparency (Accessed April 1, 2019).

Handa, C. (1990). *Computers and community*. Portsmouth, NH: Boynton/Cook.

Heater, B. (2017). As Chromebook sales soar in schools, Apple and Microsoft fight back. *Tech Crunch*. Retrieved from https://techcrunch.com/2017/04/27/as-chromebook-sales-soar-in-schools-apple-and-microsoft-fight-back/ (Accessed April 1, 2019).

Hill, K. (2019). I cut the "Big Five" tech giants from my life. It was hell. *Gizmodo*. Retrieved from https://gizmodo.com/i-cut-the-big-five-tech-giants-from-my-life-it-was-hel-1831304194 (Accessed April 1, 2019).

Keltner, J. (2007). In A. Guess (Ed.), When email is outsourced. *Inside Higher Ed*. Retrieved from http://www.insidehighered.com/news/2007/11/27/when-e-mail-outsourced (Accessed April 1, 2019).

Nichols, S. (2018). Your phone is listening and it is not paranoia. *Vice*. Retrieved from https://www.vice.com/en_uk/article/wjbzzy/your-phone-is-listening-and-its-not-paranoia and https://techcrunch.com/2017/04/27/as-chromebook-sales-soar-in-schools-apple-and-microsoft-fight-back/.

Noble, S. U. (2018). *Algorithms of oppression: How search engines reinforce racism*. New York: New York University Press.

Oberhaus, D. (2018). Why I'm quitting Google, Amazon, Microsoft, Facebook, and Apple for a Month. *Vice Motherboard*. Retrieved from https://motherboard.vice.com/en_us/article/mbxndq/one-month-without-big-five-microsoft-google-facebook-apple-amazon (Accessed April 1, 2019).

Pariser, E. (2011). *The filter bubble: How the new personalized web is changing what we read and how we think*. New York: Penguin.

Schneier, B. (2015). *Data and Goliath: The hidden battles to collect your data and control your world*. New York: W. W. Norton.

Tufekci, Z. (2017). *Twitter and tear gas: The power and fragility of networked protest*. New Haven, CT: Yale University Press.

Vaidhyanathan, S. (2012). *The Googlization of everything: (and why we should worry)*. Oakland: University of California Press.

Vaidhyanathan, S. (2018). *Antisocial media: How Facebook disconnects us and undermines democracy.* New York: Oxford University Press.

Yong Jin, D. (2015). *Digital platforms, imperialism and political culture.* New York: Routledge.

Zuboff, S. (2019). *The age of surveillance capitalism: The fight for a human future at the new frontier of power.* New York: PublicAffairs.

What is free software? (n.d.). *Free software foundation.* Retrieved from https://www.fsf.org/about/what-is-free-software (Accessed April 1, 2019).

7

Freirean Cultural Circles in a Contemporary Social Studies Class

Shelley Martin-Young

Introduction

Any discussion of Paulo Freire must begin with a look at his roots. Freire grew up in Brazil and because of the Great Depression he lived most of his life in abject poverty, knowing hunger and pain. He fell far behind in school and acknowledged that poverty and hunger affected his ability to learn. Because of his experiences growing up and spending much time with families who were poor and living in rural areas, Freire dedicated himself to searching for ways to help the poor and oppressed (Freire, 1994a; Gadotti, 1994). In his book, *A School Called Life*, Freire (1994b) tells some of his own story:

> My experience with them [poor rural families] helped me to get used to a different way of thinking and expressing myself. This was the grammar of the people, the language of the people, and as an educator of the people I devote myself today to the rigorous understanding of this language. (p. 7)

Freire's determination to help the oppressed gain freedom remained with him throughout his life and fueled his activism.

Freire (1959) openly criticized the Brazilian education system in his thesis titled "Present-day Education in Brazil," where the beginnings of Freirean pedagogy can be found. In this seminal work, Freire espoused the need for an education that matters, an education that comes directly from the lived experiences of students (Gadotti, 1994). In 1962, at a time when more than half of the population was illiterate in Brazil, Freire experimented with his pedagogy for the first time. Through a pedagogical approach that incorporated cultural circles as a means to facilitate learning, 300 peasants learned how to read in just forty-five days. Kirylo (2011) describes the emergence of cultural circles in the following way:

> It was through the adult education programs that were conducted by Freire that the notion of cultural circles and cultural centers had its beginnings, forming at such venues as soccer clubs, neighborhood associations, churches, and philanthropic organizations. Frame-worked in an approach that utilized pictures or slides to introduce topics, while at the same time encouraging dialogue with the participants, various themes such as nationalism, democracy, development, and illiteracy were discussed in these circles. (p. 41)

Indeed, the effectiveness of facilitating democratic spaces through these cultural circles was an ideal architype to teaching adult learners to read (Freire, 1996) and due to the success Freire experienced with the first cultural circles, he was invited by the Brazilian president to devise his literacy plan for adults on a national level. In 1964, 20,000 cultural circles were to begin educating more than 2 million illiterate Brazilians. However, a military coup prevented this plan from happening and Freire was exiled from Brazil. One year after being expelled from Brazil, Freire wrote his classic piece, *Pedagogy of the Oppressed*.

According to Williams (2009), "The heart of Freire's literacy framework is found in his problem posing, dialogical approach" (p. 3). That is, learners learn to read not only the word, but also their world (Freire, 1998). Participants do not begin by learning the alphabet and phonics or how to sound out words. Rather, as Freire spent time in the communities noting what was important to the people there, he used the people's own words, phrases, and sentences to teach them how to read with what he characterized as generative themes.

In that light, learning takes place in the safe spaces created by the cultural circle. In the circle, voices are heard, stories are shared, and learning happens. For Freire, education is not a neutral event, suggesting it has the capacity to liberate and to free people from oppression and marginalization (Chaib, 2010; Reyes & Torres, 2016). Gadotti (1994) mentions three distinct phases of the cultural circle, including the following:

Investigation Stage—In this stage words and themes are discovered from the participants daily lives. By spending time in the participants' environment, the facilitator becomes familiar with what is important in their lives. This can happen "through informal meetings with the dwellers of the place in which the scheme will take place—living with them, sharing their worries, and getting a feeling for the elements of their culture." (p. 22)

Thematization Stage—In the second stage of the culture circles, the themes that were uncovered in the investigation stage will be "contextualized" and a critical vision will be developed. Pictures and cards are created that will help with reading and writing.

Problematization Stage—The final stage is taking action or what Freire calls "transformative praxis". According to Gadotti (1994), "Being able to read and write becomes an instrument of struggle, social and political activity" (p. 23). The cultural circle participant becomes aware of his/her oppression and takes action to overcome their oppression (conscientization).

Despite the fact that these three stages are listed, Freire did not view this process as a static pre-fixed curriculum. His desire was that the shaping of cultural circles would be recreated from setting to setting, dictated by the needs, interests, and desires of the participants (Brown, 2011; Souto-Manning, 2010).

Cultural circles in a contemporary social studies classroom

As students make their way through a public K-12 education, the predominant mode of learning is through assigned textbooks. In 2002, the State Department of Education published a document showing that 74 percent of teachers use textbooks provided to them by their school district to aid in teaching lessons. This number was drastically higher when it came to the social studies or history classes. In this case, 94 percent of teachers used the provided history textbook as the main source of knowledge for their lessons. Many teachers rely heavily on the provided textbooks and curriculum, assuming them to be factual and filled with truths. Unfortunately, however, history textbooks are not always accurate and can be misleading and biased (Loewen, 2007; Ravitch, 2003).

For example, it is often the case that the social studies curriculum is designed to further white dominance by marginalizing others. Ways that social studies curriculum promotes the white-centered dominance are through the use of textbooks that are often full of misinformation, the promotion of a curriculum that silences "others," and choices made by teachers that are sometimes blatant and misguided. According to Litner and Macphee (2012), social studies textbooks are "contested texts in which omission offsets contribution and uniformity is touted to the exclusion of diversity. Perspectives are promoted, thus heard; perspectives are ignored, thus silenced" (p. 269). Lawrence (1997) believes that "cognizant or not, white teachers inherently obtain and thus profess a set of social, economic, and political privileges that often manifest into biases or perceptions in the classroom" (p. 110). When teachers depend heavily on textbooks, the silencing of voices is a problem.

Being cognizant of the many issues in the social studies textbook, researchers have been scrutinizing the inadequacies in these books for many years (Anyon, 1979; Gagnon, 1987; Loewen, 2007; Van Sledright, 2002). There has been a concern over how much of history is glossed over, groups and events are over-generalized, and groups are excluded (Brown & Brown, 2015). Carter G. Woodson (1933), for example, argued that "the same curriculum that tells the oppressor that he is everything and superior tells the 'Negro' that he is nothing" (p. 5). This is the danger of a single story and is still prevalent in education today.

Author James Loewen is well known for his critique of history textbooks. In his book *Lies My Teacher Told Me* (2007), Loewen takes a critical look at topics that are typically celebrated in an American history textbook and tells the "real" story of the event. Some events explored in Loewen's book include the Vietnam War, Abraham Lincoln, the absences of racism, Christopher Columbus, and Reconstruction. Loewen encourages teachers to learn how to deconstruct these single stories from the textbook, and to look critically at what we are teaching students. Bigelow and Peterson (1998) explain why critically examining textbooks is important, referring to the story of Christopher Columbus as an example, "Both the words and the images of the

Columbus myth implicitly tell children that it is acceptable for one group of heavily armed, white people from a 'civilized' country to claim and control the lands of distant non-white *others*" (Bigelow & Peterson, 1998, p. 10).

In examining these textbooks, teachers like theorists need to question— Whose knowledge is important? Whose story is being told? Whose voice is being heard? And whose isn't? (Christensen, 2011; Janks, 2014; Ladson-Billings, 2018; Leland & Harste, 2005) As Ladson-Billings (2018) succinctly states, "What intellectual information and experiences students have access to, what they are denied access to, and what distortions of information they encounter can serve as powerful funders of our racial ideology" (p. 97). When we teach children only one side of the story, we are presenting to them what we value most as a society. AnneMarie Brosnan (2016) states that embedded in the curriculum are "our values, our beliefs about human nature, our visions of the good life, and our hopes for the future. It represents the truths that we have identified as valued and worth passing on" (Brosnan, 2016, p. 719). In leaving out other voices and perspectives, we are saying their story isn't important.

To that end, I propose a critical theoretical perspective through a Freirian cultural circles model to teach social studies. From a critical theoretical perspective, literacy is viewed as having social, political, and historical meaning. With critical literacy, students are encouraged to "pay attention to what a particular text is doing to them, how it is positioning them, and whose interests are being served by how the text is written" (Leland & Harste, 2000, p. 3). Critical literacy questions power structures and the status quo. All texts are written from the perspective of the author.

By learning to read from a critical perspective, students question the perspective presented by the text and decide for themselves their positionality in the world. A critical perspective acknowledges that reading, like all of education, is not a neutral event. Instead of following a script or manual, teachers of critical literacy become advocates for students, helping them to critique their classroom, school, curriculum, society, and their world.

Critical conversations take place in a cultural circle. Instead of answering scripted questions at the end of the story, students dialogue with each other about the books they are reading. Instead of reading the history textbook as the only source of information, history students are introduced to literature that brings other perspectives to the forefront. Leland, Harste, Ociepka, Lewison, and Vasquez (1999) feel that readers need to be able to question the texts that they read, assumptions that are made, and how the text positions them. Questions that students need to ask include, "Whose story is this? Who benefits from this story? and What voices are not being heard?" (p. 71).

Critical conversations about books are important because "they highlight diversity and difference while calling attention to the nature and role of literacy in our society" (Harste, 2000, p. 507). These critical conversations about books build students' awareness of life as they transact with quality literature. Leland and Harste (2000) put it this way regarding the notion of quality:

> Don't make difference invisible, but rather explore what differences make a difference.
>
> Enrich our understanding of history and life by giving voice to those who have traditionally been silenced or marginalized.
>
> Make visible the social systems that attempt to maintain economic inequities.
>
> Show how people can begin to take action on important social issues.
>
> Explore dominant systems of meaning that operate in our society to position people and groups of people.
>
> Help us question why certain groups are positioned as "others." (p. 4)

Engaging students in critical conversations about the books they read, and in this case relative to social studies books that are assigned to them, encourages questioning their own assumptions, insists on pushing back against the status quo, and fosters a desire to action. Critical literacy leads to conscientization or a critical consciousness, which leads to the understanding of one's world and being able to take action against oppressive forces (Freire, 1970). Not teaching critically is helping to maintain the status quo that is particularly harmful to children of color. Davis and Sumara (1999) put it this way, "For us, complicity compels acknowledgement by those who dwell in the sacrosanct, unquestioned center that they too are thoroughly implicated in the unfolding of our cultural world—with all its inequities, injustices, and scabrous edges" (p. 28).

How it works

Cultural circles in the social studies classroom can happen at any grade level from kindergarten all the way to the university level. Following the structure of Freire's circles, students learn to investigate, thematize, and problematize the social studies textbook. After exploring a topic in the social studies textbook, students are invited to investigate the historical event from other perspectives. By using a variety of texts including newspaper articles, journals, eyewitness accounts, photographs, interviews, and a variety of children's and young adult literature, students will gain a more complete story of the historical event.

In the cultural circle, students dialogue about what themes are emerging and perspectives that may be new to them. As students wrestle with the historical topic in the safe space of a cultural circle, a new understanding may emerge. Through critical analysis and critical questioning, students, instead of memorizing facts to regurgitate on a high-stakes test, move toward the earlier-mentioned place of conscientization or a critical consciousness. They become individuals who interrogate their assumptions—assumptions in the textbook, the classroom, their society, and their world.

Examples of this work could include reading the picture book *Encounter* when studying Christopher Columbus at a primary or elementary grade level. In this book, the perspective of a young Taino Indian's point of view is explored. Instead of the narrative told in the textbooks, students are exposed to another side of the story. In another example, when studying the Tulsa Race Massacre, which has been completely left out of most textbooks, students can examine photographs, listen to survivor stories, and tour, including virtually, the original site of Black Wallstreet. Another topic often not talked about is the internment of Japanese Americans during the Second World War. By reading *A Place Where Sunflowers Grow*, students get a first-hand look at the experiences of people who lived in these internment camps.

While only three historical topics have been mentioned here, there are a wide variety of texts that offer an alternative to the social studies textbook. The important thing is to get students talking about what really happened. Until we acknowledge the past, we are bound to repeat it.

Conclusion

Paulo Freire began using cultural circles in the 1960s to teach peasants in Brazil to read the word and read the world. Today, these same circles can be used to critique the single story often told in the social studies textbook. By progressing through the stages, first used by Paulo Freire, students are taught to investigate, thematize, and problematize the "political and economic interests behind the production of textbooks, of the hidden agendas propagated by academic and business leaders through these political texts, and of subjugated knowledge and accomplishments and contributions of the Other that tend to be omitted from mainstream texts" (Hickman & Porfilio, 2012, p. xx). In so doing, not only do students read their world, but they also learn to critique their world, their classrooms, and the textbooks they are often forced to use.

References

Anyon, J. (1979). Ideology in United States history textbooks. *Harvard Educational Review, 49*(3), 361–386.

Bigelow, B., & Peterson, B. (Eds.) (1998). *Rethinking Columbus: The next 500 years.* Milwaukee, WI: Rethinking Schools.

Brosnan, A. (2016). Representations of race and racism in the textbooks used in southern black schools during the American Civil War and Reconstruction era, 1861–1876. *Paedagogica Historica, 52*(6), 718–733.

Brown, A. (2011). Consciousness-raising or eyebrow raising? Reading urban fiction with high school students in Freirean cultural circles. *PennGSE Perspectives on Urban Education, 9*(1), 1–12.

Brown, A. L., & Brown, K. D. (2015). "A spectacular secret": Understanding the cultural memory of racial violence in K-12 official school textbooks in the era of Obama. *Race, Gender & Class Journal, 17*(3/4), 111–125.

Chaib, D. M. (2010). Music listening circles: Contributions from development education to democratising classical music. *Policy & Practice: A Development Education Review, 10*, 42–58.

Christensen, L. (2011). Finding voice: Learning about language and power. *Voices from the Middle, 18*(3), 9–17.

Davis, B., & Sumara, D. (1999). Another queer theory: Reading complexity theory as a moral and ethical imperative. *Journal of Curriculum Theorizing, 15*(2), 19–38.

Freire, P. (1959). *Present-day education in Brazil.* (Doctoral thesis).

Freire, P. (1970). *Pedagogy of the oppressed.* New York: Continuum.

Freire, P. (1994a). *Pedagogy of hope: Reliving pedagogy of the oppressed.* New York: Bloomsbury Academic.

Freire, P. (1994b). *A school called life.* Brazil: Attica Language.

Freire, P. (1996). *Letters to Cristina: Reflections on my life and work* (D. Macedo with Q. Macedo and A. Oliveira, Trans.). New York: Routledge.

Freire, P. (1998). *Pedagogy of freedom: Ethics, democracy and civic courage.* Mitchellville, MD: Rowan & Littlefield Publishers.

Gadotti, M. (1994). *Reading Paulo Freire: His life and work.* New York: State University of New York Press.

Gagnon, P. (1987). *Democracy's untold story: What world history textbooks neglect.* New York: Freedom House, Inc.

Harste, J. C. (2000). *Supporting critical conversations in classrooms.* Bloomington: Indiana State University.

Hickman, H., & Porfilio, B. J. (2012). *The new politics of the textbook: Problematizing the portrayal of marginalized groups in textbooks.* Rotterdam, Netherlands: Sense Publishers.

Janks, H. (2014). Critical literacy's ongoing importance for education. *Journal of Adolescent & Adult Literacy, 57*(5), 349–356.

Kirylo, J. D. (2011). *Paulo Freire: The man from Recife.* New York: Peter Lang.

Ladson-Billings, G. (2018). The social funding of race: The role of schooling. *Peabody Journal of Education, 93*(1), 90–105.

Lawrence, S. M. (1997). Beyond racial awareness: White racial identity and multicultural teaching. *Journal of Teacher Education, 48*(2), 108–117.

Leland, C. H., & Harste, J. C. (2000). Critical literacy: Enlarging the space of the possible. *Primary Voices K-6, 9*(2), 7.

Leland, C. H., & Harste, J. C. (2005). Doing what we want to become: Preparing new urban teachers. *Urban Education, 40*(1), 60–77.

Leland, C. H., Harste, J. C., Ociepka, A., Lewison, M. & Vasquez, V. (1999). Exploring critical literacy: You can hear a pin drop. *Language Arts, 77*(1), 70–77.

Litner, T., & Macphee, L. (2012). Selecting history: What elementary educators say about their social studies textbook. In H. Hickman & B. J. Porfilio (Eds.), *The new politics of the textbook: Problematizing the portrayal of marginalized groups in textbooks* (pp. 259–270). Rotterdam, Netherlands: Sense Publishers.

Loewen, J. W. (2007). *Lies my teacher told me: Everything your American History textbook got wrong*. New York: The Free Press.

Ravitch, D. (2003). *The language police: How pressure groups restrict what students learn*. New York, NY: Knopf Publishing.

Reyes, L. V., & Torres, M. N. (2016). Decolonizing family literacy in a culture circle: Reinventing the family literacy educator's role. *Journal of Early Childhood Literacy, 7*(1), 73–94.

Souto-Manning, M. (2010). *Freire, teaching, and learning: Culture circles across contexts*. New York: Peter Lang.

VanSledright, B. (2002). *In search of America's past: Learning to read history in elementary school*. New York: Teachers College Press.

Williams, D. (2009). The critical cultural cypher: Remaking Paulo Freire's cultural circles using hip hop culture. *International Journal of Critical Pedagogy, 2*(1), 1–29.

Woodson, C. G. (1933). *The Miseducation of the Negro*. Washington, DC: Association Press.

8

The Liberatory Potential for Teacher Mindfulness

Amy E. Laboe

In the first year of my doctoral studies, I was introduced to Chris Higgins's book, *The Good Life of Teaching* (2011), which affirmed quite poignantly a kind of struggle I have always felt as a public-school teacher: the friction between my inner and outer lives. I continually held back from releasing my authentic self in the classroom in favor of maintaining control, and meeting the external expectations of my work. Higgins (2011) addresses this lack of agency through the following point:

> Selfhood is contagious. In order to cultivate selfhood in students, teachers must bring to the table their own achieved self-cultivation, their commitment to ongoing growth, and their various practices, styles, and tricks for combatting the many forces that deaden the self and distract us from our task of becoming. (p. 2)

As a practitioner of meditation and mindfulness, I worked to maintain a sense of presence and attention, and was sometimes able to ward off some of the "many forces that deaden the self" (Higgins, 2011, p. 2). In my experience, some of these forces included: top-down teacher evaluations, overly prescriptive curriculum, test-based accountability, and disengaged students. Although I often found many moments of joy and connection in the classroom, I ultimately began to feel disconnected and detached.

Introduction

In the first year of my doctoral studies, I was introduced to Chris Higgins's book, *The Good Life of Teaching* (2011), from which the above quote comes.

This book affirmed my internal struggles as a public-school teacher, and subsequently provoked me to engage in the scholarly discourse on teacher mindfulness, particularly from a Freirean perspective. During my twelve years of teaching, as a practitioner of meditation and mindfulness, I regularly struggled with the conflict between the outer conditions and responsibilities of my job, and my inner conditions as a human being. I battled to maintain a sense of presence and attention, while also warding off what Higgins (2011) calls "the many forces that deaden the self" (p. 2). In my experience, some of these forces included stressful teacher evaluations, overly prescriptive curriculum, test-based accountability, and disengaged students.

Although I am presently moving away from K-12 teaching and into a new phase of my career, I write this chapter with current and future public-school teachers in mind. My intent is to add to the scholarly discussion on teacher mindfulness by going beyond the commonly discussed psychological benefits for teachers, such as emotional self-regulation or stress relief (Jennings et al., 2017), to consider the liberatory and self-transformative potential of mindfulness. My argument is that while the documented psychological benefits to teachers are significant, using contemplative practices merely as interventions focused on changing behavior or reducing stress limits the potential of what mindfulness can bring to a teacher's life. Rather, I see the potential for teacher mindfulness to be considered an act of agency that leads a teacher toward Freirean notions of liberation and transformation.

Teacher mindfulness in the mainstream

In the literature on mindfulness in education, a teacher is described as in great need of stress relief and burnout prevention, and mindfulness programs are offering a strategy to combat such reactions to the environment and build emotional resiliency (Jennings et al., 2017; Mindful schools, n.d). I do not find supporting teachers' well-being and resiliency problematic; in fact, it is very much needed. Yet, in my view, approaching mindfulness as an intervention to respond to the environment of schooling and making it a *what works* tactic ultimately erode the depth of what could be the potential for teacher mindfulness (Ergas, 2015). Nevertheless, I acknowledge that this exploration into mindfulness for teachers has been valuable, and has acted as a gateway for me and other educators and scholars to consider using alternative pedagogies of teaching and learning, particularly in terms of incorporating contemplative traditions (Ergas, 2015). Therefore, in the next few sections, I will reexamine the characteristics and definition of mindfulness and then apply it to Freirean notions of liberation and transformation (Freire, 1970).

Re-defining mindfulness

Most mindfulness programs and research designs use Jon Kabat-Zinn's (2005) definition of mindfulness—"paying attention in a particular way: on purpose, in the present moment, and non-judgmentally" (part 1, location 185). While it is beneficial for psychological studies to maintain consistently defined constructs for research purposes, I would like to expand this definition using Ergas (2015) and Dreyfus (2010, 2011), to include a connection to both the cognitive and embodied aspects of mindfulness. According to Dreyfus (2011):

> Mindfulness is not just present-centered nonjudgmental awareness but involves the mind's ability to attend to and retain whatever experience one is engaged in so as to develop a clear understanding of the experience and the ability to recollect such experience in the future. (p. 48)

Dreyfus (2011) goes on to state that this retention of information, which is integrated into the temporal flow of life, allows a person to make sense of one's experiences—which is the primary job of the mind. He further flips mindfulness from a "bottom-up" process (Kabat-Zinn definition) to a "top-down" process, beginning in the mind and moving downward (p. 47). As the attention moves downward, it acquires an embodied dimension which allows for a fuller experience of the present moment (Dreyfus, 2010).

A deeper seeing or an embodied observation is thus initiated, and includes a bidirectional attention to what Ergas (2015) calls "in here" and "out there" (p. 210). The "in here" refers to the inner experience of oneself, including bodily sensations, emotions, and thoughts, and the "out there" refers to the surrounding world and other beings (Ergas, 2015, p. 210). This kind of finer attention's primary goal is understanding both ourselves and our situation, not to attain higher consciousness or simply a calm or focused state (Dreyfus, 2010). It is this understanding, gained from one's bidirectional attention, which initiates transformation, albeit as a by-product of such deep attention (Dreyfus, 2010; Ergas, 2015). Mindful attention can thus aid a teacher in "reclaiming the self," shaking her free from a socially reproduced image of a teacher, one which holds tightly to conformity, and distancing her from a path of self-cultivation (Ergas, 2017a, p. 219).

However, it is important to recognize at this point that the practice of mindful attention is in fact a practice, one that develops over time, and that has a depth and quality much different than just "paying attention." The quality and nature of the attention must go further than just a surface-level awareness and become a process in which we suspend our desire to outright name our experience, and instead, become acquainted with our habits and recurring, and often unexamined, mental and emotional processes and reactions (Segal et al., 2002, as cited by Hyland, 2014). This practice of repeatedly creating space for a bidirectional attention helps to develop a capacity to free ourselves from both the inner and outer processes that constrict our natural selves.

Teacher positioning and regulation

Teachers as helpers

It is no secret that a teacher's life is fraught with a level of stress and exhaustion that often leads to burnout (O'Brennan, Pas, & Bradshaw, 2017). Higgins (2011) engages the topic of teacher burnout from multiple philosophical perspectives, but particularly the claim that teaching as a helping profession greatly affects a teacher's societal position and working conditions. A helping profession, in sociological terms, refers to professions that are usually done by women under difficult working conditions and tend to focus on the receiver's (student, patient, etc.) well-being and development rather than the provider's (Higgins, 2011).

Furthermore, a helper is subjected to a position with lower pay, prestige, and freedom, and must forcibly consider the altruistic nature of the profession to be the reward in itself. Altruistic aims as the center of a profession create an unsustainable endeavor in which helping others replaces self-cultivation (Higgins, 2011). Lastly, helpers are located at the bottom of a hierarchy of power which regulates and controls the institutions, the content, and therefore the helpers themselves.

Teachers as regulated

In *The Teacher's Soul and the Terrors of Performativity*, Stephen Ball (2003) describes the reform and standards movement as a process of "re-regulation" (p. 217). This re-regulation of schooling means that not only have curricula and assessments been re-regulated into a system focused primarily on productivity and performance, but the teachers have as well (Ball, 2003). The constant judgment of a teacher's outward performance, stemming primarily from evaluations that focus on accountability standards, creates a sense of instability and insecurity for the teacher (Ball, 2003). What often results are fabricated performances that exist to meet the standards but result in a loss of the teacher's inner self (Ball, 2003). These performances do not represent a teacher's true self, but rather a self that exists to be accountable to the system. As Ball (2003) states, "These technologies (of market, management, and performativity) have potentially profound consequences for the nature of teaching and learning and for the inner-life of the teacher" (p. 226). Thus, as a teacher attends to the outer demands on her performance, she loses a connection to her inner self and her inner energy—the energy behind her reason for becoming an educator.

Applying a Freirean framework

Teachers as oppressed

Applying a Freirean framework to the notion of teachers as altruistic helpers and overregulated workers allows us to consider teachers as oppressed in the sense that they are bound to the conditions and regulations under which they are required to operate, and are thus prevented from developing their own sense of being (Freire, 1970). The focus on promoting productivity and performance has changed and even undermined what it means to be a teacher, particularly because the "field of judgment and its values" are determined from the outside (Ball, 2003, p. 216). This is what Freire (1970) terms "cultural conquest" (p. 153)—a means by which the oppressed are invaded, and their own value systems and standards are replaced by those of the oppressor. When this happens, one's invaded self is shaped by outer sociocultural forces, and thus programmed to conform to the "values, standards, and goals of the invaders" (Freire, 1970, p. 153).

Therefore, performance and accountability expectations act as invading forces, determining what teaching and learning look like, and thus replace a teacher's own knowledge, intuition, and insight. This is further exacerbated by the conceptualization of a teacher's job as a reward in itself, a reward that only comes from highly regarded outer performances and results, or expressions of gratitude for one's sacrifices. The unsustainability of these circumstances begets a place where mindfulness could act to renew a teacher's sense of agency, leading her toward a more liberated experience and on a transformative path.

Mindful attention as liberation

With a bidirectional attention on both oneself (*in here*) and the world around (*out there*), a teacher can begin to see her situation (Ergas, 2015). A teacher who brings a mindful attention into the classroom will be able to see that she is submerged under all the outer conditions of control and begin to look for ways to emerge—the first step toward liberation (Freire, 1970). When one begins to perceive the reality of the present, one can no longer ascribe to the "fragmented view of reality" from which she was previously operating (Freire, 1970, p. 73). This state is described by Freire (1970) as a reflection from action, and it provides an opportunity "to intervene in reality as it is unveiled," which comes directly as a result of the development of one's *conscientizaçao*, or critical consciousness (p. 109).

Thus, I see Freire's concept of reflection from action as strikingly similar to embodied, mindful attention. From this place of observation and attention, a teacher can engage in the curriculum, the classroom, and the process of teaching in a way that is *not* prescribed from the outside, but from a top-down, bidirectional attention of oneself and one's surroundings (Dreyfus, 2010; Ergas, 2015; Freire, 1970). Engaging in an experience apart from the stream of unexamined habitual actions, thoughts, and emotional responses is a movement toward freedom, with mindfulness acting as the "cognitive glue" that provides this broader vision (Dreyfus, 2011, p. 49). It is a freedom from being driven by external conditioning and permits space for the questions: Who am I? Why am I here? (Ergas, 2015).

When opened to these questions, while attending to one's inner sense of self, the meaning of teaching is freed from our "habituated tendency to attribute meaning to that which is out there" (Ergas, 2015, pp. 206–207). In other words, the teacher will no longer confuse "the map for the territory" (Ergas, 2017b, p. 151). This discovery means that a teacher can begin to see herself as a "transformer of reality," and the primary "subject" in her own transformation (Freire, 1970, p. 174). Therefore, mindful attention is a self-initiated act of agency that begins a progression toward greater self-knowledge and understanding that ultimately frees a teacher, and opens her to transformation.

Mindful attention as transformation

Transformation, in the Freirean sense, is the means by which people remake their worlds in order to become "beings for themselves," freed from oppressive conditions (Freire, 1970, p. 161). This remaking, coming from an attention to "in here" and "out there," puts teachers in a position from which they can intervene as "subjects in expectancy" (Ergas, 2015; Freire, 1970, p. 131). They do so by becoming learners themselves, engaging in dialogue with their students, and freeing themselves from attending to simple outcomes (Freire, 1970). The greater awareness developed from this attention and reflection brings a type of consciousness described by Greene (1988) as "embodied," "inevitably engaged with others," and with the "capacity to pose questions to the world" (p. 21).

This greater engagement in one's position as both teacher and learner, freer from external conditioning, and engaged with one's own inner personal growth creates a space in which a teacher may feel she has a stake in the educational process, and may begin to reconsider theory and practice (Ergas, 2015, 2017a). As Freire (1970) says, "People are fulfilled only to the extent that they create their world, and create it with their transforming labor" (p. 145). Therefore, a practice of attention and mindfulness, which initiates a process of liberation for teachers, can then serve to help them redefine or remake who they are. In Freirean terms, they will construct a praxis of liberation, which is "the action and reflection of men and women upon their worlds in order to transform it" (Freire, 1970, p. 79). Thus, mindfulness results in an initial movement toward freedom from outer conditioning, and ends in teachers transforming themselves and their experience of teaching.

Furthermore, considering Freire's (1970) description of unfulfilling work as work that is "totally dependent, insecure, and permanently threatened" (p. 145), could we not equate that teachers' work? If so, could a mindfulness practice that focuses on an agentic engagement with one's being and liberation actually address these circumstances? Or, would any mindfulness initiative for teachers inevitably exist at the intervention level due to the propensity of creating methodologies of *what works*?

I propose these questions as recognition that in most cases trying something new in education means it will inevitably end up as a research-based intervention aimed at fixing rather than exploring. However, I remain hopeful that perhaps there is an opening we have yet to discover, and that mindfulness and the wisdom of contemplative traditions can guide us in how we can begin to transform education and ourselves from the inside out. Finally, I acknowledge that not all teachers are oriented (or perhaps even ready) toward this type of inner work, but I write this for those who are. Knowing that contemplative practice is very individual, and each person's "transformation occurs in his/her own existential time," this chapter represents just one direction for mindfulness-practicing teachers (Freire, 1970, p. 161). However, I agree with mindfulness scholar, Richard Davidson (2017), that one direction we should take is to more deeply engage with the nature and philosophical underpinnings of mindfulness practices in order to guard against a loose adaptation that is often "overused" or "diluted."

Moving mindfulness from intervention to transformation

In an educational context focused primarily on finding *what works*, teacher mindfulness programs and studies have created an opening for further theorizing about the potential for mindfulness due to their research-based evidence on how mindfulness improves both teachers' lives and classrooms. With this opening, I aimed to add to the discourse by proposing that we go beyond stress relief and improved well-being to see mindfulness more from its contemplative tradition as a practice that engages a teacher in a process of coming to know and inhabit herself. This process of attentiveness to oneself begins to unravel that which has conditioned one's inner and outer selves. Or, as Ergas (2017b) states, we begin to "probe the game in which we are being played and within which we are players" (p. 161).

Change thus occurs, not as the primary goal, but rather as a by-product of the deeper engagement of one's attention inherent in mindfulness practices. As Thich Nhat Hanh (1999) states, "when mindfulness ... embraces all our mental formations ... (it) shines its light upon them and helps them to transform" (p. 75, as cited by Hyland, 2014). Mindful attention, therefore, acts through a person, provoking new understandings about one's inner and outer conditions, and naturally causes transformation. In Freirean terms, mindful teachers develop a critical consciousness that helps them to see oppressive conditions, provoking them to work toward liberation and transformation (Freire, 1970). I believe that such a transformation has the potential to support teachers in redefining the profession and eliminating the "many forces that deaden the self" (Higgins, 2011, p. 2).

References

Ball, S. J. (2003). The teacher's soul and the terrors of performativity. *Journal of Education Policy, 18*(2), 215–228. DOI: 10.1080/0268093022000043065.

Davidson, R. (September 26, 2017). In L. Krauze (Ed.), The untold story of America's mindfulness movement. *Tricycle*. Retrieved from https://tricycle.org/trikedaily/untold-story-america-mindfulness-movement/ (Accessed April 3, 2018).

Dreyfus, G. (2010). Is mindfulness present-centered and non-judgmental? A discussion of the cognitive dimensions of mindfulness. Retrieved from https://info-buddhism

(Accessed April 24, 2018).com/Mindfulness_Present-Centered_Nonjudgmental-Attention_Introspection-A-Discussion_Dreyfus.html.

Dreyfus, G. (2011). Is mindfulness present-centered and non-judgmental? A discussion of the cognitive dimensions of mindfulness. *Contemporary Buddhism, 12*(1), 41–54.

Ergas, O. (2015). The deeper teachings of mindfulness-based "interventions" as a reconstruction of "education." *Journal of Philosophy of Education, 49*(2), 203–220.

Ergas, O. (2017a). Reclaiming "self" in teachers' images of "education" through mindfulness as contemplative inquiry. *Journal of Curriculum and Pedagogy, 14*(3), 218–235. doi.org/10.1080/15505170.2017.1398698.

Ergas, O. (2017b). *Reconstructing "education" through mindful attention.* London: Palgrave Macmillan.

Freire, P. (1970). *Pedagogy of the oppressed.* New York: Continuum.

Greene, M. (1988). *The dialectic of freedom.* New York: Teachers College Press.

Higgins, C. (2011). *The good life of teaching: An ethics of professional practice.* West Sussex, UK: Wiley-Blackwell.

Hyland, T. (2014). Mindfulness, free will and Buddhist practice: Can meditation enhance human agency? *Buddhist Studies Review, 31*(1), 125–140.

Jennings, P. A., Brown, J. L., Frank, J. L., Doyle, S., Oh, Y., Dave, R., Rasheed, D., DeWees, A., DeMauro, A. A., Cham, H., & Greenburg, M. T. (2017). Impacts of the CARE for teachers' program on teachers' social and emotional competence and classroom interactions. *Journal of Educational Psychology, 109*(7), 1010–1028.

Kabat-Zinn, J. (2005). *Wherever you go, there you are: Mindfulness meditation in everyday life* (Kindle Version). Hachette Books. https://www.hachettebookgroup.biz/titles/jon-kabat-zinn-1/wherever-you-go-there-you-are/9781401394677/.

Mindful Schools (n.d.). Why mindfulness is needed in education. Retrieved from https://www.mindfulschools.org/about-mindfulness/mindfulness-in-education/ (Accessed March 12, 2018).

Nhat Hanh, Thich. (1999). *The heart of the Buddha's teaching.* New York: Broadway Books.

O'Brennan, L., Pas, E., & Bradshaw, C. (2017). Multilevel examination of burnout among high school staff: Importance of staff and school factors. *School Psychology Review, 46*(2), 165–176. DOI: 10.17105/SPR-2015-0019.V46-2.

Segal, Z. V., Williams J. M. and Teasdale J. D. (2002). *Mindfulness-based cognitive therapy.* New York: Guildford Press.

9

Who's in Charge? Teacher Authority and Navigating the Dialogical-Based Classroom

A. J. Tierney

It has been over fifty years since Paulo Freire's revolutionary work *Pedagogy of the Oppressed* was originally released, providing us an opportunity to reimagine and reinvent how his work can be applied in twenty-first-century classrooms. Since the publication of that landmark book, the educational landscape has changed vastly and in other ways has not changed much at all.

To the latter, the current educational system looks much like Freire described fifty years ago—a "banking system" where students are empty vessels to be filled with knowledge. In this scenario, teachers do not enter into a dialogue with students, suggesting that learning becomes a transactional process often with little or no meaningful impact on the student or teacher. Freire was echoing the same criticism voiced by John Dewey (1916/1966) when he opined "Why is it in spite of the fact that teaching by pouring in, learning by a passive absorption, are universally condemned, that they are still entrenched in practice?" (p. 38). Over twenty years later, Dewey (1938/1963) was still espousing the detriment of excluding students from the construction of their learning in his work, *Experience and Education*.

Just as Dewey's criticisms of the educational system were not fully embraced at the time of his writings, so too Freire's revolutionary vision has not been fully appreciated up to this day. This lack of fully valuing Freire's thought signals a call to action that needs to be picked up by every educator who believes in humanizing the world through education. As Donaldo Macedo (2000) writes in the introduction in the Anniversary Edition of *Pedagogy of the Oppressed*, "Paulo Freire did not realize his dream of entering the twenty-first century full of hope for 'a world that is more round, less ugly, and more just'" (p. 26). While Freire may not be continuing the journey into the twenty-first century, we have the wisdom of fifty years of his writings to help guide us into an exciting time in education where teachers and students have the opportunity to work together to create a new vision as to what it means to create a collaborative learning space.

Negotiating the balance between student engagement and authority

The ways in which we engage with students look different than it did fifty years ago with the introduction of technology such as tablets, computer, and virtual learning as just a few examples. In my own experience, I have had the honor to teach high school students, traditional and non-traditional college students, and even incarcerated students. Initially, my approach in both high school and college classrooms had taken an authoritarian stance where I stood in a place of authority because of my advanced education and content expertise; I am not alone in this style of teacher authority. That is, historically, authority was derived from a person's particular skill, training, or knowledge (Peters, 1963). Because of this competence or success in particular areas, a person became an authority and was seen as having a "right" to make pronouncements and further take a position of superiority (Peters, 1963).

Within that historical context, teachers established authority by completing teacher preparation programs, becoming experts at a skill, or developing knowledge in a particular area (e.g., art, music, dance, literature, mathematics). The teacher became the expert and shared the wisdom with those who were "less enlightened." Much like my teachers before me, my authority as a teacher set me apart in a superior role to impart knowledge to my "inferior" students. The power dynamic was set up in such a way to ensure an acceptable and comfortable level of distance. However, this described authoritarian stance I took as a teacher was severely challenged when I began teaching a widely adopted financial literacy program in an adolescent pregnancy prevention program at the high school level.

The students questioned and challenged my "superior" content knowledge and offered examples from their own lives that contradicted the lessons I was teaching, and in many ways displayed a depth and breadth of knowledge of race, class, and justice that I honestly had no justifiable reason to reject as "inferior" to what I was attempting to teach. The tensions heightened when they wanted to be heard, all the while when I attempted to "get back on track" to the prescribed curriculum. Ultimately, we were lacking a dialogical classroom setting. As Darder (2018) asserts, "Freire considers pedagogical dialogue as *indispensable* to developing relationships of cooperation and collective action within schools and society" (p. 113).

To that end, I started to critically reflect more on my role as a teacher. Indeed, Freire (2000) advocated for a revolutionary practice that is rooted in teachers grappling with their role in the classroom—specifically as an authority figure. It's as if he knew I would find myself in this place, a place where a teacher can struggle in finding that space of fostering authentic dialogue between teacher and student (Darder, 2017; Freire, 2000). Slowly, and certainly through trial and error, a dialogical environment began to emerge in my classroom setting with students, which worked to reorient my ideas about teacher authority and student engagement.

Rethinking teacher authority

With a traditional view of teacher authority, there are some assumptions made about the learning environment. The teacher is considered competent and knowledgeable in the area of the content.[1] Other aspects of perceived teacher authority may be that the teacher is the person whose opinions matter above all else; he or she establishes the "right" and "wrong" understanding of material, as well as a classroom oriented to the teacher's beliefs and perspective. Clearly, this problematic point of view of teacher authority dismisses and even delegitimizes whatever musings, opinions, or thoughts the students bring into

---

[1] While most teachers can be considered knowledgeable and competent, it is not always true as many under-trained teacher-candidates are entering the profession through ill-conceived alternative or fast-tracked routes.

the classroom. By disregarding the knowledge students bring into class such as languages, customs, rituals, and conclusions about the world, teachers act as an oppressor in an environment where students have little to no control and whose only option is to set aside their experiences to appease the one person who controls their lives.

While good and just teachers would agree that our goal is not to oppress our students, in subtle and not so subtle ways, we, nevertheless, silence their voices in our classrooms. This silencing of student voices can happen in not so subtle ways such as teaching curriculum that aligns with the goals of the dominant culture to reproduce class, gender, and racial structures or by demanding obedience from students. More subtle ways of silencing students can manifest as withholding praise and acknowledgment of students who are perceived as troublemakers.

Teacher authority is always present regardless if a teacher decides to pursue the revolutionary praxis advocated by Freire and develop a dialogical approach in the classroom. At the forefront of a teacher's duty remains a necessity to impart the knowledge required of the course and curriculum. However, Freire (1987) encourages teachers to imparting knowledge as more than just transmitting information:

> Teaching from a progressive point of view is not simply transmission of knowledge ... which is intended to be mechanically memorized by students ... [but] ... that the learners penetrate or enter into the discourse of the teacher, appropriating for themselves the deepest significance of the subject being taught. (p. 213)

Through this lens of teaching from a progressive point of view, we begin to see that teacher authority becomes a both/and proposition. Teachers are to be both content expert and dialogue participant which means at certain times in class the teacher will also take on the role of the student as a learner.

From a socio-cultural theoretical perspective, teachers can honor the lives and experiences students bring to the classroom by actively and authentically engaging them in the learning process. Substantively acknowledging and valuing a student's lived experience is not for the sake of some superficial attempt at diversity and inclusion, but rather is foundational to liberative teaching that according to Freire (2000) is paramount to shifting the oppressed–oppressor relationship. In other words, through a dialogical-based classroom focused on an openness to students' lived experiences, teachers and students can benefit from a deepened mutual understanding of instructional material and its impact on their lives. Blending the greater good of teachers' academic training and students' lived realities to construct a brand of teaching and learning that is culturally responsive and inclusive is what will foster Freire's vision for education into the twenty-first century.

Despite arguing for a classroom that seeks to bring teacher and student closer through the cultivation of a horizontal relationship through dialogue, Freire (2000) also recognized the necessity of directives in a classroom. Directives need not be shunned in an attempt to realize a dialogical-based classroom. Directives that shape and move content knowledge forward are what should be the goal. Examples include working with classes to develop themes of interest and building curriculum and lessons around those themes.

In addition, teachers can design courses that include the study of groups with different values and histories, providing students with valuable knowledge to potentially combine with their own. While Freire (1993) conceded the necessity of those directives, he saw the role of the progressive educator as to "diminish the distance between what they say and what they do so as not to allow a directivity to turn into authoritarianism or manipulation" (p. 116). Freire (1993) also warns that while attempting to avoid authoritarianism, teachers may lack directivity and slip into a "laissez-faire approach" (p. 116), which some students may internalize as a teacher who doesn't care.

In that light, therefore, how do educators find the balance between directives that guide and honor student lives yet not perpetuate an authoritarian stance? Freirean scholar Antonia Darder (2017) agrees with Freire that teaching requires teachers to give directives and these are both "legitimate and necessary" (p. 98). Of particular interest to teachers in the twenty-first century, she makes clear that in terms of revolutionary practice we are not to be concerned about worksheets, lectures, and vocabulary list, but rather look closely at the underlying intent and how we propose to use the knowledge that we present (Darder, 2017). Understanding our intent and purpose of knowledge we share requires critical reflection and oftentimes a change in course of how we deliver content and engage with students. Regardless of how we move forward, we remain an authority in classrooms with directives but these need not be rote directives that are standardized for the masses. If our directives perpetuate the oppression of our students, to keep the systems of oppression intact, we have a problem.

When students' experiences differ from our own, it may be difficult to understand the impact of those experiences, for example, on classroom behaviors or inability to relate to and engage with the curriculum. When the values and lived experiences of students conflict with curriculum being taught in the class, those students may be silenced (Darder, 2015). And ultimately, they are not learning ways to translate the material they are learning in the classroom to their lives and communities. This is where the structural formation of classrooms produces different kinds of responsibilities for different participants.

As the teacher, I am *responsible* for creating an educative environment, for creating the conditions for learning and meaningful study. We move toward progressive teacher authority by focusing on creating what Darder (2015) calls "pedagogical conditions for students to engage freely across their lived histories in the process of knowledge construction" (p. 20). Within our classrooms, we must create spaces that encourage students to connect with the curriculum in ways that include their past and current experiences as well as hopes and dreams they have for their lives and communities. It is in this revolutionary act that shifts the power dynamic where historically excluded students have the freedom to participate in a space where their voices are not only heard but also liberated to such an extent that they begin to make critical decisions that affect their lives in and out of the classroom.

Conclusion

Where does this leave the K-12 educators as well as college educators of the twenty-first century who embrace Freire's call to dialogue in our classrooms? How do we share power in the classroom? In short, how do we go about realizing the dialectical interweaving of Freirean praxis in our classrooms, particularly in a time that is hooked on rigid standardization, positivistic accountability measures? These questions present great challenges for the K-12 educator who embraces a Freirean perspective. Yet, "teachers must critically utilize their power in the interest of democratic life 'on the side of freedom'" (Freire, 2002, p. 74).

In addition, teachers must always be mindful of the principal intent of shared authority, which is "to restructure education into something done *by* and *with* students rather than *by* the teacher *for* and *over* them" (Shor, 1996, p. 148). As for me, in the attempt not to reduce Freire's ideas into a set of methodological guidelines, I have re-shifted my approach with students with respect to negotiating the construction of syllabi and assignments, have looked to the students in establishing class norms, and have promoted a dialogical pedagogical space. Within this new praxis in my classroom, I more meaningfully work with my students in discovering the contradictions that impact their worlds that are both social and material (Darder, 2018).

As teachers, we must work to have meaningful conversations about topics that are impacting students' lives. And within that frame, we are responsible for creating a structure in which the dialogical exchange can be productive and liberating. In this context, teacher authority can be seen as empowering for both student and teacher, which works to diminish the distance between what we say and what we do, creating a synergy of respect between teacher and student. This synergetic energy assumes there is a "profound trust in people and their creative power" (Freire, 2000, p. 75).

In the end, the process of incorporating a Freirean approach to teacher authority is not easy and formulaic; rather, it demands a commitment and an understanding of its process and purpose and is much needed for the twenty-first-century schooling.

References

Darder, A. (2015). *Freire and education*. New York: Routledge.

Darder, A. (2017). *Reinventing Paulo Freire: A pedagogy of love*. New York: Routledge.

Darder, A. (2018). *The student guide to Freire's pedagogy of the oppressed*. London: Bloomsbury Academic.

Dewey, J. (1916/1966). *Democracy and education*. New York: Free Press.

Dewey, J. (1938/1963). *Experience and education*. New York: Collier.

Freire, P. (1987). Letters to North American teachers. In Ira Shor (Ed.), *Freire in the classroom* (pp. 211–214). Portsmouth, NH: Boynton/Cook.

Freire, P. (1993). *Pedagogy of the city*. New York: Continuum.

Freire, P. (2000). *Pedagogy of the oppressed*. New York: Bloomsbury Academic.

Freire, P. (2002). *Pedagogy of hope: Reliving pedagogy of the oppressed*. New York: Continuum.

Macedo, D. (2000). Introduction. In *Pedagogy of the oppressed* (pp. 11–27). New York: Bloomsbury Academic.

Peters, R. (1963). *Authority, responsibility, and education*. London: George Allen and Unwin Ltd.

Shor, I. (1996). *When students have power: Negotiating authority in a critical pedagogy*. Chicago, IL: The University of Chicago Press.

Part Three

The Intersection of Paulo Freire and Myles Horton, Martin Luther King, Jr., and Simone de Beauvoir

10

"To Speak a Book": Lessons from Myles Horton and Paulo Freire's *We Make the Road by Walking*

Jon Hale and Alexandra Bethlenfalvy

Myles Horton and Paulo Freire: Intersecting backgrounds

As two of the editors of *We Make the Road by Walking*, John Gaventa and John Peters noted, "While [Horton and Freire] shared, in some ways, a family background and intellectual heritage, they chose very different paths to begin to pursue their beliefs" (Gaventa & Peters, 1988, p. 5). Myles Horton preceded Freire in this world and the fields of adult education and educational reform for equity and justice. Born in Savannah, Tennessee, in 1905, Horton was born to white, working-class parents who were without formal education yet worked various jobs, often wherever employment was to be found. Although the family was poor, Horton's parents "never accepted the fact that they were inferior to anybody or that anybody was inferior to them" (Gaventa & Peters, 1988, p. 8).

The experience of frequent unemployment was characteristic of most people living in Appalachia during this time period. Indeed, as a child growing up in rural America, Horton was exposed to a lack of necessary material goods and a general poverty common to rural Appalachia (Adams, 1975; Horton & Freire, 1990). Horton internalized values under these conditions that would come to define his general educational philosophy, and internalized an almost unquestioned antipathy toward exploitive practice and a positive identification and respect for the poor. Consequently, he developed a harsh critique of the American wage and labor system. In his words, "My first feeling about [the wage system] was that it was very unjust for somebody to have to work so hard and get so little, and for somebody else to have so much" (Horton, 1990, p. 2). This inherent belief would lead a teenaged Horton to organize a strike and interracial meetings in a region deeply opposed to such values (Adams, 1975; Hale, 2007).

Against a backdrop of poverty and a commitment to social justice, Myles Horton articulated and implemented his ideas on establishing a new social order based on principles of justice and equity. Horton was searching for ideas and examples that could not necessarily be found in Appalachia. As Horton stated, "I had grown up in a religious world and was trying to get beyond that to understand the broader economic, cultural, and social contexts in which things happened" (Horton, 1990, p. 26). This led Horton to pursue graduate studies in New York City and Chicago where he researched not only the intellectual history behind radical reform, but also the practical knowledge on how to apply these ideas.

Horton articulated his ideas on education and social change in early 1932 upon reflection of a trip to observe the Danish Folk Schools that was a part of his graduate education. "I can't sleep but there are dreams," Horton noted in 1931 as he recorded his ideas for a school that would serve as "a stopping place for traveling liberals and a meeting place for Southern radicals" (Jacobs, 2003, p. 3). After his trip abroad, Horton and two other southern progressives, Jim Dombrowski and Don West, founded the Highlander Folk School in 1932. Located in the southern mountain region of Tennessee, Highlander was a central force in popular struggles (Adams, 1975; Glen, 1996; Hale, 2007; Horton & Freire, 1990; Jacobs 2003).

Paulo Freire was born in Recife, the capital city in the state of Pernambuco, in the northeastern part of Brazil in 1921. Alhough born into the middle class, the region Freire was born and raised was one of the poorest in the country, and the international economic depression introduced him to the reality of poverty and the oppression generated by hunger, exploitive working conditions, and restricted access to education. For Freire, the depression introduced to him "a real and concrete hunger that had no specific date of departure" and the poverty that precipitated it inspired a "solidarity with the children from the poor outskirts of town" (Macedo, 2002, p. 13).

He never forgot the lessons of poverty and economic hardship as he furthered his own education. Freire enrolled in the Universidade do Recife in 1943, where he studied philosophy and the psychology of language. He became a secondary school teacher of Portuguese. He eventually became the director of the Department of Education and Culture in Pernambuco and later the director of the Department of Cultural Extension of Recife University (Bradley & Ford, 2015; Gadotti & Torres, 2009). In these positions, Freire engaged in comprehensive adult literacy campaigns in the field that allowed him to test his theories on adult learning, literacy, and social and political theory.

The campaigns developed under the administrations of Getúlio Vargas and João Goulart, who implemented widespread adult literacy programs for poor rural communities and farmers as part of the modernizing campaigns to increase participation of the rural poor in self-government (Kee & Carr-Chellman, 2019). His work experienced unprecedented success. In one campaign, it was claimed that Freire and his team successfully educated 300 rural sugarcane workers in less than fifty days through a problem-posing method in which participants would first decipher images specific to the students. Such images or depictions were designed after in-depth observations and interactions with the community and served as the basis of a critical dialogue between students and teachers about larger social, political, and economic structures that defined their society (Gadotti & Torres, 2009; Kee & Carr-Chellman, 2019).

The process was inherently political as the methods were pedagogical in teaching literacy, but also a form of consciousness raising or "conscientización," in following the critical or Western Marxist tradition (Gadotti & Torres, 2009; Kee & Carr-Chellman, 2019). When the Brazilian Armed Forces, who received support from the US government, toppled the government in a military coup, Freire was branded as a subversive and a Communist by the new dictatorship. The military junta arrested and imprisoned Freire for seventy days, then exiled him. Freire first relocated to Bolivia, then Chile and the United States for sixteen years before returning to Brazil in 1980. It was while in Chile that Freire published the revolutionary text, *Pedagogy of the Oppressed* (Bradley & Ford, 2015; Gottesman, 2010; Kee & Carr-Chellman, 2019).

A meeting of the minds

Although familiar with each other's work, it is recorded that Horton and Freire met only briefly in 1973, when they were both invited to an adult education conference in Chicago. Horton himself did not attend, though members of the Highlander staff attended a conference at the Historic Penn Center on St. Helena Island in South Carolina, a conference titled, "Learning and Change Workshop with Dr. Paulo Freire," in January 1974 (Horton & Freire, 1990; "Learning and Change Workshop," January, 1973). During the "Brazilian Workers Discussion" in March 1978, Horton learned in more detail of "Paulo Freire's ideas and books [that] were prohibited in Brazil" ("Brazilian Trade Union," March 12, 1978). They crossed paths again in New York, California, Nicaragua, and, later, Latin American-based conferences (Glen, 1996; Horton, Kohl, & Kohl, 1998; Horton & Freire, 1990; "O'Leary to Myles Horton," October 23, 1979).

A fortuitous meeting in California during the summer of 1987 led to formal collaboration. Freire was in Los Angeles to partake in a memorial conference for his late wife, Elza. Horton was there visiting his daughter who was recovering from surgery necessitated by colon cancer. It was after more intimate conversations that Freire proposed to Horton the possibility of "talking a book," a method Freire himself used in publishing numerous texts. John Peters, a professor of adult education at the University of Tennessee, orchestrated with Highlander staff a visit with Paulo Freire in the fall of 1987. Freire gave a series of lectures and talks with students, faculty, and the public that were hosted at the University of Tennessee, titled "A Symposium on Education for Social Change" ("Paulo Freire Visit," 1987 and "Symposium on Education," 1987; Peters, personal communication, 2019).

After the visit in Knoxville, Freire spent time at Highlander for the conversations that constituted the bulwark of *We Make the Road by Walking* (Horton, 1998; Horton & Freire, 1990). John Peters and Brenda Bell, a graduate student of Peters, and John Gaventa, a professor of sociology and a co-director of research at Highlander Folk School, agreed to help transcribe, edit, and submit for review what was published as *We Make the Road by Walking* (Peters, personal communication, 2019).

Their work affirmed the rights of the poor to identify their own solutions or, at least, to be an integral part of the process to addressing the immediate problems. Horton's views on adult education ostensibly preceded Freire's ideology. In an interview, Horton credited Freire for "considerable progress made in the direction of getting working people to assume responsibility for their own education" ("Brazilian Trade Union," March 12, 1978, p. 1). Horton believed that while battling oppressive regimes was a collective effort, people must first consider what measures they can take separate from the group. Horton explains, "Learning to make decisions on problems effecting their lives is difficult and dangerous. The most valuable and lasting learning, we have found, comes from action; and sustained action is only possibly by people who have developed confidence in their group judgment and pride in who they are" ("Horton to Geraldine O'Leary," December 14, 1977, p. 1).

Although parallel and deeply intertwined, Freire and Horton's work diverged in meaningful ways. Highlander's trajectory and longevity by 1987 provided alternative narratives to Freire's well-publicized approach of solely involving working-class people. As Freire said, "It isn't from the universities or the theological seminaries but from the struggles of people against oppression that revolutionary consciousness comes" ("Brazilian Trade Union," March 12, 1978, p. 1). Freire believed that to effect societal change, individuals ought to be from the working class to confront socioeconomic and educational issues, though this does not account for his modest economic background. Horton's experiences supported the claim, noting that "our experience [at Highlander] is that people are conditioned by topdownsim to being given facts and told what to think" ("Horton to Geraldine O'Leary," December 14, 1977, p. 1).

Yet Horton in some ways disagreed with Freire's perception of class identity, or the belief that change agents can only be found among the poor. Horton suggested instead that the combined efforts of individuals from various classes are essential to fighting oppressive forces, acknowledging that "until people learn together and struggle together against repression, there is no hope for democracy" ("Horton to Geraldine O'Leary," December 14, 1977, p. 1). By the late 1980s, class identity at Highlander was important but not a determining factor when it came to remaking the social and political order.

Programmatic differences between the two shaped their collaboration as well. Geraldine O'Leary, an American educational worker located in Nicaragua, explained that the Nicaraguan Institute for Human Development relied on the "Paulo Freire method of conscientización," for their Adult Education programs ("O'Leary to Myles Horton," October 5, 1977). She acknowledged that Freire's most effective model at the time was "an audio-visual method using drawings, photos or slides to stimulate small groups to discuss a series of themes and leads them to self-awareness, self-respect and motivation to change their lives and the reality" ("O'Leary to Myles Horton," October 5, 1977).

While Highlander utilized audiovisual methods as well, Horton believed that residential workshops were a critical component. The workshops were to be led in a manner that draws on the personal experiences of individuals (Horton, 1990). Therefore, when Freire visited Highlander in 1988, Horton enhanced his outlook on adult education. Not only did Highlander use audiovisual materials, but they organized workshop participants in a way unfamiliar to Freire.

Historical review of *We Make the Road by Walking*

Reviewers of *We Make the Road by Walking* emphasize the significance of human connections, rather than the pedagogical parallels or contrasts between Horton and Freire. In their co-authored review, Stacy Kaser, Kathryn Miller, and Thomas Keyes collectively suggest that "the book might easily have been titled *We Make the Road by Talking*," as two humble intellectuals discuss the trajectory of "processes of social change" (Kaser, 1993, p. 144). Richard Blaustein (1995) also acknowledges this potential title change because the rhetoric in this book forces the reader to confront shifting notions of the "disenfranchised and the impoverished" (p. 30).

A powerful book indeed, *We Make the Road by Walking* draws on the value of intimately discussing methods of participatory education. Annelle Huggins (1991) underscores that "love for people, respect for people's abilities to shape their own lives, and the capacity to value others' experiences," are central elements to Horton and Freire's shared view on education (p. 98). The book has been taught around the world and was translated into two languages, Spanish and Hindi (John Peters, personal communication, March 5, 2019). Much like *Pedagogy of the Oppressed*, the collaborative project with Freire and Horton gained wide appeal among critical pedagogues and scholars.

The collaborative history behind *We Make the Road by Walking* illustrates a broader historic context that deepens our understanding of Freire and Horton. The release of *We Make the Road by Walking* through the network of Highlander Folk School helped facilitate the growing popularity and acceptance of Freire, particularly in the southern United States. As a site of political incubation, Highlander provided a foundation for a regional network that cultivated activist ties, developed organizational strategies, and raised a collective consciousness.

By providing an established network for the dissemination of Freire, his work could be incorporated into a region that was not renowned for critical pedagogy or transformative educational practice. The publication of *We Make the Road by Walking* aided the work of Highlander, too. As Horton noted, Freire "got academicians to read something that is based on the study of people. Few of them had ever done it before" (Jacobs, 2003, p. 55).

This history demonstrates that the road they sought to make is still incomplete. Isaac Gottesman demonstrated that Freire's impact in the United States was greatest not with the publication of *Pedagogy of the Oppressed* when it was released in 1970. The greater impact was not felt until the early to mid-1980s, over a decade after the translated text was published (Gottesman, 2010).

As *We Make the Road by Walking* generated an impact into the 2000s, the text provides a critical link to an activist past. In addition, since much of this work took place in the American and global South, it highlights these regions as historically activist spaces or inclined to educational activism. More than just a meeting of the minds, the book ushered in a new understanding of reform and a text through which to read the shifting nature of education for social change. The book continues to compel us to not only travel the road they paved, but also continue to "speak the book" today.

References

Adams, F. (1975). *Unearthing seeds of fire: The idea of Highlander.* Winston-Salem: John F. Blair.

Blaustein, R. (1995). [Review of the book *We make the road by walking: Conversations on education and social change* by Myles Horton and Paulo Freire]. *In Trust, 7*(1), 30.

Brazilian Trade Union. (March 12, 1978). *"Brazilian workers discussion."* [Transcription] Highlander Research and Education Center Records. (M2004-203, Box 7, Folder 57). Wisconsin Historical Society, Madison, Wisconsin.

Gadotti, M., & Torres, C. A. (2009). Paulo Freire: Education for development. *Development and Change, 40*(6), 1255–1267. Published on behalf of the Institute of Social Studies (Oxford: Blackwell Publishing).

Gaventa, J., & Peters, J. (1988). "The lives and conversations of Paulo Freire and Myles Horton." [Book Proposal]. Highlander Research and Education Center Records. (M2004-203, Box 9, Folder 15). Wisconsin Historical Society, Madison, Wisconsin.

Glen, J. (1996). *Highlander.* Knoxville: University of Tennessee Press.

Gottesman, I. (2010). Sitting in the waiting room: Paulo Freire and the critical turn in the field of education. *Educational Studies, 46*(4), 376–399.

Hale, J. (2007). Early pedagogical influences on the Mississippi Freedom Schools: Myles Horton and critical education in the deep south. *American Educational History Journal, 34*(2), 315–330.

Horton, M. (December 14, 1977). "Letter to Geraldine O'Leary." [Letter]. Highlander Research and Education Center Records. (MSS831, Box 8, Folder 5). Wisconsin Historical Society, Madison, Wisconsin.

Horton, M. (May 4, 1988). "Letter to Moacir Gadotti." [Letter]. Highlander Research and Education Center Records. (MSS831, Box 7, Folder 7). Wisconsin Historical Society, Madison, Wisconsin.

Horton, M., & Freire, P. (1990). *We make the road by walking: Conversations on education and Social Change.* Philadelphia, PA: Temple University Press.

Horton, M. with Kohl, J., & Kohl, H. (1998). *The long haul: An autobiography.* New York: Teachers College Press.

Huggins, A. R. (1991). [Review of the book *We make the road by walking: Conversations on education and social change* by Myles Horton and Paulo Freire]. *Library Journal, 116*(5), 98.

Jacobs, D. (Ed.) (2003). *The Myles Horton reader: Education for social change.* Knoxville: University of Tennessee Press.

Kaser, S., Keyes, T., & Miller, K. (1993). [Review of the book *We make the road by walking: Conversations on education and social change* by Myles Horton and Paulo Freire]. *The Oral History Review, 21*(1), 143–146.

Kee, J. C., & Carr-Chellman, D. J. (2019). Paulo Freire, critical literacy, and indigenous resistance. *Educational Studies, 55*(1), 89–103.

Learning and Change Workshop with Dr. Paulo Freire (January 5–8, 1973). Highlander Research and Education Center, Box 24, folder "Mike Clark Attends Freire Workshop."

Macedo, D. (2002). Introduction in P. Freire, *Pedagogy of the oppressed*, 11–27. New York: Continuum.

"Myles Horton's Speaking Engagements in São Paulo." (May 1988). Highlander Research and Education Center Records. (MSS831, Box 7, Folder 7). Wisconsin Historical Society, Madison, Wisconsin.

O'Leary, Geraldine. (October 5, 1977). "Letter to Myles Horton." [Letter]. Highlander Research and Education Center Records. (MSS831, Box 8, Folder 5). Wisconsin Historical Society, Madison, Wisconsin.

O'Leary, G. (October 23, 1979). "Letter to Myles Horton." [Letter]. Highlander Research and Education Center Records. (MSS831, Box 8, Folder 5). Wisconsin Historical Society, Madison, Wisconsin.

Peters, J. (March 5, 2019). [interview with the author].

"Paulo Freire Visit" (1987). Highlander Research and Education Center Records. (M2000-186, Box 10, Folder "Freire Returns"). Wisconsin Historical Society, Madison, Wisconsin.

Porfilio, B. J., & Ford, D. (2015). *Leaders in critical pedagogy: Narratives for understanding and solidarity* (Rotterdam: Sense Publishers).

"Symposium on Education for Social Change." (1987). Highlander Research and Education Center Records. (M2000-186, Box 10, Folder "Paulo Freire invitation; schedule 1987"). Wisconsin Historical Society, Madison, Wisconsin.

11

The Beloved Community and Utopia: Hope in the Face of Struggle as Envisioned by Martin Luther King, Jr. and Paulo Freire

Drick Boyd

Hope for the future, lessons from the past

In his book *The Discipline of Hope*, Herbert Kohl (1998) wrote, "Providing hope to young people is the major challenge of teaching. Through engaging the minds and imaginations of children, teachers can help children develop the strength, pride and sensitivity they need to engage the world, and not despair when things seem stacked against them" (pp. 9–10). As a college professor teaching graduate and undergraduate students, I have always perceived my role in similar terms. That is, as a teacher I am preparing the next generation to carry on the struggles for peace, economic equity, racial justice, and social inclusion that I have engaged in for the 40+ years of my adult life. Yet in this age of capitalist exploitation, migrant masses seeking refuge, war, and white supremacy, hope can sometimes seem like a pipe dream. At such times it is helpful to draw on the lessons of the past to find guides who can lead us through this maze of fear and despair. Two such guides are Dr. Martin Luther King, Jr. and Paulo Freire.

If Martin Luther King's life had not been cut short by an assassin's bullet, one can only wonder if he and Paulo Freire would have eventually joined efforts in a movement for peace and justice among the world's oppressed peoples. It is this speculation that leads me to examine the respective visions of hope articulated by Freire and King. King's vision of hope was embodied in the idea of the Beloved Community, whereas for Freire it was captured in the concept of Utopia.

King's view of hope

For King, hope involved a faith in the future with justice as the ultimate goal. In his 1961 address "Love, Law, and Civil Disobedience," King (1986) described the Civil Rights Movement as "a movement based on faith in the future. It is a movement based on a philosophy, the possibility of the future bringing into being something real and meaningful. It is a movement based on hope" (p. 52). In that same speech he went onto say even though he knew that many would have to suffer before their hope would be realized, his faith in the future was tied to the conviction that ultimately *truth* and *justice* would win out over *falsehood* and *evil*.

In a sermon entitled "The Meaning of Hope," King (1967) said: "Genuine hope involves a recognition ... that what is hoped for is already there ... that it is a power which drives us to fulfill that which we hope for ... [and] is based on willingness to face the risk of failure and embrace an in-spite-of quality" (p. 3). He stressed that hope was not something one held individually or in isolation but had a "we quality" that connected one to others. King further emphasized that hope was necessary for life and that the hopeless person was spiritually dead, even if physically living. Finally, he underscored that for him the "ground of hope is the eternality of God" (p. 9) who upholds the basic morality of the cosmos.

Howard Thurman and the Beloved Community

King's conception of hope was most clearly embodied in his vision of the Beloved Community. It is widely acknowledged that the concept Beloved Community was first articulated by philosopher Josiah Royce who lived and wrote near the turn of the twentieth century (Herstein, 2009). Royce conceived of the Beloved Community as a community of individuals committed to a higher cause characterized by relationships of "super-human form of love" that resembled the divine love. The key to this love, or what Royce called "loyalty," is an all-encompassing social cause that requires self-sacrifice and a renunciation of self-centeredness in pursuit of a higher good (Jensen, 2016).

Although King may have been exposed to Royce's work while earning his PhD from Boston University, most likely King's acquaintance with Royce's came through his mentor, Howard Thurman.

Thurman (1971) acknowledged Royce's influence on his thought and characterized the Beloved Community as a "harmony that transcends all diversities and in which diversity finds its richness" (p. 6). However, for Thurman (1966) desegregation and integration by themselves were not sufficient; there had to be a quality of relationships between individuals that made the community a "living confirmation" of the transforming power of the Divine. Moreover, Thurman, as well as King, suggested the idea of the Beloved Community originated in the Black Church tradition.[1]

Thurman's ideas were further crystallized when he pastored the intentionally integrated congregation in San Francisco he co-founded in 1944, *The Church for the Fellowship of All Peoples*. It was there that Thurman realized bringing people of different races together was not sufficient; there had to be an authentic quality of relationships that balanced freedom to be oneself with a commitment to mutuality, "an achievement of the human spirit as [people] seek to fulfill their high destiny as children of God" (Thurman, 1966, p. 11).

Martin Luther King, Jr. and the Beloved Community

King's vision of the Beloved Community expanded on Thurman's view to embrace the global community. For King, this community did not just consist of like-minded individuals but embraced friend and foe alike. This is why he claimed that the purpose of his boycotts, nonviolent actions, and other efforts was ultimately "reconciliation and redemption" of all people regardless race, ideology, or nationality (Jensen, 2016, p. 251).

King further believed that any vision of the Beloved Community needed to include certain key elements. First, there needed to a commitment to nonviolence which epitomized the spirit of the redemptive power of love

---

[1] It should be noted that in addition to any influence Royce and Thurman had on King's "integrationist" rhetoric, this was also integral to the Black Church tradition in which King was raised. As James Cone (1986, 2007) stresses, the Black Church Integrationist tradition precedes the twentieth century and can be documented as far back as Frederick Douglass and the abolitionist movement.

(Inwood, 2009). Second, like Thurman, he believed there needed to be a deep level of integration that went beyond people simply being together, but rather the development of authentic relationships that formed true community across race and class. There also needed to be the eradication of economic inequity, whereby every person had the spiritual and material necessities of life. Finally, he saw the Beloved Community as the concrete yet imperfect representation of the Kingdom of God in human life. Even though societies might not fully realize the vision of the Beloved Community, it would be a reminder that God is at work in the affairs of human life (Smith & Zepp, 1974).

For King the Beloved Community existed on three levels. The first level is the achievement of integration and the alleviation of economic and racial inequities. The second level is reached when people of different races and backgrounds find their full personhood through community with one another. The third and deepest level exists in the recognition that the diverse community committed to a common cause lives out of a divine overflow of unconditional love (Greek "agape"). For King the ultimate goal of his commitment to nonviolent direct action was to draw the adversary into that community through the power of Divine Love working through persons and the community of which they are a part (Jensen, 2016).

Paulo Freire and Utopia[2]

For Freire, hope was not so much a choice as it was a basic human need. In *Pedagogy of Hope* (1996), he wrote that hope is a natural human response to injustice and corruption. While acknowledging the hopelessness that some people feel in the face of oppression, he countered: "There is hope, however timid, on the street corners, a hope in each every one of us." He went on: "I do not understand human existence, and the struggle needed to improve it, apart from hope and dream. Hope is an ontological need. Hopelessness is but hope that has lost its bearings." He concluded: "I am hopeful, not out of mere stubbornness, but out of an existential, concrete imperative" (Freire, 1996,

[2]   Much of this section comes from the author's book *Paulo Freire: His Faith, Spirituality and Theology*, co-authored with James D. Kirylo (Sense, 2017).

p. 8). In other words, for Freire hopelessness was not an option as hopefulness is a driving necessity for those suffering injustice and oppression.

Like King, Freire's concept of hope involved the Divine. In a letter to a friend, Freire (1972) discussed God's involvement in history. He wrote that he did not believe God brought about peace and justice apart from the work and struggle of the people. He put it this way: "In the final analysis, the Word of God is inviting me to re-create the world, not for my brothers' domination, but for their liberation." People must "make themselves subject, agents of their own salvation and liberation" (p. 1).

Utopia

Freire's ideas about hope were captured in his concept of Utopia. He characterized Utopia as "the aspiration for radical changes in society in such as areas as economics, human relationships, property, the right to employment, to land, to education and to health" (Freire, 1998, p. 6). To understand Utopia, one has to use the power of imagination. He wrote: "There is no change without dream, as there is no dream without hope" (Freire, 1996, p. 91).

Freire's conception of the new society drew on the personalism of Mounier and Marx's belief in the human capacity to change the course of history, but his ideas of Utopia largely derived from his interaction with the liberation theologian Gustavo Gutiérrez. Like Freire, Gutiérrez (1971) believed Utopia consisted of two subversive forces in history: denunciation and annunciation. A commitment to Utopia "necessarily means a denunciation of the existing order … a repudiation of a dehumanizing situation" (p. 233). At the same time Utopia announces the new order "the forecast of a different order of things, a new society" (Gutiérrez, 1971, p. 233). This dynamic of denouncing and announcing leads to action whereby people both imagine and voice their dream for a new society while working to bring it into being.

Freire (1998) asserted that this work of denunciation and annunciation must be led by the oppressed. And while this work involves political action, at its deepest level it is also the work of faith and the humanization of the individual (Gutiérrez, 1971). As the oppressed work for sociopolitical change, through faith they bring into concrete being God's Reign on the earth. As Gutiérrez (1971) writes, "If utopia humanizes economic, social and political liberation, this humanness—in light of the Gospel—reveals God" (p. 239). Webb (2008) suggests Gutiérrez's (and by extension Freire's) concept of hope is transformative because it leads to the creation and establishment characterized by justice fellowship and solidarity.

However, for Freire (1975/2000), utopia was not only a political and theological concept, but it was the orientation one must have in their approach to teaching. He called his pedagogical philosophy "a utopian pedagogy" because "it is filled with hope" as it engages students and their teachers in a collaborative process of denunciation and annunciation: analyzing their dehumanizing reality, fostering a commitment to change that reality, and working concretely for that change. Utopian pedagogy is not only "realistic" because it sees the world as it truly is, but also "risky" because it challenges individuals to challenge the status quo and work toward creating a more just, equitable, and liberating future in the face of fierce opposition from those who benefit from the status quo (pp. 28–29).

Comparisons and contrasts

So, what do the Beloved Community and Utopia have in common, and in what ways can they add understanding to the nature of hope in these troubled times? First, both the Beloved Community and Utopia point to a positive, constructive vision of a just and equitable sociopolitical society. As King (1967) said, hope arises out of "a tension between present and future" (p. 5). King characterized hope as a faith in the future and belief in the basic moral foundations of the universe. Freire referred to hope as an "untested feasibility"—something possible yet not tested (Kirylo & Boyd, 2017).

Second, both King and Freire saw hope as bringing about the full humanity and personhood of the individual and the creation of a community of people bound together by a common political or social agenda, as well as deep and meaningful relationships. Third, in both visions of the hoped-for future, faith in God plays a significant role. Both Freire and King believed the realization of hope came about in cooperation with God. For Freire, God's role was to cast the vision, while the people work to bring the vision into reality. For King, God provided the very foundation for hope at all; one's faith in God provided the energy to live in hope and work for a better future. Even if that better future is not fully realized, the vision moves people to make concrete changes for justice in their setting.

Fourth, Freire's incorporation of the process of denunciation and annunciation, while not as clearly articulated by King, was certainly demonstrated by the movement he led. So often the Civil Rights Movement found itself vehemently, and nonviolently, confronting the injustices of segregation in its many forms (denunciation), while at the same projecting a vision of a new society (annunciation). Even in King's last sermon in Memphis, where he had gone to support resistance to a violent and oppressive city regime, he spoke of a "promised land" (annunciation) to which he saw the movement was headed (King, 1986, p. 286).

Finally, the realization of the Beloved Community and Utopia is primarily the work of the oppressed. King often spoke of the inspiration he got from all those who boycotted, marched, went to jail, sat at lunch counters, and rode the buses on the Freedom Rides (King, 1986). By living into and out of their divine hope, the oppressed not only achieve their freedom but also will set their oppressors free from their need to oppress. In a similar fashion, Freire (1970/1993/2018) believed that the oppressed, working in solidarity with non-oppressed, can free their oppressor from the need to use violence and dehumanize the people.

The differences between King and Freire were more nuanced than substantive. For King hope was a choice to believe in the moral foundation of the universe, whereas for Freire hope was an ontological need without which one could not live. Freire believed that even the most despairing persons have a measure of hope regardless of how hopeless they feel. King seemed to reflect Freire's sentiment when he recounted the stories of his slave ancestors who persisted in the face of terrible atrocities and said, "hope refuses to give up" (King, 1967, p. 7).

Conclusion

Teachers at all levels of education are charged with providing their students with a reason for hope. If we—who claim a critical pedagogical mantle—only provide information and skills without seeking to infuse our students with a reason for engaging and improving the world, we have failed them. We must enable them to think critically about the issues facing them as current and future citizens, denouncing injustice and announcing a new vision of the world. One only has to think of the students of Parkland, Florida, who used the tragic shootings at Marjory Stoneman Douglas High School to begin the March for Our Lives movement. While taking nothing away from the power and initiative of those students, I suspect that there were teachers in that school practicing a pedagogy of hope that empowered those students could be catalysts for change in the laws and policies regarding the use of guns in this country.

When students, whether at Parkland or any school, look back at the teachers who significantly impacted their lives, it will not be the math or English or science they learned. It will be those teachers who instilled in them a love of learning and gave them a reason to believe they could make a positive difference in the world, because they too lived out a vision of hope for a better world. As Herbert Kohl (1998) writes, "To teach hope you yourself must be hopeful" (p. 10). Dr. King's vision of the Beloved Community and Freire's vision of Utopia are two images we can embrace, learn from, and live into as we prepare the next generation for the challenges facing them now and in the future.

References

Cone, J. (1986). The theology of Martin Luther King, Jr. *Union Seminary Quarterly Review, 40*(4), 21–39.

Cone, J. (2007). *Martin & Malcolm & America: A dream or a nightmare*. Maryknoll, NY: Orbis Books.

Freire, P. (1970/1993/2018). *Pedagogy of the oppressed, 50th Anniversary Edition*. New York: Bloomsbury Academic.

Freire, P. (1972). The third world and theology. *LADOC* 2.29a, 13–15.

Freire, P. (1996). *Pedagogy of hope: Reliving pedagogy of the oppressed.* New York: Continuum.

Freire, P. (1998). *Pedagogy of freedom: Ethics, democracy and civic courage.* Lanham, MD: Rowman & Littlefield.

Freire, P. (1975/2000). *Cultural action for freedom, 2000 Edition.* Harvard Educational Review, Monograph Series, No. 1, Revised edn. Cambridge, MA: Harvard College.

Gutiérrez, G. (1971). *A theology of liberation.* Maryknoll, NY: Orbis Books.

Herstein, G. (2009). The Roycean roots of the beloved community. *The Pluralist,* 4(2), 91–107.

Inwood, J. F. J. (2009). Searching for the promised land: Examining Dr Martin Luther King Jr.'s concept of the beloved community. *Antipode, 31*(3), 487–508.

Jensen, K. (2016). The growing edges of beloved community: From Royce to Thurman and King. *Transactions of the Charles S. Pierce Society, 52*(2), 239–258.

King, M. L. (1967). The meaning of hope. The King Center. Retrieved from http://www.thekingcenter.org/archive/document/meaning-hope# (Accessed July 2, 2018).

King, M. L. (1986). I see the promised land. In J. Washington (Ed.), *A testament of hope: The essential writings of Martin Luther King, Jr.* (pp. 279–286). San Francisco, CA: Harper and Row Publishers.

Kirylo, J., & Boyd, D. (2017). *Paulo Freire: His faith, spirituality and theology.* Boston, MA: Sense Publishers.

Kohl, H. (1998). *The discipline of hope: Learning from a lifetime of teaching.* New York: New Press.

Smith, K., & Zepp, I. (1974). Martin Luther King's vision of the beloved community. *The Christian Century,* April 3, 1974, 361–363.

Thurman, H. (1966). Desegregation, integration and the beloved community. *The Howard Thurman Papers Project of Boston University.* Retrieved from https://www.bu.edu/htpp/files/2017/06/Desegregation-Integration-and-the-Beloved-Community.Sept_1966.pdf (Accessed November 26, 2019).

Thurman, H. (1971). *The search for common ground: An inquiry into the basis of man's experience of community.* New York: Harper.

Webb, D. (2008). Christian hope and the politics of hope. *Utopian Studies, 19*(1), 113–144.

12

Less Certain But No Less Committed:
Paulo Freire and Simone de Beauvoir on
Ethics and Education

Peter Roberts

We live in a time of exaggerated certainties. Extremism, across the religious and political spectrum, is on the rise, with fanatical conviction, intolerance, and ignorance sometimes leading to horrific acts of violence. Capitalism, in its current neoliberal, globalized form, appears to have trumped all other modes of production and is invariably touted as the only possible way forward for "developed" and "developing" nations alike. The current president of the United States makes almost daily declarations via Twitter with an expressed definitiveness that brooks no doubt. We are told, in no uncertain terms, what makes us happy, and products and services are marketed aggressively by those seeking to sell their version of the good life to us.

In education too, we have witnessed the emergence of new discourses of certainty. Funding agencies expect initiatives in education to be "evidence-based," as if questions relating to what counts as evidence, for whom, in what ways, and under what circumstances require no further discussion. Science is frequently seen as the only legitimate arbiter on matters of educational debate, and developments such as "brain-based" education are promoted as the answer to a host of pedagogical problems. There is also a widespread belief in the educational importance of new technologies, and it is assumed that if children are to flourish in the twenty-first century, computers and other digital devices must become an integral part of classroom life. Policy-makers in almost every country of the Western world take it as given that economic advancement should be a key aim of education.

We have, or think we have, greater certainty than ever before in considering how best to structure our societies, what to prioritize in education, and how to live our lives. The work of Paulo Freire suggests we should be a little less certain than we appear to be. Freire argues that our certainties should always be considered *provisional*. It is impossible, he says, "to be absolutely certain, as if the certainty of today were the same as that of yesterday and will continue to be the same as that of tomorrow" (Freire, 1997, pp. 30–31). Another thinker with much to offer in addressing questions of certainty and uncertainty is the French existentialist philosopher and novelist, Simone de Beauvoir.

Existentialism had a notable influence on Freire's thought (Darder, 2018; Mackie, 1980; Webster, 2016). This is most apparent in *Pedagogy of the Oppressed* and other early publications, where references to writers such as Sartre, Jaspers, Buber, and Marcel are not difficult to find (Freire, 1972a, b, 1976). But some of the central philosophical concerns that preoccupied twentieth-century existentialists continued to leave their mark on Freire throughout his intellectual and pedagogical life. Those animating concerns are captured particularly well by Beauvoir in her principal philosophical work, *The Ethics of Ambiguity* (Beauvoir, 1948).

Beauvoir and Freire remind us that doubts and uncertainties are fundamental to our existence as human beings and that excessive certainty can be dangerous, oppressive, and misleading. They show that uncertainty need not impede our ability to make decisions and take action; on the contrary, it can provide the basis for a renewed sense of commitment to education and social change.

Ambiguity, freedom, and responsibility: The work of Simone de Beauvoir

Beauvoir (1948) argues that there is an inherent *ambiguity* in our human condition. This is a source of both hope and despair. As conscious, thinking beings, we can interpret and experience the world in ways that are not possible for other forms of life; yet we cannot free ourselves from that world; we remain *of* the world while reflecting on it. We assert our power to determine our own destinies, yet also find ourselves "crushed by the dark weight of other things" (p. 7). We perceive ourselves as unique, sovereign subjects in a world of objects; yet, as objects for others, we are merely individuals in a greater collectivity. We believe we know that we exist, yet "between the past which no longer is and the future which is not yet, this moment when ... [we exist] is nothing" (p. 7).

Over the ages, philosophers have endeavored to eliminate the ambiguity of the human condition "by escaping from the sensible world or by being engulfed in it, by yielding to eternity or enclosing oneself in the pure moment" (p. 8). We may try to confine the most troubling aspects of our existence to the shadows, or to create a sense of order that will provide the security we think we need. But such efforts simply serve to highlight the "disorder from which we suffer" (p. 8). The sense of mastery that emerges from advances in technology and science is also accompanied by a crushing fear of being subject to forces beyond our control. As rational beings, we have the capacity not only to create but also, as the example of atomic weapons has shown, to destroy.

Beauvoir proposes that rather than fleeing from the truth of our ambiguity, we should look it in the face and embrace it. It is in ambiguity, in imperfection, that the terrain for ethical investigation is to be found. This is not a rules-based ethics, where abstract principles can be specified in advance as the basis for human conduct. We should not look to an "impersonal universal man who is the source of values" (p. 17); instead, we should focus on particulars, on individual men and women as they negotiate the situations in which they find themselves. We form ourselves as ethical beings through the process of existing, and in doing so we discover a world characterized not by certainties and predictability but by uncertainty and complexity.

It is not a matter of being pessimistic or of being optimistic but of acknowledging contingency as a fundamental feature of human existence. We cannot turn to sources higher than ourselves in seeking a warrant for our activities. We have to decide, to act, in the face of situations that provide no easy answers. As human beings, we must, Beauvoir argues, accept responsibility for the world we create. Our destiny is not given to us; rather, it is up to us to give our lives meaning and significance. This carries inherent risks, and can be intimidating, for we typically do not like to feel in danger. Yet, as Beauvoir points out, "it is because there are real dangers, real failures and real earthly damnation that words like victory, wisdom or joy have meaning" (p. 34).

For Beauvoir, we remain free beings not despite the ambiguity of our human condition but precisely because of this. Beauvoir embraces a concept of freedom that is intimately connected with the idea of existence. Freedom is "the source from which all significations and all values spring"; it is "the original condition of all justification of existence" (p. 24). Freedom for Beauvoir is not the same as license or unfettered liberty; rather, it is the ground on which moral life is established. In exercising our freedom, we also form ourselves as moral beings. Freedom is more than spontaneity, for all spontaneity, on closer examination, is "pure contingency" (p. 25). Free moral decisions can only be made when we have the capacity to place our actions in historical perspective, and to recognize ourselves in the past and imagine ourselves in the future. Freedom requires willing and perseverance, and if the choices we make are to be genuine, "patience, courage, and fidelity" will be necessary (p. 27).

Failures earlier in life, if viewed with bitter regret, can blight our ability to face obstacles in the future. We can become discouraged and disillusioned. Fear of further failure can prevent us from taking on any substantial new challenges, but as Beauvoir sees it, "gloomy passivity" is not the answer, and nor is Stoic indifference (p. 29). Instead, facing life's difficulties, aware of the contingent nature of our existence, and hence of constraints that hamper us in our pursuits, affirms our existence as free beings. Freedom does not "trap" being; it discloses it. This disclosure, Beauvoir says, is "the transition from being to existence" (p. 30).

Paulo Freire on education, uncertainty, and commitment

The theme of uncertainty has an important place in Freire's work (Roberts, 2005). Uncertainty for Freire has ontological, epistemological, ethical, and educational dimensions. The starting point for Freire's ontology and ethic is the notion of humanization (Freire, 1972a). As humans, we exist both *in* and *with* the world. We humanize ourselves through *praxis*: critical, dialogical reflection and action for transformation. Freire stresses that we are *unfinished* beings, with the capacity to become *more* fully human but always with more work to do. The reality that emerges as we transform ourselves and the world presents its own, fresh challenges, requiring further reflective action from us. In a world that is constantly changing, knowledge too is necessarily incomplete. In seeking to know, we can at best come *closer* to grasping the essence of the object under investigation; we can never attain absolute, final, or full knowledge.

In keeping with Beauvoir's views, Freire contends that to be human is to exist as an ethical being (Freire, 1998a). As reflective beings facing an uncertain world, *we must decide* what to do; we must exercise the distinctive responsibilities we have as humans and commit, even though we can never be certain of quite what will happen as we act in the world. As Beauvoir recognized, and as Freire also acknowledges, this can be unsettling and distressing, but it is also the basis of our freedom. The ethical dimension of human existence is, Freire would add, also the foundation for our formation as educational beings. Freire, like Beauvoir, does not equate freedom with license; he speaks of the need for limits to freedom, consistent with the principle of ensuring, as far as reasonably possible, that our actions as free beings do not to impede the pursuit of humanization by others. Addressing constraints to freedom is, for Freire, an important educational task, requiring of us that we place personal and immediate problems in their broader social, cultural, and historical contexts (Shor, 1980).

Freire argues against both authoritarian and "anything goes" pedagogical approaches, stressing the need for structure, purpose, and direction in liberating education (Freire & Shor, 1987). In the second chapter of *Pedagogy of the Oppressed*, Freire's primary concern was not "teacher talk" but rather the authoritarian and oppressive nature of banking education (Freire, 1972a). Banking education relies on excessive certainties. It takes it as given that the teacher holds all the worthwhile knowledge and that students are ignorant. It also assumes that the social system to which education contributes should be supported and retained. It was the discouragement of questioning, the suppression of dissent, and the implicit acceptance of inequities and injustices in banking education that troubled Freire the most. Teachers have a responsibility to know their subject domains well, but they should also be open to having their views challenged by students. Critical reflection, dialogue, and debate should be welcomed and actively encouraged. Freire wanted to foster critical engagement with not just texts but also *contexts* (Freire & Macedo, 1987; Roberts, 1996).

Those who work with students in classrooms should not, Freire argues, see themselves as mere facilitators; they should embrace the term "teacher" and work hard to live up to all that this term implies (see Freire & Macedo, 1995). Teaching, whether in formal or informal educational settings, is always an *interventionist* activity, but this does not mean it has to be *impositional* (Roberts, 2003). There is, as Freire sees it, no way to be "neutral" in taking on such a task; educating others is always a political process (Freire, 1985, 1994, 2004; Kirylo, 2011; Mayo, 1999; Schugurensky, 2011). We must know what we stand for and why, while remaining open to the possibility of change. Teaching is one of the most difficult but also most rewarding tasks a human being can take on. It involves long hours of preparation, a deep sense of care for those with whom one works, and a constant readiness to examine one's ideas afresh. To be a good teacher takes great courage (Freire, 1998b).

The same is true of education more generally. Freire's work shows that education does not make life "easier" for us; it is an uncomfortable, demanding, lifelong process. This is consistent with Beauvoir's observation that exercising our freedom as existing human beings requires willing and perseverance. Education is not something that is "given" to us; rather, it is "created" through persistent human effort and struggle. To commit to education is to risk the possibility of suffering and despair as well as joy and fulfillment (Freire, 1994, 1996; Roberts, 2013). Education gives us a fuller, more nuanced and complex, more balanced understanding of what it means to exist as a human being. It is, Freire insisted, not merely an intellectual endeavor but a profoundly emotional process.

All education is, in effect, a form of work on the self, but the self as Freire and Beauvoir understand it is not "self-contained." We are *social* beings, and our formation through education always depends on others, even if the connections we establish and the relationships we develop may sometimes be less direct than an immediate face-to-face pedagogical encounter. We can, Freire maintains, have a dialogical connection with authors and texts separated from us great distances of the passing of many years (cf. Freire, 1976). Freire, like Beauvoir, does not adopt a posture of passivity. To the contrary, his pedagogy proceeds from the premise that while dehumanization is a reality, it is not an inevitability, and a commitment to building better worlds is, for Freire, one of the key aims of education (Freire, 1972a, 1994, 2007; Horton & Freire, 1990; Roberts & Freeman-Moir, 2013; Torres, 2014).

Freire's later work emphasizes the importance of becoming less certain than we sometimes tend to be. Freire does not reject the idea of certainty altogether; he *qualifies* it. He is not an advocate for either complete certainty or total uncertainty. Being "less" certain implies a comparison with something else, and for Freire, a key contrast in his later years was between his own position and the views adopted by neoliberals. By the 1990s, neoliberalism had become political orthodoxy, and those who adhered to its creed acted as if any other direction for economic and social reform was unthinkable. Freire regarded neoliberalism as fatalistic and dehumanizing, too closed to alternatives, too dismissive of other ideas (Freire, 1996, 1998a, 2004).

While he was most heavily critical of those on the right of the political spectrum, Freire also expressed dismay at the excessive certainties exhibited by some on the political left. As far as he was concerned, dogmatism and an inability to work constructively rather than destructively with difference hampered progress in addressing pressing social problems and played into the hands of those who sought to rule via "divide and conquer" policies (cf. Freire, 1996, 1997).

Freire encouraged us, as teachers and learners, to develop—through reflection, reading, listening, dialogue, and investigation—*sufficient* certainty to act, without being so certain that we are unable to seriously consider competing points of view. Seen in this light, education implies a kind of restlessness in our existence as human beings. We may recognize that if some things are to be questioned, other things must be accepted, but we must also acknowledge that what we accept, and why, may change over time. We must remain open, humble, and ever ready to learn as we make our way in the world.

Conclusion

The need to engage the work of thinkers such as Simone de Beauvoir and Paulo Freire has never been more apparent than at our current moment in world history. The excessive certainties that characterize our age are deeply worrying from an ethical and educational point of view. Beauvoir and Freire teach us that such tendencies run counter to the capacities we have as reflective, restless beings. The task of seeking to more deeply understand ourselves and the world we inhabit is necessarily incomplete, and the knowledge we gain in undertaking this work must always be regarded as partial and provisional.

We can, and should, still draw distinctions between "better" and "worse" ways of living and making sense of the world, but in making such judgments we must always be open to the prospect of being convinced otherwise in the future. For both Beauvoir and Freire, uncertainty is not something that is merely espoused as an abstract philosophical notion; it is *lived*, and constantly renegotiated, as we make decisions, take action, and join with others in dialogue and solidarity. By becoming less certain of our certainties and acknowledging our fragilities, while still being prepared to commit ourselves to others and to the ideals we espouse, we affirm our existence as ethical and educational beings.

References

Beauvoir, S. de (1948). *The ethics of ambiguity* (B. Frechtman, Trans.). New York: Citadel Press.

Darder, A. (2018). *The student guide to Freire's Pedagogy of the oppressed*. London: Bloomsbury.

Freire, P. (1972a). *Pedagogy of the oppressed*. Harmondsworth: Penguin.

Freire, P. (1972b). *Cultural action for freedom*. Harmondsworth: Penguin.

Freire, P. (1976). *Education: The practice of freedom*. London: Writers and Readers.

Freire, P. (1985). *The politics of education*. London: Macmillan.

Freire, P. (1994). *Pedagogy of hope*. New York: Continuum.

Freire, P. (1996). *Letters to Cristina: Reflections on my life and work*. London: Routledge.

Freire, P. (1997). *Pedagogy of the heart.* New York: Continuum.

Freire, P. (1998a). *Pedagogy of freedom: Ethics, democracy, and civic courage.* Lanham, MD: Rowman and Littlefield.

Freire, P. (1998b). *Teachers as cultural workers: Letters to those who dare teach.* Boulder, CO: Westview Press.

Freire, P. (2004). *Pedagogy of indignation.* Boulder, CO: Paradigm Publishers.

Freire, P. (2007). *Daring to dream.* Boulder, CO: Paradigm Publishers.

Freire, P., & Macedo, D. (1987). *Literacy: Reading the word and the world.* London: Routledge.

Freire, P., & Macedo, D. (1995). A dialogue: Culture, language, and race. *Harvard Educational Review, 65*(3), 377–402.

Freire, P., & Shor, I. (1987). *A pedagogy for liberation.* London: Macmillan.

Horton, M., & Freire, P. (1990). *We make the road by walking: Conversations on education and social change.* Philadelphia, PA: Temple University Press.

Kirylo, J. D. (2011). *Paulo Freire: The man from Recife.* New York: Peter Lang.

Mackie, R. (1980). Contributions to the thought of Paulo Freire. In R. Mackie (Ed.), *Literacy and revolution: The pedagogy of Paulo Freire* (pp. 93–119). London: Pluto Press.

Mayo, P. (1999). *Gramsci, Freire and adult education: Possibilities for transformative action.* London: Zed Books.

Roberts, P. (1996). Critical literacy, breadth of perspective, and universities: Applying insights from Freire. *Studies in Higher Education, 21*(2), 149–163.

Roberts, P. (2003). Epistemology, ethics and education: Addressing dilemmas of difference in the work of Paulo Freire. *Studies in Philosophy and Education, 22*(2), 157–173.

Roberts, P. (2005). Freire and Dostoevsky: Uncertainty, dialogue and transformation. *Journal of Transformative Education, 3*(1), 126–139.

Roberts, P. (2013). Happiness, despair and education. *Studies in Philosophy and Education, 32*(5), 463–475.

Roberts, P., & Freeman-Moir, J. (2013). *Better worlds: Education, art, and utopia.* Lanham, MD: Lexington Books.

Schugurensky, D. (2011). *Paulo Freire.* London: Continuum.

Shor, I. (1980). *Critical teaching and everyday life.* Boston, MA: South End Press.

Torres, C. A. (2014). *First Freire: Early writings in social justice education.* New York: Teachers College Press.

Webster, S. (2016). The existential individual *alone* within Freire's socio-political solidarity. In M. A. Peters (Ed.), *Encyclopedia of educational philosophy and theory.* (pp. 781–786). Singapore: Springer.

Part Four

Policy, the Environment, and Liberation Theology

13

Ley de Reforma Educativa de Puerto Rico: A Freirean Perspective

Patricia Virella and Jennie Weiner

In his seminal text, *Pedagogy of the Oppressed*, Freire (1972) explains how traditional forms of schooling fundamentally oppress those through a "banking approach." This approach positions teachers as having all the knowledge and "pouring" this knowledge into students' empty "glass" (i.e., their minds). The result of this orientation is a system that elevates the voice, beliefs, and norms of the powerful while simultaneously obviating these same attributes of oppressed populations. As an antidote, Freire argued for a new crop of teachers oriented toward, and operating from, a place of liberation. He saw teaching as an inherently political act, working not only to denounce unjust practices and policies, but also to announce a more thoughtful, democratic approach to the teaching and learning process (i.e., pedagogy), illuminated through a problem-posing approach (Freire, 1985, 1972).

Freire's arguments have never been so poignant. With the rise of neoliberal policies elevating concepts of "performativity" (Day & Gu, 2007) and competition to "reform" all parts of the public sector including schools (Anderson & Cohen, 2015, 2018), and, under the Trump Administration, the elevation of white supremacy Coates (2017), xenophobia (Rosa & Bonilla, 2017), and other forms of discrimination in civil society—Freire would have called for resistance of these oppressive forces.

And yet, as seen with the misappropriation of concepts like "social justice" by groups seeking neoliberal educational reforms (e.g., Lahann and Reagan's [2011] work on Teach for America; Kershen, Weiner, and Torres's [2019] piece on "care" in No Excuses charter schools, etc.), we argue Freire's concepts of liberation too have been co-opted by such groups. In this way, Freirean discourse itself may be contorted as the powerful attempt to use his words to validate policies that promote and uphold the type of oppression Freire asks us to fight against.

As we discuss in this chapter, nowhere does this co-option appear to be truer than in Puerto Rico where the legislature just passed a systemic overhaul of their education system. While a critical understanding of Freire suggests he would view these neoliberal policies as continuing oppressive structures to maintain power, those promoting these reforms used his words to justify them. Given the island's schools' long history of being a tool of colonization, this misappropriation seems tone deaf at best and ethically bankrupt at worst.

Puerto Rico's history as a colonized territory and education

In 1904, Puerto Rico's education system was overhauled by the United States. Key to these efforts was a push for Puerto Ricans to become "American" and for its people to assimilate (Negrón, 1977). For example, in the early 1900s, stateside American education officials declared English language and American culture acquisition as essential components of Puerto Rico's schools' goals and curriculum. In short, teachers in Puerto Rico were taught to instruct in ways to aid the newly colonized territory to become more "American" and ignore traditions and cultures of native Puerto Ricans (Negrón, 1977).

Moreover, in letters during this time, Puerto Rico's education secretaries reflected views of the "nobility of imperialism" (Caban, 2002), detailing how these reforms aligned to that of stateside education systems. The letters detail new teacher evaluations and, most importantly, the plan to Americanize Puerto Rico by depositing American traditions and knowledge into students. While most of these colonizing enculturation efforts failed to some degree, they left a legacy of economic stratification and heavily regulating public schools (Negrón, 1977); indeed, the continued effort to "Americanize" Puerto Ricans remains a key feature of its contemporary school system.

Fast forwarding to the 1990s, we find educational reformers focused on the same choice policies popular in the United States. During this time-frame, the then Governor Rosello proposed, what was ultimately a failed legislation, to bring school vouchers and charter schools into Puerto Rico's educational system. And yet, despite what seemed the public's disinterest in such approaches, the Puerto Rican government continued to introduce legislation focused on these same neoliberal policies. These efforts culminated in 2018, with *Ley de Reforma Educativa de Puerto Rico* (LRE). In this way, and despite their numerous negative impacts (Lakes & Carter, 2011), neoliberal education reforms, influenced by the US government (i.e., a colonizing force on the island), continue to oppress Puerto Rico's people, a population still without the necessary voting rights to legislatively challenge the United States' influence over their schools.

Ley De Reforma Educativa de Puerto Rico

LRE, passed in March 2018, was created to reform education in Puerto Rico. The law stipulated the closures of numerous traditional public schools (deemed as "failing" schools) and the introduction of charter schools and school voucher programs. The law also includes new department of education positions, such as a regional superintendent, and encourages reevaluating teacher certification stating a need to enhance educator quality across the island (LRE, 2018).

The bill's passage was and continues to be contentious. Proponents assert the law will provide Puerto Ricans with rigorous education to help them become global citizens (LRE, 2018). Alternatively, opponents claim closing 283 schools limits the possibility of rural populations in Puerto Rico from accessing high-quality schools near their municipalities. Furthermore, opponents have sought legal action in blocking the school voucher program.

While the opposition to the LRE has fought hard to respond to the bill itself, we argue, by responding to the bill's pieces rather than its underlying assumptions misses an opportunity to highlight how these assumptions themselves uphold, rather than dismantle, an oppressive educational system.

Therefore, the assertion here is that employing a Freirean lens is an important tool to analyze this bill as its progenitors drew upon Freire words to justify its introduction and elements. As stated in the bill:

> For Freire, education has to be liberating in order for human beings to discover and overcome themselves, as agents of their own historical destiny. Education is also a humanizing process where human beings rediscover themselves as citizens who are completely free, aware that they are agents of their own destiny, and makers of their history with the strength and capability to transform their social, financial, and political reality, making them fit to live an authentic and real participatory democracy where they have agency, not just a democracy in theory. There are various notable concepts in Freire's liberating theory; however, the most notable concept was Freire's proposal of a pedagogy of the oppressed as a form of hope, a means to achieve freedom, and as an education that embraces autonomy. He also expressed his opposition to the banking concept of education which is oppressive to human beings. Rote learning is emphasized in the banking model and students become "receptacles" where knowledge is "deposited." A humanistic educator identifies with his students and guides them toward practices that liberate both the student and the educator, as Freire claimed. (LRE, 2018, p. 15)

This quote, used to justify the legislation's pedagogical foundation, reveals how policy-makers situated their education reform in the larger context of Freire's words. Yet, critically examining it more closely, we find the bill serves not to elevate or address, but to reduce, Freire's concepts of "banking education" and liberation in various and deeply problematic ways. For example, in the case of this quote to conflate oppression with "rote memorization" and to ignore the historical/contextual nature of their argument is flawed. In that light, using a Freirean lens, we discuss these issues and others in more detail below.

A Freirean analysis of LRE

Despite the language in the law stating how Freire's theory of liberatory education is implemented in the law, we analyze how the language corrupts Freire's intent. Thus, we offer our analysis as a reclaiming of Freire's intentions and as a means to highlight how the timing of this bill—legislated after Hurricane Maria, a time of total devastation on the island—allowed those in power to pass legislation without those most affected by it—the working class—to advocate for their needs. To enact a law when the majority of the population was without consistent food, water and/or electricity and say LRE will liberate them contort Freire's notion of liberation almost entirely. This is not liberation; rather, by legislating without consensus from the majority of Puerto Ricans, power was further taken from them and given to those stationed in the "ivory tower" (Freire, 1972).

In this, and myriad other ways, the law does not align to the criticality of Freire's thought. Specifically, the law largely fails when analyzed through a Freirean lens because (1) while criticizing "banking education" the actions within the law reinforces this approach; (2) solutions relied on neoliberal approaches, and specifically choice as the avenue for liberation; and (3) the justification for the bill is decontextualized, and excludes authentic liberatory practices.

Legislation as reinforcement of "banking education"

In *Pedagogy of the Oppressed*, Freire (1972) explains banking education as when "the educated individual is the adapted person, because she or he is better 'fit' for the world. Translated into practice, this concept is well-suited to the purposes of the oppressors, whose tranquility rests on how well people fit the world the oppressors have created, and how little they question it" (p. 76). This latter quote, originally applied to Brazil in the 1960s and '70s, equally reflects on contemporary neoliberal education reforms implemented globally, and for our purposes, in Puerto Rico.

Many education reform policies have sought privatization of education as a means to create "justice" and/or "equity." However, while cloaked in the language of liberation, such efforts can be understood as new forms of oppression. To liberate a society, education must ensure "a moment or process or practice where we challenge the people to mobilize or organize themselves to get power" (Shor & Freire, 1987, p. 34). Therefore, while Puerto Rico's citizens must be liberated, the legislation stands as an example of Freire's banking education. For example, the law states a goal of increasing citizens' engagement in their communities. In reality, however, the law falls short in explaining how Puerto Ricans will become empowered to support their authentic vision of the island and instead provides a laundry list of vague attributes grounded in what appears to be growing productive workers for today's global economy.

> Human beings that are educated in the public education system must become humanists that feel empathy with the realities and needs of others and the communities where they live, work, grow, and become enterprising professionals capable of integrating themselves into a dynamic global economy. The goal is to develop sensible and deep critical thinkers; selfless, resilient, steadfast, and genuine men and women of the state committed to the progress and sustainability of an Island that needs them. (LRE, 2018, p. 3)

In addition to their emphasis on production and a commitment to "progress" as the primary motivators for enhancing the education system, these characteristics are described in what will be deposited into students as a result of this law, not what will be co-created with Puerto Ricans based on what they deem critical for their society. As Freire (1972) argues, "Liberation education consists in acts of cognition, not transferrals of education" (p. 79). Education in Puerto Rico must empower students to move the world to make room for their culture and experiences, not the other way around (Freire, 1985). If this bill was intended to liberate, there would be an expression of liberation and cultural inclusion within. To provide students with the education to truly be liberated, policy-makers must understand knowledge is a communal and iterative process.

Another example which demonstrates how this law is situated in the concept of "banking education" is the constriction of public schools and their regulations. In the bill, school principals are given a one-year contract to improve outcomes in public schools. Their contracts are reviewed annually at first and then granted for longer tenure after proven success. In contrast, charter and private schools participating in the school voucher program are guaranteed "operational and academic freedom" (LRE, 2018). This reveals freedom in education is given to private entities and not to the public.

In addition, the lack of inclusion of Puerto Ricans in decision-making or opportunities to learn from their own history belies the banking orientation of the bill. Although the law states Freirean educational theory includes learning from one's own historical context, the law's focus has an aim on how Puerto Ricans can learn to be in the oppressors' society. This is stated in the areas of focus for the public schools such as STEM education. Freire asserts it is important for children to learn the world around them; however, it becomes "banking" when policy-makers define a narrow set of educational goals to serve the oppressors as was done in this law. The law states:

> Education's general purpose is to develop the students' maximum potential and ensure that they are prepared in STEM disciplines upon their graduation to be able to compete in the global economy. Moreover, students shall be allowed to develop their personalities to the fullest and strengthen their appreciation for human rights. (LRE, 2018, p. 34)

Thus, this policy pays lip service to liberatory education, while simultaneously constricting liberation of education by placing silos around what students will learn for one singular purpose: the assimilation into a neoliberal society.

Choice positioned as liberation

School choice is often presented by education reformers as a way to bring equity to the educational landscape (Gauri & Vawda, 2004). LRE is no different and stipulates the allowance of school choice reform (e.g., charter schools and school vouchers) to increase high-quality schools in Puerto Rico. An additional benefit to this approach, as stated in the law, and aligned with foundational ideas on school competition and choice more broadly (Chubb & Moe, 1991), is an enhancement to the general quality of education on the island as public schools must now keep their students from enrolling in private schools and charter schools. In this way, school choice and competition are frequently positioned by reformers as democracy in action as parents are giving back the "right" to choose their child's school. However, studies show such systems often do more to stratify demographics, leading to greater levels of segregation and inequity and do little, if anything, to liberate the oppressed (Gauri & Vawda, 2004).

However, in its failure to address or acknowledge the differential access of those within the educational "marketplace" (i.e., native Puerto Ricans) who have to make such choices, this model is in opposition to Freire's views of true liberation of education—that liberation comes when the oppressed are given opportunity to engage in the processes prior to the system being in place (Freire, 1994). In the case of school choice, this would mean that, before the system is introduced, all Puerto Rican families would have equal access to information, transportation, social capital, and any other features of the school choice process. Of course, this was not the case and it is therefore likely that school choice will do little to address existing disparities and may even worsen them (Holme, 2002). Thus, as Shor and Freire (1987) argue, these reforms are likely to further reify the education system as "a complicated and indirect agency through which corporate interests are promoted in the public sector" (p. 76).

Problems are narrowly defined and decontextualized

Finally, this bill is also problematic as it narrowly defines the problems of the education system in Puerto Rico as situated in the economic results of Hurricanes Irma and Maria. "Currently, Puerto Rico is undergoing one of the worst fiscal and economic crises in its history" (LRE, 2018, p. 2). Decontextualizing these problems and relating them primarily to capitalist interests ignore the problematic history of Puerto Rico's education system. For instance, the law excludes mention of the colonization of Puerto Rico by the United States and never references its occupation. Therefore, colonization, the central reason why Puerto Rico's education system has been in shambles for decades, is excluded from the problem definition and thus how solutions are constructed. Again, we argue that rather than align himself with the progenitors of the bill, Freire would assert this law further oppresses Puerto Ricans as only the views of the oppressor are valued and included.

Discussion: Real liberation in Puerto Rico's education system

Freire's concept of "humanizing education" (Freire, 1972) is front and center in LRE. It is the only portion of Freire's critical theory stated. By selecting this portion of Freire's work, it suggests the policy's authors wanted the law to allude to liberation. It is alarming that Puerto Rico's Department of Education called on Freire to support their vision of education. Yet, much of the law is situated in the concept of "banking," further limiting the opportunities for the liberation of Puerto Rico's people. Lacking is the authentic voice of Puerto Ricans to create an education system which is particular to the "orgullo" of Puerto Rico. Together, we must not be distracted by notions of school choice or mired down in controversy. Instead, we must heed Freire's call and address the oppressive system as a whole and reclaim his legacy.

References

Anderson, G., & Cohen, M. I. (2015). Redesigning the identities of teachers and leaders: A framework for studying new professionalism and educator resistance. *Education Policy Analysis Archives, 23*(85).

Anderson, G. L., & Cohen, M. I. (2018). *The new democratic professional in education: Confronting markets, metrics, and managerialism.* New York: Teachers College Press.

Caban, P. (2002). The colonizing mission of the U.S. in Puerto Rico. *Latin American, Caribbean, and U.S. Latino Studies Faculty Scholarship.* 26.

Coates, T. (2017). The first white president. *Atlantic.* Retrieved from https://www.theatlantic.com/magazine/archive/2017/10/the-first-white-president-ta-nehisicoates/537909/September 28, 2017 (Accessed September 13, 2019).

Chubb, J. E., & Moe, T. M. (1991). *Politics, markets, and America's schools.* Washington, DC: Brookings Institution.

Day, C., & Gu, Q. (2007). Variations in the conditions for teachers' professional learning and development: Sustaining commitment and effectiveness over a career. *Oxford Review of Education, 33*(4), 423–443.

Freire, P. (1972). *Pedagogy of the oppressed.* New York: Herder and Herder.

Freire, P. (1985). *The politics of education: Culture, power, and liberation.* South Hadley, MA: Bergin & Garvey.

Freire, P. (1994). *Pedagogy of hope: Reliving Pedagogy of the oppressed*. New York: Continuum.

Gauri, V., & Vawda, A. (2004). Vouchers for basic education in developing economies: An accountability perspective. *The World Bank Research Observer, 19*(2), 259–280. http://doi.org/10.1093/wbro/lkh017 (Accessed April 2, 2019).

Holme, J. J. (2002). Buying homes, buying schools: School choice and the social construction of school quality. *Harvard Educational Review, 72*(2), 177–206.

Lahann, R., & Reagan, E. M. (2011). Teach for America and the politics of progressive neoliberalism. *Teacher Education Quarterly, 38*(1), 7–27.

Lakes, R. D., & Carter, P. A. (2011). Neoliberalism and education: An introduction. *Educational Studies, 47*(2), 107–110.

LexJuris de Puerto Rico (c)2018 1, Pub. L. No. 85 (2018). Puerto Rico: LexJuris de Puerto Rico. Retrieved from http://www.lexjuris.com/LexLex/Leyes2018/lexl2018085.pdf (Accessed May 2, 2019).

Negrón, M. A. (1977). *La americanización de Puerto Rico y el sistema de instrucción pública, 1900-1930*. Río Piedras: Editorial Universitaria, Universidad de Puerto Rico.

Rosa, J., & Bonilla, Y. (2017). Deprovincializing Trump, decolonizing diversity, and unsettling anthropology. *American Ethnologist, 44*, 201–208. DOI: 10.1111/amet.12468 (Accessed September 20, 2019).

Rosado, T. T. (2018). Puerto Rico's children mired in poverty. Retrieved March 29, 2019, from https://www.aecf.org/m/databook/2018KC_newsrelease_PR.pdf (Accessed April 1, 2019).

Shor, I., & Freire, P. (1987). *A pedagogy for liberation: Dialogues on transforming education*. South Hadley, MA: Bergin & Garvey Publishers.

Weiner, J. M., Cyr, D., & Burton, L. J. (2019). Microaggressions in administrator preparation programs: How Black female participants experienced discussions of identity, discrimination, and leadership. *Journal of Research on Leadership Education*, online first.

14

Overcoming (In)Difference: Emancipatory Pedagogy and Indigenous Worldviews toward Respectful Relationships with the More-Than-Human World

Jennifer Markides

Reading the world

Nowadays, one can scarcely open up a news feed or observe media that does not portray an image and caption about the dire state of climate change—from catastrophic weather events to the rapidly melting polar icecaps: images of polar bears—mothers with cubs—afloat on small pieces of ice amid the vast seas, and heart-wrenching clips of emaciated polar bears unable to find food as their territory disappears.

Famous environmental activists, such as David Suzuki, have been talking about the problem of climate change for years; now, popular television personality, Bill Nye, the Science Guy, drops f-bombs in a desperate and angry plea for change (O'Brien, 2019), adding that the significant trouble posed by climate change is not 50–75 years away, but 10–15 years, at most (Torres, 2019).

Humans' mass development, industry, resource extraction, globalization, pollution, consumption, and waste have put the planet into great peril. As an educator, activist, mother, student, researcher, Métis[1], flood survivor, resident of High River in southern Alberta, and citizen of the Earth, I feel the crushing

---

[1] Métis are a distinct people whose society emerged during the time of the fur trade in North America. Men—mainly French, but also of English, Scottish, and other European origins—married Indigenous women and established settlements, Michif language, cultural traditions, and commerce, that set them apart as a Nation (Shore, 2018).

weight and urgent need for action, as society must look for answers to the world's biggest problems.

With the state of the planet becoming increasingly bleak, I contend that we are in dire need of an education for environmental revolution. Through critical theory I understand the dialogic relationship between knowledge creation and action necessary to bring about transformative change (Freire 1970/1993; Kincheloe et al., 2018). Paulo Freire's *Pedagogy of the Oppressed* (1970/1993) stands as the preeminent educational text on emancipatory teaching. Critical scholars have long taken up Freirean practices in work with oppressed groups to speak back to power in actionable ways.

How can Freire's formative work be re-imagined to empower the planet and all its inhabitants in the face of the greed and entitlement that is destroying it. What if we re-thought Freire's original position on animals and the Earth, moving from merely living, to also existing in states of becoming? How can we better contribute to the emancipation of all beings, living and non-living? How can we apply Freirean pedagogy in new ways to promote change and trouble dominance over the land, water, animals, and other natural resources?

Listening to Mother Earth

The call to address the issues of the state Mother Earth's well-being is not new. Richard Atleo (2011) acknowledges:

> Ḥaw'iłume, Wealthy [where "wealth" signifies both the material and the non-material] Mother Earth, the home of biodiversity, is currently under abnormal duress. Her immediate problem is a global warming that has produced a "dis-ease" evident in her convulsions in the form of violent storms and earthquakes. Other threats to Ḥaw'iłume and her inhabitants include, but are not limited to, a looming energy crisis, rampant diseases, the possibility of nuclear war, and terrorism. What has gone wrong? (p. 1)

In the discussion that follows the above quote, Atleo candidly remarks that "it doesn't seem that long ago when certain people spread throughout the world carrying the good news about civilization and the promise of a better life"

(p. 1); yet, the ill-health of the Earth is likely the by-product of civilization's progress. Further to his point, Atleo suggests that "there is a suspicion that the main origin story provided by the dominant peoples of the globe, who have prevailed for the past five hundred years, may be contributing to our current global crisis" (p. 2).

With the need to spread dominion and providence, the swift hand of colonial rule forced new ideologies and values onto Indigenous peoples around the world. Alternatively, the widely accepted scientific origin story has produced problems of its own, with the "unblinking assumption that science has cornered the market on truth" (Kimmerer, 2013, p. 160). Darwinian thought supports a hierarchal view of species, races, and societies, which has led to the oppression of various peoples and non-humans alike. From religion to science, it may seem a leap to consider cosmology as the root of hegemonic discourses about the Earth and its inhabitants, but the stories we live by—our truths—influence the ways we interact with each other and the more-than-human world.

Different societal groups ascribe to different origin stories. Creation stories that describe the Earth as being created for human beings set up a sense of ownership over the Earth and all of its inhabitants. Renowned storyteller Thomas King (2003) contrasts a Native American creation story, where a curious pregnant woman falls from the sky and lands on an Earth that is covered in water. The swimming and flying animals work together to save the woman. They retrieve mud from the bottom of the ocean to create land on the back of the turtle, so that the woman and her children can survive. The children help to shape the landscape—one favoring order, and the other favoring chaos—in a synergistic relationship. King notes that the Christian origin story of Genesis introduces a hierarchy with a single deity responsible for all creation; while in the story of the *Woman Who Fell from the Sky*, the Earth is co-created by the animals and the humans.

Consequently, differing origin stories contribute to differing worldviews. Leroy Little Bear (2000) distinguishes that a Eurocentric worldview is centered around hierarchies that put God at the top, then man in God's image—who is perpetually struggling between good and evil—followed by the rest of creation: plants, animals, and non-living things, at the bottom; Little Bear offers that

Aboriginal values privilege relationships where all beings—living and non-living—are considered sacred, noting that a wholly Indigenous worldview no longer exists due to the influences of colonization.

I do not share these examples to be reductionistic, nor to essentialize creation stories. Instead, I hope to offer insight into the way worldviews—often, influenced in differing beliefs about the creation of the Earth—shape one's interactions with and perceptions of the more-than-human[2] world (Abram, 1996). By critically attending to the problematic elements of both Western/Eurocentric and scientifically based worldviews, I hope to provoke a paradigmatic turn to Indigenous ways of reading the world.

Turning to Indigenous—taken broadly—worldviews

At the onset, I must acknowledge that using the word "Indigenous" as a standalone term is problematic. I do not wish to perpetuate notions of pan-Indigeneity by suggesting a singular Indigenous worldview, ontology, epistemology, axiology, or cosmology (Battiste, 2013; Grande, 2004; Smith, 1999/2012); rather, I draw upon the work of a variety of Indigenous scholars whose insights speak back to the prevailing hegemonic discourse and open up conversations of possibility. As such, it is important to note that the groups of First Peoples in North America are as diverse as the myriad geographies they inhabit(ed).

Despite the harsh influences of colonization, there are several hundred distinct Indigenous groups that continue to live on Turtle Island[3] to this day. Colonization saw the end of many traditional ways of living, as Indigenous groups were intentionally obliterated, persecuted, relocated, infantilized, romanticized, and undermined in the name of imperial expansion and industrialized progress.

---

[2]   Abram (1996) introduces the term "more-than-human" in his writings on animism, as a recognition that all things are sentient beings—imbued with souls—be they rocks or blades of grass.

[3]   As mentioned in the Native American creation story (King, 2003) shared above, the world was formed on the back of a turtle. Hence, many Indigenous groups in North America refer to the continent as Turtle Island.

While communities can never be restored to a precolonial time or existence, many Indigenous ways of being, knowing, and doing are in resurgence (Simpson, 2014, 2011), and language and cultural revitalization efforts are underway (Morris, 2018; Smith, 1999/2012). As Willie Ermine (1995) states, "Our Aboriginal languages and culture contain the accumulated knowledge of our ancestors, and it is critical that we examine the inherent concepts in our lexicons to develop understandings of the self in relation to existence" (p. 104).

Both Ermine (1995) and Little Bear (2000) caution against the adverse influence of Western and Eurocentric worldviews, as they stand in direct opposition to widely held Indigenous understandings that humanity exists in a web of relations with all other living and non-living beings. If one sees themselves as a distinct entity—set apart from other forms of life—then one can compartmentalize and justify the use of resources—rocks, minerals, plants, animals, water, and air—as consumable for themselves without crisis of conscience.

The Western/Eurocentric, fragmented and jagged worldviews do not align with an Indigenous epistemology that sees the *self-in-relation* to all other beings. Rather than focusing on the incongruences between competing worldviews, Ermine (2007) would suggest operating in an "ethical space of engagement" where dialogue may disrupt existing ways of thinking toward new possibilities. Further to this, Dwayne Donald (2009) conceptualizes "ethical relationality" from an ecological standpoint, where differing perspectives—informed by experience, history, culture, and societal circumstance—are mutually sought and valued. By acknowledging inter-connectivity amid difference and maintaining a respectful and responsive counter-hegemonic stance, ethical engagement and relationality may open up possibilities to shift dominant discourses away from human supremacy toward interdependency.

Many Indigenous communities from around the world have land-based, place-specific knowledge systems (Grande, 2004; Sheridan & Longboat, 2006; Simpson, 2014; Smith, 1999/2012), learning from their environments and aspiring to nurture harmonious—respectful and balanced—relationships with the Earth. Specific to a Korean ontology, the atma of oneness, within Han philosophy, values a striving toward "unity through harmony, balance, and cooperation" (Kim, 2019, p. 138). Speaking to Hawaiian epistemology,

Manulani Aluli Meyer (2001) describes, "Relationships or interdependence offered Hawaiians opportunities to practice reciprocity, exhibit balance, develop harmony with the land, and generosity with others" (p. 134).

While I prefer to avoid sweeping generalizations, my survey of the Indigenous literatures referenced within this chapter suggests an overwhelming consensus that relationships—with the land, and all living and non-living entities—are axiomatically central in many Indigenous epistemologies and ontologies. Within Haudenosaunee territory and consciousness, the animals and the sentient lands are revered as teachers and spiritual helpers (Sheridan & Longboat, 2006); an Indigenous worldview that holds the more-than-human world as sacred provides a sharp contrast to views held by the dominant, Western culture.

What if we saw *all* things as *becoming*?

With Freire's *Pedagogy of the Oppressed* just past the fiftieth anniversary of its original release, I am not surprised to find that others have written responses to the same points in the text that I take issue with myself. Akin to the perspective taken by Lauren Corman (2011), I have not agreed with Freire's discussion of animals as ahistorical beings, incapable of risk-taking, devoid of self-awareness, merely living but never becoming (see Freire, 1970/1993, pp. 78–80). Corman (2011) thoroughly problematizes Freire's anthropocentric and speciesist contentions, which position animals as Other. Moreover, Corman and others (see Bowers, 2005; Kahn, 2002) highlight the ways that Freirean conceptions (1970/1993) of the non-human—beings and environments—negatively contribute to the current state of ecological crisis.

While many responses have been written to address the ideas presented in *Pedagogy of the Oppressed*—arguably Freire's most widely read and referenced work—it is important to note that he began speaking differently about the world in his later writing, positing that "ecology has gained tremendous importance at the end of the century. It must be present in any educational practice of a radical, critical, and liberating nature" (Freire, 2004, p. 47). Faced with the grim state of the world, Freire (2004) urges us to avoid fatalism, and instead lean into the dream of a utopian world, such that it can be manifested as real, as follows:

> Therefore, embracing the dream of a better world and adhering to it imply accepting the process of its creation. It is a process of struggle that must be deeply anchored in ethics. It is the process of struggle against all forms of violence—violence against the life of trees, of rivers, of fish, of mountains, of cities, against the physical marks of historic and cultural memories. It is also the process of struggle against violence toward the weak, the defenseless, the wounded minorities, violence toward those who are discriminated against for any reason. It is a process of struggle against impunity, which at the moment encourages crime, abuse, disrespect for the weak, and blatant disrespect for life among us. (p. 121)

There is a lot packed into Freire's statements; unfortunately, Freire passed away before he could expand on these ideas more fully. As such, I find cause to revisit and re-imagine Freire's (1970/1993) earlier position on plants, animals, and the environment, in service of the oppressed more-than-human world.

The notion of kinship circles extends to all beings: entities seen as inanimate from a Western worldview are understood to be imbued with life and spirit within a traditional Indigenous belief system (Donald, 2009; Sheridan & Longboat, 2006). In Robin Kimmerer's (2013) ruminations on the grammar of animacy, she problematizes the language of domination and species supremacy; for example:

> In English, we never refer to a member of our family, or indeed to any person, as *it*. That would be a profound act of disrespect. *It* robs a person of selfhood and kinship, reducing a person to a mere thing. So it is that in Potawatomi [an Anishinaabe language] and most other indigenous [*sic*] languages, we use the same words to address the living world as we use for our family. Because they are our family. (p. 55)

Allying with Kimmerer creates an entry for considering the more-than-human inhabitants as kin. With this radical turn, Freire's (1970/1993) words—re-imagined—become:

> Dialogue further requires an intense faith in [all kinship relations— living and non-living], faith in their power to make and remake, to create

and re-create, faith in their [innate ability] to be more fully [themselves, without risk of degradation or oppression] (which is not the privilege of an elite [human race], but the birthright for all). (p. 71)

By considering the prospect of a dialogue with the more-than-human world, it becomes the responsibility of humans to learn the language of the world (Kimmerer, 2013, p. 160). Entering into the conversation:

It is not our role to speak to [all entities] about our own view of the world, nor to attempt to impose that view on them, but rather to dialogue with [all entities] about their view and ours. We must realize that their view of the world, manifested variously in their action, reflects their *situation* in the world. (Freire, 1970/1993, p. 77)

While the re-written passage reads contradictory to Freire's initial assertions—that distinguished humans from all other animals—his later work (2004) suggests a substantial shift in thinking in response to the world. Similarly, Henry Giroux (2013) states that the inherent nature of critical pedagogy is to be ever evolving—a movement in response to struggle.

Entering into dialogue with the more-than-human world

The voices of the more-than-human world have been neglected. The Earth and its inhabitants are crying out—their call necessitates sustained action and consciousness raising on behalf of all beings, living or otherwise. I contend that humanity must begin by listening in order to better understand the view and situation of the world; then, proceed with actions marked by care.

For too long, humans have participated in a one-sided, self-interested conversation with the Earth. Entering into the dialogue, anew—by embracing a critical and open-minded perspective—humankind may initiate practices of "*radical* listening to everyday places" (Ackerman et al., 2016, p. 91), opening eyes, ears, hearts, and minds to different ways of coexisting. As Freire (1970/1993) explains, the oppressor cannot emancipate the oppressed; but instead, the oppressor can support the conditions for the oppressed to liberate themselves. The same is true for non-human beings. If people can create and sustain the conditions for a healthier planet—whereby all parties can work together to support life and protect the interests of all living and non-living entities—then the environment and animal species may experience resurgence and revitalization.

To set up the conditions for all beings to become self-liberating, humans have a responsibility to enter into caring relations with the more-than-human world. Nel Noddings (2012, 1984) describes that an *ethic of care* is a relationship where care is demonstrated by the carer and experienced by the cared-for. Thus, society may perform radical enactments of care for the Earth. It is not enough to hope for change, or to simply click the angry emoji when someone shares yet another example of the degradation of the Earth: dead sea creatures with stomachs filled with plastic bags and other garbage, remote communities with astronomical cancer rates caused by the by-products of resource extraction, or urban and rural centers with people unable to access the basic necessities for life, such as safe drinking water and nutritious food. The radical enactments of care—by the carer—must be tangibly appreciated by the cared-for. This is not to say that sea life will know that people kept garbage out of the ocean; but instead, their lives will not be hampered by it in the future as a result of the carers' actions.

In order to address the complex environmental issues and prolonged impacts on the Earth, a paradigmatic shift is needed—moving away from ideologies that objectify the natural world, to worldviews that necessitate ethical relationality inclusive of all beings—living or existing. Today, Western colonial capitalist agendas have superseded an ethic of care for the Earth, seeing earthly inhabitants persistently subjugated. To counter the narrative of human supremacy over the non-human world, people might benefit from re-imagining ecological relationships in ways that push beyond hierarchies of oppression, engaging in radical listening as a means of dialogue with the more-than-human world, and responding with care for others such that the cared-for may exist unencumbered in the liberation of their whole selves.

When it comes to environmental issues, it can be difficult to navigate societal rhetoric and industry-constructed roadblocks; but, the need for transformative change is overwhelmingly clear. It is my great hope that by applying Freire's (2004) position on animals and nature to his earlier work

(1970/1993), humanity might begin to reconnect and dialogue with the more-than-human world toward greater respect, voice, and balance for all.

References

Abram, D. (1996). *The spell of the sensuous: Perception and language in a more-than-human world*. New York: Pantheon Books.

Ackerman, J., Druschke, C. G., McGreavy, B., & Sprain, L. (2016). The skunkwork of ecological engagement. *Reflections on Sustainable Communities and Environmental Communication, 16*(1), 75–95.

Atleo, Umeek E. R. (2011). *Principles of Tsawalk: An Indigenous approach to global crisis*. Vancouver, BC: UBC Press.

Battiste, M. (2013). *Decolonizing education: Nourishing the learning spirit*. Saskatoon, SK: Purich.

Bowers, C. A. (2005). How the ideas of Paulo Freire contribute to the cultural roots of the ecological crisis. In C. A. Bowers & F. Apffel-Marglin (Eds.), *Rethinking Freire: Globalization and the environmental crisis* (pp. 131–148). Mahwah, NJ: Lawrence Erlbaum.

Corman, L. (2011). Impossible subjects: The figure of the animal in Paulo Freire's *Pedagogy of the Oppressed*. *Canadian Journal of Environmental Education, 16*(1), 29–45.

Donald, D. (2009). Forts, curriculum, and Indigenous métissage: Imagining decolonization of Aboriginal-Canadian relations in educational contexts. *First Nations Perspectives, 2*(1), 1–24.

Ermine, W. (1995). Aboriginal epistemology. In M. Battiste & J. Barman (Eds.), *The circle unfolds: First Nations education in Canada* (pp. 101–112). Vancouver, BC: UBC Press.

Ermine, W. (2007). The ethical space of engagement. *Indigenous Law Journal, 6*(1), 193–203.

Freire, P. (1993). *Pedagogy of the oppressed*. (M. B. Ramos, Trans.). London: Penguin Books. (Original work published 1970).

Freire, P. (2004). *Pedagogy of indignation*. Boulder, CO: Paradigm Publishers.

Giroux, H. (February 6, 2013). Henry Giroux: The necessity of critical pedagogy in dark times (J. M. Barraso Tristán, Interviewer). *Global Education Magazine*. Retrieved from https://truthout.org/articles/a-critical-interview-with-henry-giroux/ (Accessed June 7, 2019).

Grande, S. (2004). *Red pedagogy: Native American social and political thought.* Lanham, MD: Rowman & Littlefield.

Kahn, R. (2002). Paulo Freire and eco-justice: Updating *Pedagogy of the Oppressed* for the age of ecological calamity. *Freire Online Journal, 1*(1). Retrieved from https://www.academia.edu/167231/Paulo_Freire_and_Eco-Justice_Updating_Pedagogy_of_the_Oppressed_for_the_Age_of_Ecological_Calamity (Accessed June 7, 2019).

Kim, J. A. (2019). Han—Korean—Ontology: Similarities and difference from Indigenous ontologies. In J. Markides & L. Forsythe (Eds.), *Research journeys in/to multiple ways of knowing* (pp. 135–145). New York: DIO.

Kimmerer, R. W. (2013). *Braiding sweetgrass: Indigenous wisdom, scientific knowledge, and the teachings of plants.* Minneapolis, MN: Milkweed Editions.

Kincheloe, J. L., McLaren, P., Steinberg, S. R., & Monzó, L. D. (2018). Critical pedagogy and qualitative research: Advancing the bricolage. In N. K. Denzin & Y. S. Lincoln (Eds.), *The Sage handbook of qualitative research* (5th ed.) (pp. 235–260). Thousand Oaks, CA: Sage.

King, T. (2003). *The truth about stories: A native narrative.* Toronto, ON: House of Anansi.

Little Bear, L. (2000). Jagged worldview colliding. In M. Battiste (Ed.), *Reclaiming Indigenous voice and vision* (pp. 77–85). Vancouver, BC: UBC Press.

Meyer, M. Aluli (2001). Our own liberation: Reflections on Hawaiian epistemology. *The Contemporary Pacific, 13*(1), 124–148.

Morris, Kāshā J. A. (2018). Using language nests to promote the intergenerational transmission of Tāłtān. In J. Markides & L. Forsythe (Eds.), *Looking back and living forward: Indigenous research rising up* (pp. 73–80). Leiden, NL: Brill | Sense.

O'Brien, C. (May 14, 2019). Bill Nye drops the F-bombs in exasperated climate change plea. *CTV News.* Retrieved from https://www.ctvnews.ca/sci-tech/bill-nye-drops-the-f-bombs-in-exasperated-climate-change-plea-1.4421456 (Accessed June 7, 2019)

Noddings, N. (1984). *Caring: A feminine approach to ethics and moral education.* Berkeley: University of California Press.

Noddings, N. (2012). The language of care ethics. *Knowledge Quest, 40*(4), 52–56.

Sheridan, J., & Longboat, D. R. "He Clears the Sky." (2006). The Haudenosaunee imagination and the ecology of the sacred. *Space and Culture, 9*(4), 365–381.

Shore, F. J. (2018). *Threads in the Sash: The Story of Métis People.* Winnipeg, MB: Pemmican Publications.

Simpson, L. Betasamosake (2011). *Dancing on our turtle's back: Stories of Nishnaabeg re-creation, resurgence and a new emergence.* Winnipeg, MB: ARP Books.

Simpson, L. Betasamosake (2014). Land as pedagogy: Nishnaabeg intelligence and rebellious transformation. *Decolonization: Indigeneity, Education & Society, 3*(3), 1–25.

Smith, L. Tuhiwai (2012). *Decolonizing methodologies: Research and Indigenous peoples* (2nd ed.). New York: Zed Books. (Original work published 1999)

Torres, A. (May 16, 2019). Bill Nye on climate change: "It's not 50 to 75 years away—it's 10 or 15." *MSNBC.* Retrieved from http://www.msnbc.com/velshi-ruhle/bill-nye-climate-change-its-not-50-75-years-away-its-10-or-15 (Accessed June 6, 2019)

15

We Write on the Earth as the Earth Writes on Us: Paulo Freire the (Post)Humanist

Tricia Kress and Robert Lake

After fifty years, *Pedagogy of the Oppressed* (Freire, 2000a) continues to warrant social struggle to change the material conditions of people's lives to alleviate suffering. For all the verbiage of the dangers of neoliberal free market capitalism, increasing wealth disparity around the globe, creeping authoritarianism, and continual disregard for the health of the planet we inhabit (Evans & Giroux, 2015), somehow, people's materiality and the need to address fundamental conditions of biological existence tend to evaporate amid conversations of "what to do about teaching and learning for future generations of young people?"

In the US context, technocratic tendencies of institutionalized schooling that envisages learning as something that is done to young people's brains still drive the agenda for what ought to be done to "fix" schooling. In this chapter, we force a rupture in this institutionalized agenda. We leverage Paulo Freire's philosophy from a place of ontology, considering teachers and learners as being and becoming as sentient creatures in a material world, in order to shift the conversation toward what we see as necessary directions for thinking about sustainable futures, not just of people but also of the world and all its entities.

In the sections that follow, we position Freire in dialogue with posthumanism (Braidotti, 2013) and consider the ways that people simultaneously write on and are written on by the world. This recursive relationship necessitates, as Freire says, learning to read both the word and the world. We pay specific attention to how Freire's notion of humanization, which at first appears at odds with posthumanism's priority of decentering the human, can work in partnership with posthuman philosophies to defuse human arrogance and the destruction it yields. Moreover, we highlight passages from Freire's later works to illustrate how the plight of oppressed peoples is intertwined with the plight of the earth. In these texts humanization does not constitute an end goal of establishing a superior "enlightened Man" where people are *above* or *beyond* the earth and its creatures. Rather, humanization recognizes that *all* people are in and with the earth *at all times*. Imagining that some people exist outside of a relationship with the earth is a precondition for maintaining classist ideologies and oppressive socioeconomic and political arrangements that are toxic for the earth and all its inhabitants.

In Jabotão when the rivers were still alive

When we arrived in Jabotão, the rivers had not yet been degraded in the name of a perverse notion of development and as a function of the power of the powerful. The rivers were still alive. We used to bathe in them without any fear; on the contrary, their waters were clear and warm, rarely cold, they almost caressed us ... [T]hey were free of all the dirt that has now taken over so many Brazilian rivers, free of those white foamy borders that increasingly form on the banks of condemned rivers.

There was life in them, fish, shrimp, lobster, and fresh-water weeds. And in the rivers we experienced intense life. (Freire, 1996, p. 52)

In *Letters to Cristina: Reflections on My Life and Work*, Paulo Freire (1996) recalls his childhood and details what it was like when his family saw financial hardship and was compelled to leave their home in the city of Recife and move to Jabotão, a smaller city on the outskirts of Recife. His story is one of juxtapositions. On the one hand, Freire expresses a deep sadness from being pushed away from Recife; yet, on the other hand, he expresses a profound love for Jabotão and its water and lands that welcomed and nurtured him.

This particular chapter of that 1996 text spills over with life, sensuality, learning, and exploration as Freire recounts his relationship with the Duas

Unas river, which snaked through Jabotão. He refers to it as a "water road," and it was along the river's edge where he grew from a boy into a young man. For Freire, the river, its fish, water fowl, and Ingá trees were alive, and his body and mind grew as the river and the many beings that dwelled in its waters and on its shores changed too. He became a "river-bank dweller" and the river changed his "whole psychology" (Freire, 1996, p. 52). His family's economic circumstances in concert with life by the river compelled him and his brothers to make their own toys—fishing rods from sticks, fish hooks from safety pins—they lived and learned through exploration. The river was alive around and within him, and it played a fundamental role in shaping who he was and how he understood the world.

The quote that begins this section is striking to us because in a brief passage just as Freire displayed his biophilic connection to the river and its inhabitants, he also illustrated the necrophilic effects of power when through his retrospective gaze he notes the river's state of degradation at the time when he was writing the story. The river-bank dwellers, the Duas Unas river, the fish, fowl, and trees were intertwined in their fate as industry and development poisoned the water and land. The toxic runoff from the paper mills and sugar cane refineries, the primary industries of the region that also exploited the working people of Jabotão, degenerated the relationship between the river-dwellers and the river into something toxic.

Instead of invoking the caress of the water, the foamy banks signaled a reason for river-dwellers to fear the water that flowed through their lives. This fear suggests a different kind of sensibility than is typically thought of when considering the term "humanization," and it is notable for its post-anthropocentric leanings. Braidotti (2013) explains from a post-anthropocentric perspective, in the neoliberal world all animals (people included) are "equally inscribed in a market economy of planetary exchanges that commodifies them to a comparable degree and therefore makes them equally disposable. All other distinctions are blurred" (p. 71). Toxic capitalism does not discriminate in its treatment of human and non-human, living and non-living entities. It exploits and discards, in the process, divorcing people from water, land, creatures, and foliage that they might otherwise live with in communion. This thread, that humanization is an impossibility if humans are understood as separate from the world, weaves through Freire's work in several places, as we will demonstrate in the upcoming sections.

Rearticulating "humanization" in a disposable world

> We were walking, Danilson Pinto and myself, with our souls open to the world, curious, receptive, along the trails of a slum where early on one learns that a life, where it is almost absent or negated, can only be woven through much stubbornness against need, threat, injury, and pain. [...] We stopped midway across a narrow bridge that made it impossible to cross over to a less run-down part of the popular district. From above, we looked at a polluted, lifeless stretch of river whose mud, not whose water, drenched the huts immersed in it. "Beyond the huts," Danilson told me, "there is something worse. There is a great big dump where the public garbage is deposited. The residents of this entire area 'research' the garbage for something to eat, to wear, for anything to keep them alive." (Freire, 2004, p. 58)

Freire's work was, first and foremost, rooted in people's lived realities. It is common in conversations about critical pedagogy for Freire's philosophy to be recognized for its abstract concepts like dialogue, subject–object, banking, praxis, conscientization, and humanization. Yet, unless one reads beyond *Pedagogy of the Oppressed* it is less common to be exposed to how these abstract ideas were the outgrowth of his work in concrete places where people experienced immense suffering.

Abstraction of Freire's philosophical concepts is not in and of itself a bad thing—abstraction makes it easier to apply his ideas to contexts that are quite different from when and where they were originally generated. In this regard, Freire's call for people to "reinvent" his work in their own places is made realizable as his abstract concepts come to life in novel ways when transplanted into new spaces and places. Yet, when we read passages like the above from *Pedagogy of Indignation* (Freire, 2004), we cannot help but recognize humanization as more than just an idea. Through Freire's memories we watch as "disposable" people (Evans & Giroux, 2015), who are dispossessed of necessities like food, clean water, adequate shelter, and clothing, seek out disposed of materials to afford their continued existence.

Dehumanization is not abstract. As the mud from the dead river floods people's homes, and as the refuse of a society becomes their source of life, dehumanization is tied to material conditions of deprivation because the economic and social structures that shape their material lives *require* excess for some and deprivation for others. This excess–deprivation dynamic is the nature of capitalism as a socioeconomic structure, and hence, why Marxist critique was so foundational to Freire's philosophy.

However, as demonstrated in later writings, Freire's philosophy was not *only* a Marxist critique of the inequities of class-based social relationships created and maintained by capitalism. Rather, Freire's philosophy also raises questions about the relationship between people and world by identifying the material conditions of people's lives as living articulations of socioeconomic and political structures. Moreover, we take this idea a step further by positing: the ways in which people connect to and/or are disconnected from the natural world indicate the degree to which society reifies various people's presumed quantities of "humanness" and therefore stratifies their positioning in unequal socioeconomic and political arrangements.

Braidotti (2018) offers a way of moving beyond the human–non-human binary that rests at the center of Humanism's penchant for categorizing and stratifying the world with "rational Man" positioned at the apex of the universe. From a posthumanist perspective, "human nature," the unifying Humanist construct against which all "others" are measured and which feeds "contemporary bio-genetic capitalism" (Braidotti, 2013, p. 50), is replaced by "a 'naturecultures' continuum" (Braidotti, 2018, p. 4). This "brings an end to the categorical distinction between life as *bios*, the prerogative of the *Anthropos*, as distinct from the life of animals and non-humans, or *zoe*" (Braidotti, 2018, pp. 4–5). Instead, through ever-shifting and reorganizing geo-political–economic arrangements, humans, non-humans, and other worldly entities are mutually constitutive. Humanization is therefore bound up in people's relationships to non-human others and the natural world.

While all humans are connected to the plight of the earth, some humans are positioned in closer proximity to the effects of toxic capitalism than others. In the excerpt above from *Pedagogy of Indignation*, privileged people discard their waste in a place removed from their homes but nearer to the homes of the peoples who have also been discarded by society. Toxic waste from industry flows into the communities where poor people live.

For wealthier and more powerful groups, such toxicity would be met with outrage and a demand for action. If action were impossible, these same people would have the financial capacity to move elsewhere. For people who do not have financial privilege and social power, humanization as a material reality and not just an abstract notion requires attending to the health of the environment and all its living and non-living entities in order to address dehumanization. It is not possible to speak of humanization without first addressing toxic environmental conditions.

Conclusion: We write on the world as the world writes on us

> When I was a child, I learned my first letters from my parents in the shade of a wonderful mango tree in the yard of the old house where I was born in Recife. The words that I first learned were the words of my child's universe. My first blackboard was the ground itself, and my first chalk a small stick.
>
> Much later, in Chile, I had similar occasion to see words written by newly literate peasants with their farm implements on the roads leading to their work fields. (Freire, 1978, p. 132)

Freire's articulation of humanization challenges tendencies toward abstraction that remove learning from material reality and divorce people from their worlds, which allows for hierarchical arrangements of peoples and natural entities alike. Dehumanization renders particular peoples along with *all* non-human entities as disposable and this disposability is marked on both the world and people's bodies. Hence, in this final section, we illuminate how reading the word and the world is not a figure of speech or a clever catch-phrase.

Freire recalls in his later works how people's expressions of literacy were part and parcel to their physical existence in the world. People literally write on the earth, while the earth also writes on people. In addition to the quote above, Freire also noted how in Chile the peasants would write words on the trunks of trees (Freire, 2005). He further recalls how in Pernambuco during the literacy movement, teachers would write meaningful phrases on walls in the workers' communities (Freire, 1996). Yet, as we consider Freire's work from a posthuman lens, we recognize the world, too, writes on people.

In cities, we see the world writing the impact of air quality on the lungs of children who experience greater rates of asthma. In agricultural regions, dust clings to workers' clothing and earth embeds itself in the lines of people's skin, and the writing of the world is available to be read by others. Freire (2005) explains:

> Issues of sociability, imagination, feelings, desires, fear, courage, love, hate, raw anger, sexuality, and so on lead us to the need to "read" our bodies as if they were texts, through the interrelations that make up their whole. [...] [A]s I exist in the world and with the world, the reading of my body, as well as that of other bodies, implies the reading of space. (p. 95)

This embodied understanding of literacy, as a lifelong process that humans do and that is also done to humans by the world, is different than thinking about literacy as simply the capacity to read print-based texts. Literacy is henceforth inextricable from the larger process of humanization which involves an axiological commitment to recognizing and then honoring the immense worth and *irreplaceability* of both person and world.

While Freire might not have approached the world as agentic as we are doing here, he recognized the need to read people's bodies because the world writes upon us as we write upon the world. By expanding Freire's notion of humanization and engaging with posthuman sensibilities we are able to make visible the conjoined plight of oppressed people and the world and advocate for new epistemologies and ontologies that are robust enough to usher forth social-eco justice. This is not a leap from what Freire was writing about already in his later works. In *Pedagogy of the Heart*, Freire (2000b) engages the axiological and ontological problems of anthropocentrism. Consider the following:

> It is urgent that we assume the duty to fight for the ethical principles of respect of life of human beings, life of other animals, the life of birds, the life of the rivers and the life of the forest. [...] And it seems a regrettable contradiction to make a radical progressive discourse, a revolutionary discourse and to have a practice that negates life—the practices of polluting the oceans, the waters, the fields, the devastation of the forest, and those which threaten the animals and birds. (Freire, 2000b, pp. 66–67)

Braidotti (2013) still leads us further by acknowledging the world as full of imagination, creativity, and desire; these capacities are not the sole domain of people. We wish to underscore this point because the previous quote from Freire could potentially lead to a stance whereby people assume they must protect the earth.

While it is true that people need to alter their ways of being to live harmoniously and lovingly with the world, a stance of protection is still a stance of superiority. This is not fundamentally different from the anthropocentrism that cleared the way for where we are now. According to Braidotti (2013), "We need a vision of the subject that is 'worthy of the present'" (p. 52), and which involves recognizing subjectivity as "both materialist and relational, 'nature-cultural' and self-organizing" (p. 51). Nature-culture reunites people with the dynamic movement of a living world and transcends the zero sum logic of Marxist structural analysis, which is predicated on systemic necrophilic–biophilic binary that at best results in people's mere materialist existence. On the contrary, the concept of zoe (life force) has the potential to "displace the exploitive and gravitational pull of advanced capitalism" (Braidotti, 2013, p. 141).

From within the horrors of the neoliberal era of disposability, we also see premonitions of the future as life persists within and among discarded peoples and places. Life refuses to be extinguished, and here we pause and remember—dehumanization is not an abstraction. As oppressive human-made structures re-form, further entrenching dispossession and disposability over time, so too the world continues to self-organize toward materialist subjectivities of thriving. And hence, humanization is real. It is material, and it is always an imminent possibility because life refuses abstraction.

References

Braidotti, R. (2013). *The Posthuman*. Cambridge: Polity Press.

Braidotti, R. (2018). A theoretical framework for the critical posthumanities. *Theory, Culture & Society*, 0(0): 1–31. https://doi.org/10.1177/0263276418771486 (Accessed April 1, 2019).

Evans, B., & Giroux, H. (2015). *Disposable futures: The seduction of violence in the age of spectacle*. San Francisco, CA: City Lights.

Freire, P. (1978). *Pedagogy in process*. New York: The Seabury Press.

Freire, P. (1996). *Letters to Cristina: Reflections on my life and work*. New York: Routledge.

Freire, P. (2000a). *Pedagogy of the oppressed*. New York: Bloomsbury.

Freire, P. (2000b). *Pedagogy of the heart*. New York: Continuum.

Freire, P. (2004). *Pedagogy of indignation*. Boulder, CO: Paradigm.

Freire, P. (2005). *Teachers as cultural workers: Letters to those who dare teach*. Boulder, CO: Westview.

16

The Postdigital Challenge of Paulo Freire's Prophetic Church

Peter McLaren and Petar Jandrić

Postdigital critical pedagogy

Paulo Freire died in 1997. In that year, world champion chess player Garry Kasparov was defeated by IBM's Deep Blue computer; the Mars Pathfinder successfully landed on Mars and started sending images in real time; the lithium-ion battery, which today powers all our mobile devices such as smartphones and tablet computers, entered commercial use; Bill Gates became the world's richest businessman; search engine Google and social network Facebook went online (Computer Hope, 2019).

Freire left us at the very brink of the age of ubiquitous digital networking, yet he had a great feeling for the future, realizing as Secretary of Education for the city of Sao Paulo in the 1990s that "computers represented society's and education's inevitable future, and thus he acted decisively to commit to the infusion of computers in all of the schools under his direction" (Kahn and Kellner, 2007, p. 437). These days, however, Freire's views toward technologies have largely remained in the shadow of his other achievements.

> While a plethora of work in English exists that looks to Paulo Freire's work for guidance on issues of literacy, radical democracy and critical consciousness, there has arguably been less interest in the fourth major platform of the Freirean program—economic development through technological modernization processes. (Kahn and Kellner, 2007, p. 434)

Since the development of Freire's views on technology, much has emerged these past few decades, leading technology into three distinct digital ages.

The First Digital Age covers relationships between human understanding of the world and the analog-digital continuum, introduces the problem of representation, and outlines some digital transformations in education and radical social action. The Second Digital Age describes the so-called Information Revolution and its aftermath with an accent to struggles over transformations in our social arrangements. These days we witness the first signs of the Third Digital Age, where digital technology has become taken for granted, and where the so-called postdigital challenge refocuses our attention from physics to biology. (Jandrić, 2019, p. 161)

According to Peter McLaren (2000), the challenges of the Third Digital Age "demand not only a vigorous and ongoing engagement with Freire's work, but also a reinvention of Freire in the context of current debates over information technologies and learning, global economic restructuring, and the effort to develop new modes of revolutionary struggle" (p. 15). Therefore, let us briefly outline critical pedagogy in and for the Third Digital Age—which, in our recent writings, we also call the age of the postdigital.

Conceived in the First and Second Digital Ages, Freire's attitudes to technology have been developed in the spirit of "using technology to *enhance/ support* critical pedagogy and economic development." Such focus to *enhancement* and *support* is far from unique—it is characteristic for mainstream educational theories in late twentieth and early twenty-first centuries on all sides of ideological spectra. As of recently, however, a growing body of literature has shown limitations to this approach: its deep links to neoliberalism, and underlying technological determinism, which cannot be counterbalanced solely by pedagogy (Jandrić and Hayes, 2018; Hayes and Jandrić, 2014).

In the words of Henry Giroux: "As the Internet opens important new public spheres, its presence presents new questions for your generation. Your generation cannot just simply learn how to read digital media critically. Your generation needs to learn how to produce digital media" (in Jandrić, 2017, p. 143). Furthermore, digital media deeply transforms our sense of what it means to be human (Fuller & Jandrić, 2019). Thus, it enters into deep interaction with the analog and creates the new concept of the postdigital. Trying to describe the postdigital condition, a group of us recently wrote:

> We are increasingly no longer in a world where digital technology and media is separate, virtual, "other" to a "natural" human and social life. This has inspired the emergence of a new concept—"the postdigital"—which is slowly but surely gaining traction in a wide range of disciplines. (Jandrić et al., 2018, p. 893)

Digital world, powered by long lines of zeroes and ones which are permanently transformed through logical operations, offers no room for non-quantifiable concepts such as feelings, intuition, and magic. Postdigital world, defined as a mashup between the digital and the analog, transcends this grave narrowness; at least in theory, it allows us to compute the incomputable, to feel the logic, and to logicize feelings. Situated between reason and emotion, logic and magic, the postdigital approach carries significant consequences for ways we deal with our reality and, as a corollary, for ways we conceive of critical pedagogy. A more detailed account of postdigital critical pedagogy would surely take up much more space than allowed in this chapter, so we will just emphasize its two main characteristics. At the theoretical level, postdigital critical pedagogy requires its own critical philosophy, as Peters and Besley (2019) describe:

> A critical philosophy of the postdigital must be able to understand the processes of quantum computing, complexity science, and deep learning as they constitute the emerging techno-science global system and its place within a capitalist system that itself is transformed by these developments. (p. 40)

At the practical level, traditional critical pedagogy must be expanded to include the critical posthumanist perspective to education "where the human teacher's agency comes up against the workings of data to conduct another, and different, kind of teaching which is neither human not machinic but some kind of gathering of the two" (Bayne in Jandrić, 2017, p. 206). It is in this uncanny gathering that liberation theology gets its space and relevance for postdigital critical pedagogy.

Paulo Freire's prophetic church

Paulo Freire was a devout Christian and sympathetic to Marx. According to Peter McLaren, the main point of convergence between Freire's teachings and liberation theology is critical consciousness, particularly in light of the poor. "In the sense that Christians come to recognize not only their preferential option for the poor but, as I would put it, their preferential obligation and commitment to the poor" (McLaren & Jandrić, 2018, p. 253). However, Freire recognized that many Christians do not share the preferential obligation and commitment to the poor. In her interview with James D. Kirylo, Paulo's wife, Nita Freire, unpacks his love–hate relationship with the Church in depth:

> Paulo was a man of authentic faith that believed in God. And while he was Catholic, he was not caught up in the "religiosity" of the faith. He believed in Jesus Christ, and in his kindness, wisdom, and goodness. He did, however, have grave concerns with the Church, particularly the contradictions of its actions, and the actions of the priests. For example, he observed, since his childhood, how so many priests ate well and gained weight, yet the poor remained poor and hungry, only to hear the priests say to them, "Don't worry, God is with you, and your reward is great in heaven." For Paulo, many priests, with their belly full, did not have authentic compassion and empathy for the poor, and were not consistent with what they had said and what they did. (Kirylo, 2011, p. 278)

According to Kirylo and Boyd (2017), this "theological perspective put him at odds with the Roman Catholic Church of his day" (p. 48)—and this theological perspective brought Freire in close relationship with liberation theology.

In 1968 in Brazil, "The bishops decided to form Christian base communities in which they would create literacy programs, and this captured the attention of Paulo Freire. The goal of the bishops was to support conditions so that the poor could liberate themselves from the 'institutionalized violence' of poverty" (McLaren & Jandrić, 2017, p. 624). In the same year, a conference in Medellín, Colombia, created foundations of contemporary liberation theology. "However, John Paul II was very much opposed to communism and he considered liberation theology a dangerous development within the Church. In the late 1970s, shortly after he was elected Pope, he began to oppose liberation theology directly and the church hierarchy moved decidedly to the right" (McLaren & Jandrić, 2017, p. 624). Freire's literacy program in Brazil had fallen out of grace immediately after it showed its first results, landing Freire in jail and years of exile; immediately after its "official" constitution, liberation theology had fallen out of grace of the Church mainstream. Critical pedagogy, in its both religious and secular versions, has always been a dangerous enterprise.

In "Education, liberation and the Church" (Freire, 1973), "Freire analyses the three main types of church: the traditionalist, the modernizing, and the prophetic church" (McLaren & Jandrić, 2018, p. 258). He attacks the first two churches for failing to fulfill the preferential obligation and commitment to the poor, and develops the notion of the prophetic church. Kirylo and Boyd (2017) put it this way:

> In Freire's view the only true role for the church is the prophetic role. The Prophetic Church rejects the otherworldliness and "halfway measures" of most established churches, and instead works for the social and spiritual liberation of oppressed people. The Prophetic Church takes a critical stance toward existing socio-political structures and engages in an ongoing process of challenging the status quo on behalf of the poor and oppressed. The role of the Prophetic Church is to be "an instrument of transformative action" and societal change. (p. 48)

Similarly, Nita Freire (2011) writes that the prophetic church is the "one that 'feels' with you; one that is in solidarity with you, with all the oppressed in the world, the exploited ones, and ones that are victimized by a capitalist society" (p. 278). In our recent work, we show:

> The prophetic church grew out of the contradictions embedded with social relations of production, relations supported by government corruption, the exploitation of the poor, and class war that exploded within a brutal comprador capitalist system (a system where local elites work on behalf of foreign governments in return for a share of the profits). It was the members of the prophetic church that risked their lives for the sake of the well-being of the poor, the exploited, those who were the targets of a brutal military

regime. But the prophetic church is at work in every community where faith, solidarity and struggle are conjugated with hope for a better world. (McLaren & Jandrić, 2018, p. 259)

The prophetic church is not a thing, or a place, or a theory—at least not in a standard academic sense. Based on Freire's other works, it is fair to say that the prophetic church is a Christian philosophy of praxis which both theorizes and lives its preferential obligation and commitment to the poor. The prophetic church is any place where people believe in God, struggle to emancipate the poor, and strive for social change. As such, the prophetic church necessarily reincarnates in the age of the postdigital.

The postdigital challenge of Paulo Freire's prophetic church

As one of us writes these words on his computer, then sends the text to the other for comments and changes, we use digital technology to collaborate between California and Croatia. Here, digital technologies are tools, which enable our work together on this chapter. In this sense, these technologies are neutral.

By this point, digital tools for personal empowerment have been used by billions of people to increase their autonomy and freedom. They are also useful to capitalists, they are useful to terrorists, they are useful to authoritarian governments—in the same egalitarian way that printing press enabled the Bible, and Mein Kampf, and The Communist Manifesto, to reach wide worldwide audiences. (Rheingold in Jandrić, 2017, p. 221)

However, the act of writing is inevitably supported by the act of reading—and our work is enabled by various sources. And how do we choose what we read? To find relevant sources, we use various "general" search engines (Google, Yahoo, Bing), academic databases (Google Scholar, Web of Science, Scopus); we sometimes find inspiration in sources brought to us by "general" social networks (Facebook, Twitter) and academic social networks (ResearchGate, Academia.edu).

Aside from reading, we sometimes use videos, podcasts, audio books, and each database of these sources uses their own search engines and recommendation tools. However, these search engines and recommendation tools are far from neutral—in a nutshell, they always reflect ideologies of their makers and users (see Jandrić, 2018; Williamson, 2019). It is here that digital technology loses its apparent neutrality—in our postdigital world, just like in previous technological eras, the technological is the political (Feenberg, 2019).

Based on two main pillars—Marxism and Christian faith—liberation theology is oriented toward a concrete praxis of liberation. Without its Marxist elements, liberation theology would not be able to develop practical steps toward liberation; without its Christian elements, liberation theology could not identify hope for a better world. Arguably the best support for this claim can be found in the concept of eschaton shared between Marxism and liberation theology. For Marx, the destruction of capital is "the immanent form for a higher principle that makes possible capitalism's ability to cede its place to a communist society. Marx's entire corpus of works is orientated towards this historical eschatology in his denunciation of the worship of the god of money" (McLaren & Jandrić, 2017, p. 627).

It is easy to agree that money is not a god—however important, money is merely a socioeconomic technology designed for efficient exchange of goods and services. In order to retain hope, however, denunciation of one god requires establishment of the other. Thus, "we cannot affirm the existence of an eschaton unless we affirm the existence of a God guiding history. The eschaton for Christ meant that injustice and exploitation will disappear once and for all" (McLaren & Jandrić, 2017, p. 628). Liberation theology shows that myth, faith, and belief are mutually constitutive with techno-scientific approaches to the world. The technological is not merely political—it is also religious.

In our postdigital world, this expands to the posthumanist and indeed postdigital approaches in which technology is not external to human existence. Human beings are inherently technological—our beliefs, just like our sciences, are shaped through complex interaction with technology. This is the postdigital challenge of Paulo Freire's prophetic church: in our postdigital world, liberation theology needs to open up toward the technological, and the technological needs to open up toward the mystical. Social and spiritual liberation is dialectically intertwined with technological liberation.

Such liberation can take various forms: liberation from technology (which allows us to complement our logic and experiment with feeling, myth, and belief) (see McLaren & Jandrić, 2014), liberation of technology (which contributes to development of technologies of liberation) (see Illich, 1973), liberation through technology (which uses technology as a tool for liberation) (see Jandrić & Hayes, 2019), and many others. In our postdigital age, we need to transcend the ancient divide between scientific and religious worldviews. While we develop Paulo Freire's prophetic church in and for our present and future, we need to embrace our technologies as an intrinsic part of our struggle for emancipation and liberation.

References

Computer Hope. (2019). Computer history—1997. Retrieved March 26, 2019, from https://www.computerhope.com/history/1997.htm.

Feenberg, A. (2019). Postdigital or predigital?. *Postdigital Science and Education*, *1*(1), 8–9. https://doi.org/10.1007/s42438-018-0027-2.

Freire, P. (1973). Education, liberation and the Church. *Study Encounter*, *1*(1973), 1–16.

Freire, N. (2011). An Interview with Ana Maria (Nita) Araújo Freire. In J. Kirylo (Ed.), *Paulo Freire: The Man from Recife* (pp. 271–289). New York: Peter Lang.

Fuller, S., & Jandrić, P. (2019). The postdigital human: Making the history of the future. *Postdigital Science and Education*, *1*(1), 190–217. https://doi.org/10.1007/s42438-018-0003-x.

Hayes, S., & Jandrić, P. (2014). Who is really in charge of contemporary education? People and technologies in, against and beyond the neoliberal university. *Open Review of Educational Research*, *1*(1), 193–210. https://doi.org/10.1080/23265507.2014.989899.

Illich, I. (1973). *Tools for conviviality*. London: Marion Boyars.

Jandrić, P. (2017). *Learning in the age of digital reason*. Rotterdam: Sense.

Jandrić, P. (2018). Post-truth and critical pedagogy of trust. In M. A. Peters, S. Rider, M. Hyvönen, & T. Besley (Eds.), *Post-truth, fake news: Viral modernity & higher education* (pp. 101–111). Singapore: Springer. https://doi.org/10.1007/978-981-10-8013-5_8.

Jandrić, P. (2019). The three ages of the digital. In D. R. Ford (Ed.), *Keywords in Radical Philosophy and Education* (pp. 161–176). Leiden: Brill/Sense. DOI:10.1163/9789004400467_012.

Jandrić, P., & Hayes, S. (2018). Who drives the drivers? Technology as ideology of global educational reform. In A. Means & K. Saltman (Eds.), *Handbook of global educational reform*. Hoboken, NJ: WileyBlackwell. https://doi.org/10.1002/9781119082316.ch15.

Jandrić, P., & Hayes, S. (2019). The postdigital challenge of redefining academic publishing from the margins. *Learning, Media and Technology*. https://doi.org/10.1080/17439884.2019.1585874.

Jandrić, P., Knox, J., Besley, T., Ryberg, T., Suoranta, J., & Hayes, S. (2018). Postdigital science and education. *Educational Philosophy and Theory, 50*(10), 893–899. https://doi.org/10.1080/00131857.2018.1454000.

Kahn, R., & Kellner, D. (2007). Paulo Freire and Ivan Illich: Technology, politics and the reconstruction of education. *Policy Futures in Education, 5*(4), 431–448. https://doi.org/10.2304/pfie.2007.5.4.431.

Kirylo, J. D. (2011). *Paulo Freire: The man from Recife.* New York: Peter Lang.

Kirylo, J. D., & Boyd, D. (2017). *Paulo Freire: His faith, spirituality, and theology.* Rotterdam: Sense.

McLaren, P. (2000). *Che Guevara, Paulo Freire, and the pedagogy of revolution.* Boulder, CO: Rowman & Littlefield.

McLaren, P., & Jandrić, P. (2014). Critical revolutionary pedagogy is made by walking: In a world where many worlds coexist. *Policy Futures in Education, 12*(6), 805–831. https://doi.org/10.2304/pfie.2014.12.6.805.

McLaren, P., & Jandrić, P. (2017). From liberation to salvation: Revolutionary critical pedagogy meets liberation theology. *Policy Futures in Education, 15*(5), 620–652. https://doi.org/10.1177%2F1478210317695713.

McLaren, P., & Jandrić, P. (2018). Paulo Freire and liberation theology: The Christian consciousness of critical pedagogy. *Vierteljahresschrift für wissenschaftliche Pädagogik, 94*(2), 246–264.

Peters, M. A., & Besley, T. (2019). Critical philosophy of the postdigital. *Postdigital Science and Education, 1*(1), 29–42. https://doi.org/10.1007/s42438-018-0004-9.

Williamson, B. (2019). Brain data: Scanning, scraping and sculpting the plastic learning brain through neurotechnology. *Postdigital Science and Education, 1*(1), 65–86. https://doi.org/10.1007/s42438-018-0008-5.

Part Five

Reflections, Experiences, and Considerations

17

Pursuing Critical Consciousness on the Tenure Track: Toward a Humanizing Praxis within the Neoliberal University

Rolf Straubhaar, Sascha Betts, and Sara Torres

To many educators drawn to teaching through Paulo Freire, moving from the K-12 classroom to a university position might seem an ideal career path for having time to reflect and build one's level of critical consciousness. Unfortunately, the dominant paradigm governing contemporary academia leans more toward what Freire (1970) called banking education. Instead of spending our time focusing on how to make our classrooms spaces of becoming for both professor and student, the messages we hear—in our case—from administration consistently focus on enrollment and graduation numbers, maximizing productivity, and promoting student "customer satisfaction."

In his seminal text *Pedagogy of the Oppressed*, Freire (1970) identifies praxis as the backbone of a more humanizing alternative to this banking model. To Freire (1970), education in its purest form is praxis, or reflection combined with action, with a conscious aim to do so for the purpose of social transformation. Only through a consistent process of reflection and action can university-based academics reach full humanity. When divorced from application, knowledge becomes banal and flavorless, a collection of publications that have no use beyond one's dissertation defense or tenure case. Yet, knowledge, when we recognize its transformative potential, is the root of all meaningful social action. When knowledge is genuinely created, through a pedagogical process that involves meaningful interaction with and reflection upon one's circumstances, education truly becomes authentically liberating. As Freire (1970) states, "Liberating education consists in acts of cognition, not transferals of information" (p. 79).

Through praxis, university-based academics can not only identify ways to more fully realize democratic, humanizing, and emancipatory ideals in the classroom, but also personally pursue what Freire calls critical consciousness, or a deeper awareness of reality that comes from the recognition of the inequalities (and privileges) that shape one's own circumstances within larger social structures. While many Freirean academics have already taken steps toward critical consciousness, it can be difficult to stay on this path in the face of the dehumanizing context of the neoliberal university. What, then, can university-based academics do to continue to pursue critical consciousness, both for themselves and for their students?

It is precisely this question which we explore here, through our personal experiences as three Freirean academics from differing positionalities at various points in our careers. All three of us work within the same department at Texas State University, a public Hispanic-serving institution in the United States. Specifically, we are a white male assistant professor (Rolf) from Central Texas, and two doctoral candidates, a Black woman (Sascha) from Detroit and a Latina (Sara) from Central Texas. We will share portions of our personal journeys toward critical consciousness here, and then discuss potential pathways forward for Freirean scholars within the neoliberal academy.

Rolf's journey

I began my career as an adult educator, teaching adult literacy during my college years in Houston. I later moved to the Northeast of Brazil (the *Nordeste*) to teach literacy and other adult education classes at a community-based organization. I was full of the idealistic, hubris-filled fire in the belly you often see in young Americans who feel they have all the answers. From my perspective, the world had problems, but I had just gone to college and learned how to fix them. If I just rolled up my sleeves, it was all fixable.

I was a privileged, white, oppressor-class young man who wanted to save the world—in other words, I was precisely who Freire (1970) was targeting in *Pedagogy of the Oppressed*. Luckily, the organization I was working with in the *Nordeste* focused extensively on Freire to orient its work. I quickly became a converted Freirean, wanting to dive into praxis and look toward growing in critical consciousness.

As you might notice, there are a lot of "I" statements here. In my early career, I tended to seek out jobs teaching in far away, exotic places where I assumed there would be need—where I assumed *I* would be needed. After Brazil, I worked in rural Mozambique, before teaching elementary school in Washington Heights in New York City and on the Navajo Nation in New Mexico. In each of these jobs, I was the hero of my story, the great white hope. I was a complete, round character, and those around me were supporting players at best. Critical consciousness was, to put it mildly, still a work in progress.

One passage that I returned to a number of times over these years was this one from *Pedagogy of the Oppressed*, which pricked my thinking and pushed me toward critical consciousness:

> Those who authentically commit themselves to the people must re-examine themselves constantly. This conversion is so radical as not to allow of ambiguous behavior .... The convert who approaches the people but feels alarm at each step they take, each doubt they express, and each suggestion they offer, and attempts to impose his "status," remains nostalgic towards his origins. (Freire, 1970, pp. 60–61)

When I would read that, it led to genuine reflection—How am I imposing? What am I assuming? How does what I'm doing (or not doing) reveal my continued nostalgia toward my origins?

These days, that oppressor–oppressed dynamic is not quite as visually stark in my current position as a tenure-track professor. Rather than working in rural villages without electricity or under-resourced elementary schools, I'm working in well-maintained buildings with other university faculty and graduate students. However, the academy is just as much a product of colonialism as the international development sector or public K-12 schools, and the remedy remains the same—a consistent praxis of reflection and action, aimed at critical consciousness.

Particularly in my work with doctoral students, even when I claim to problematize the oppressor–oppressed power dynamics named by Freire (1970), it is very easy to fall back into those same hierarchal power structures.

We are conditioned to treat students as below us, simply by virtue of degree and position, even when in a field like education our doctoral students often have decades of professional experience as educators themselves. While I am now a tenure-track assistant professor, my most basic way of being has not changed.

I am not that different from the Rolf who taught elementary school, or who led adult literacy classes in Brazil, or who was middle management at an ostensibly Freirean Mozambican nonprofit. Yet, because I am on this side of the dissertation and the job search, within academia I am elevated to a position where there is the expectation that I am somehow *more* than the students who work with me. If I do not purposefully and regularly sit to deconstruct how that hierarchical structure is reflected in my thinking and in my work, it is easy to let it creep in again.

It is striking to me how Freire maintained a focus on humanization throughout his career. To Freire (1970), education done right is the process of becoming—becoming more fully human. That process is an inherently dialogic one, which requires trust and give and take between equal parties. That kind of humanizing, dialogic relationship of equals is my goal for all of my academic relationships going forward, both with students and with other faculty.

Sascha's journey

I read Freire's (1970) *Pedagogy of the Oppressed* in my freshman year at Spelman College while taking Spelman's ADW (African Diaspora and the World) course, which was designed, in part, to cultivate global citizens. Prior to taking that course I would read assigned materials because they were required, not because I sought self-actualization; however, unbeknownst to me at the time, Freire's *Pedagogy of the Oppressed* sparked within me an orientation toward emancipation through self-advocacy. While in class, I began to ask more thoughtful, content-focused questions and advocate for more meaningful and engaging dialogue. I no longer wanted to be a receptacle, only made functional after receiving strategic deposits of knowledge. I wanted to "problem-pose," and think critically about and participate in the learning happening all around me. I wanted to be free.

Although I was becoming more strategic about my own liberation as an undergraduate, a much more significant step down that path occurred several years later when I was 23 years old. That marked the year I began teaching ninth-grade English with a clear focus on emancipation. I couldn't get behind the notion that standardized test results were the best indicator of student and/or teacher ability, so I encouraged my students to aim for what others thought was unattainable for them, and I also took the time to embrace who they were as people. Although focusing on my students and their growth fueled my fire to teach and create, I felt confined while teaching in the accountability era. I couldn't relegate myself to the four walls of a classroom under the conditions I was asked to teach, so I left K-12 teaching and embarked on my current PhD journey where Freire's *Pedagogy of the Oppressed* serves as a touchstone for my work.

As a doctoral student in a School Improvement program, I continue to employ Freire's language and consciously explore the evolution of emancipatory pedagogy. But to what end? Through my dissertation work, I plan to explore how educators in inner-city public schools can cultivate emancipatory spaces for Black students within the era of standardized testing. Can it be done, or are we too far gone? Has our "banking system" advanced to the point where a "problem-posing" style of teaching and learning is out of the question? The aforesaid questions, and others like them, are on a constant loop in my mind. Recently, though, I've been plagued with another set of questions related to personal growth and self-liberation/emancipation: questions that lead to this conversation on maintaining an emancipatory Freirean perspective within the academy.

While on my doctoral journey I've begun to see cracks in the academic system along the way—cracks that I am unable to ignore. When I see both graduate students and faculty struggling to seek and find liberation in higher education institutions, I question whether or not I want to work in an academic setting when I successfully defend my dissertation. For example, as a graduate student the rat race to publish leaves room for frustration—it at times feels like a form of academic punishment.

This frustration is not born out of hatred toward publication; rather, it is the implicit message that I have to publish more than my competition (my colleagues), or else I am not valuable (and nor are my insights). I am constantly told to "publish in top tier journals" because the academic job market is extremely competitive. However, I am hardly ever told to publish because it is a liberating exercise.

The message I receive is to publish because it will enhance my career, not because it will feed my soul and meaningfully contribute to emancipatory thinking and practice. While both these things can be true, when I am all but forced to do something if I want a job, that action is no longer liberating— it becomes oppressive. I love the idea of getting my thoughts into print and adding to the field of education, but is the academy no more than Freire's "banking system?" I am constantly told: "Read this. Write this. Publish here. Publish there. Your introduction has to look like this. Have you cited theory? While this thought is interesting, your word on it is not enough—we need in-text citations from scholars in the field to validate your experience." Are we not feeding the beast each time we submit a course paper, submit a publication, or present at a conference out of obligatory duty rather than authentic desire?

Regarding the professoriate, the same questions haunt me. It is no secret that professors also have to publish their work in top-tier journals, receive rave evaluations from their students, present at conferences, and sometimes bring in a certain amount of grant dollars per year in order to keep their positions. While some can do this and still maintain their genuine desire to teach, create, and liberate, the hoops that academics have to jump through seem like significant distractions from that emancipatory work. This is why the tenure track is not as desirable as it once was for me. At the same time, I do not know how to get my head around the notion of becoming a PhD *without* securing an academic position.

While the climate and culture from one academic setting to another is varied, I, nevertheless, have this fear that I will run into the same issues of confinement and oppression in academia that I found when teaching in K-12 settings. Can I really become Freirean in approach when the "ready-to-wear" ways of thinking prescribed by the dominant minority onto the majority only serve to "obviate thinking?" (Freire, 1970, p. 76).

Sara's journey

I was born in Lockhart, Texas, in 1972. My parents were very hard working and humble people. We lived a simple life. My life as a child unrolls in images in my head: images of the small two-room home my father could afford to rent; of myself in clothing made at home by my mother. We didn't have many material things, and most months we would have to get by on *fideo* (noodles) and beans at the end of the month until payday. We did, though, have the wealth of each other, our company together, and family stories.

Much of my childhood was filled with time spent with family—my grandparents *Ama* and *Apa*, and an abundant number of aunts and uncles. We spent countless hours sitting in the kitchen and talking, and working together *en las labores* (in the fields) as my grandfather shared stories from when he was a boy. Many of his stories were of oppression he faced in his lifetime. Listening to my grandfather's stories made me proud, grateful for my family, and thankful for our way of life.

I attended a segregated elementary school where we were divided into the "smart" class and the "other" class. As a Native Spanish speaker and a Latina, I was in the "other class" all through elementary school. When I completed high school and began college, I struggled to make sense of my course work and found myself in academic turmoil. My school experience since childhood had been banking education (Freire, 1970), and as a result I had not developed the skill set or motivation to do well in my college courses—especially math and history.

In 2014, while working as a K-12 teacher, I was accepted into a Master's program in Educational Leadership at Texas State University, and it transformed my life. It was in this program that I first encountered Freire. After reading the first two chapters of *Pedagogy of the Oppressed*, I was able to make sense of my school and life experiences as a young child. I realized that my school experience as a child in the "other class" had social power and impact that oppressed me, but did not define who I was. This nascent development of critical consciousness transformed the way that I worked and lived my life. I could never go back to the educator or person I had been before.

I had always considered myself a good teacher and good person, but after reading Freire I found myself in this newfound space of respect, awareness, and appreciation for the present moment and for the person standing before me at any given time.

I'm embarrassed to say that prior to my introduction to Freire, I thought that I was doing a fine job as a teacher, prescriptively providing an invaluable experience for my students. After reading Freire I felt shaken awake, no longer sure that I knew what was best for my students and their families—in fact, I was now sure of the opposite, that I didn't know what was best for them. Rather, I learned what was best for them through conversations with families, in which I closed my mouth and opened my ears. I began to hear students' families' stories and learn what their hopes and dreams were for their children.

As I reflected on some of the stories that lingered within me from childhood, I realized my family had lived Freire. Learning to become more fully human, as charged by Freire (1970), was part of the legacy of what my family had already taught me.

Today as I have transitioned to my current position as a doctoral student and STEM research faculty member at Texas State University, my personal mission is rather simple. I serve as a bridge between the university and the community and public K-12 schools. Every day I face a choice: I can bury my head in books and fall to the pressures to publish for the sake of my career[1], or I can choose to find ways to develop community STEM programs that inspire and initiate hope that our Latinx children will achieve their dreams making our community and world a better place. I choose the latter.

The journey forward

In all three of our narratives, despite the fact that we come from such different personal histories and positionalities, it is striking to see the common challenges we identify as standing in the way of pursuing a humanizing, emancipatory,

---

[1] To be clear, I am not suggesting that the notion of scholarship and community activism is exclusively a binary dynamic. Rather, what I am questioning is the notion of publishing simply for the sake of publishing in which its only motive is to advance one's career.

Freirean praxis as university scholars in the neoliberal academy. In the current banking university system, we define "good" undergraduate students by their ability to receive and repeat what they are taught (Freire, 1970), and we similarly define "good" graduate students and faculty by what they are able to produce: peer-reviewed articles in high-impact journals, externally funded research projects, and positive course evaluations.

While, on one hand, graduate students and faculty are ostensibly able to authentically pursue their own interests and actively create knowledge through their scholarship, university administrators, on the other hand, oftentimes superficially focus on a scholar's number of publications and the impact factor of each journal than on the actual content of their writing. Both graduate students and faculty in this system are dehumanized—defined by their productivity rather than their humanity. As Freire (1970) framed it, in such a setting we are made into objects rather than subjects unto ourselves. Indeed, all three of us feel this pressure, and experience the way in which it dehumanizes us and reduces our motivation to engage in truly emancipatory work.

Freire's work, though, gives us the tools to not only name this dehumanization, but also work against it. All three of us have shared how the notion of Freirean praxis has pushed us on a path toward critical consciousness, reminding us of our own humanity, and the humanity of those with whom we work. For two of us (Sascha and Sara), this has meant embracing the strength and power of our heritage, even when that heritage is not given value by society at large. For one of us (Rolf), it has meant realizing that our oppressor-class heritage did not imbue us with special power and privileges above others, despite that being an implicit message we had received our whole lives. For all of us, Freire (1970) has been an important touchstone for the steps to take toward "becoming more fully human" (p. 44), and avoiding dehumanizing pitfalls in the neoliberal academy.

Reference

Freire, P. (1970). *Pedagogy of the oppressed*. (M. B. Ramos, Trans.). New York: Continuum.

18

Living in the Contradictions: LGBTQ Educators and Critical Pedagogy

Dena Lagomarsino

Over fifty years ago, Brazilian educator Paulo Freire outlined his conceptualization of education as a dialectical process of teaching and learning, offering possibilities for a critical pedagogy of the people—an anti-colonial pedagogy with the potential to subvert power structures and discursive constructions of race, class, and other identity markers that contribute to multiple material oppressions for marginalized groups.

Since its publication in English in 1970, *Pedagogy of the Oppressed* has been central to critical pedagogy in the United States, with a number of theorists taking it up particularly in the mid-1980s, such as Stanley Aronowitz, Antonia Darder, Henry Giroux, Donaldo Macedo, and Peter McLaren. Freirean pedagogy continued to gain prominence in the early 1990s into the twenty-first century, with the critique and expansion of feminist theory by black feminist/lesbian theorists, such as Audre Lorde, Patricia Hill Collins, Kimberlé Crenshaw, and bell hooks.

Queer theorists such as Adrienne Rich, Eve Kosofsky Sedgwick, and Judith Butler marked a shift from theorizing about the status of women to theorizing gender and sexuality as systems of social stratification, often relying on the postmodern tradition to question the limiting frames of feminism and gay/lesbian studies. Like queer theory, critical theory destabilizes the notion of natural identity categories but looks more explicitly at intersecting issues, considering how individuals are raced, classed, gendered, sexualized, and more.

To that end, this chapter explores how Freirean pedagogy and queer theory inform and enhance one another by listening to the philosophies and pedagogical anecdotes of current middle and high school educators who teach in large American cities and openly identify as lesbian, gay, bisexual, and queer.[1] In their commitments to not only being "out" in their schools but actively engaged in socially just pedagogies and in local and national struggles, these educators demonstrate the possibilities of moving beyond the dichotomous notion of being in or out of the closet to a consideration of "bridging" as a queer, embodied critical pedagogy.

The closet and the classroom

Freire (2011) is interested in how, within structures of domination, schools "function largely as agencies which prepare the invaders of the future," privileging and producing dominant discourses and ways of being (p. 154). A foundational contribution to queer theory identifies "the closet" as both product and producer of "modern Western culture and history at large" (Sedgwick, 1990, p. 46). In her critique of the lesbian and gay rights movement's uncritical adoption of the hegemonic metaphor, Sedgwick discusses our education system, pointing to seminal court cases like *Acanfora v. Board of Education of Montgomery County* (1973), in which eighth-grade earth science teacher Joseph Acanfora, III was removed from the classroom when administrators discovered that he was gay.

The federal district court supported the Board of Education's decision to move Acanfora to a non-teaching position by claiming that he had brought "undue attention" to himself by speaking to the media, which would in turn negatively impact the educational environment should they return him to his position (p. 47). The Fourth Circuit Court of Appeals overruled the rationale of the lower court, acknowledging his First Amendment right to free speech, but claimed that he did not have a right to bring a suit in the first place, as

---

[1] The research this chapter builds from consisted of multiple semi-structured interviews with eight middle and high school educators. While the study called for LGBTQ educators, the participants identified as cisgender lesbian, gay, bisexual, and queer men and women at the time.

he had not properly disclosed previous involvement in a college "homophile organization" on his original job application, which would have prevented him from being hired on the spot. Notably, both courts failed to acknowledge that he would have had no need to exercise the right to protected speech in the media had he not been removed from his position in the first place.

In Sedgwick's (1990) interpretation, the two separate rulings in *Acanfora* demonstrate the double binds that serve as organizing structures of sexuality, power, and oppression in heterosexist society at large. While both courts stated that Acanfora's sexuality "itself" could not be grounds for removal, they effectively punished the dissemination of such information. From this, Sedgwick posits that sexuality is located in labeled speech acts, and coming out is not an inherently liberatory act, but one that often produces and enforces dichotomous categories. In this aspect, Sedgwick (1990) builds on Foucault's work around sexuality and power, questioning the "natural self-evidence" (p. 55) of the opposition between gay and straight and demonstrating how self-policing and societal surveillance maintain our dichotomies and reinforce power imbalances in different institutional settings.

Today's educational landscape

In more recent years, efforts to combat bullying and increase LGBTQ representation within schools tend to focus on the creation of gay-straight alliances, inclusion of texts in libraries and syllabi, creation of anti-homophobia trainings and programs, and the encouragement of openly LGBTQ educators as role models for youth (Rofes, 2005). And while these efforts have had an impact, we still have a way to go as attacks on queer and gender nonconforming people have increased in local schools and at the federal level (Kosciw, Greytak, Zongrone, Clark, & Truong, 2018).

Today's educators teach in an era where public education is under acute attack, in which resources continue to be unequally distributed. In a nation without federal protections against employment discrimination based on sexual orientation or gender identity, advancements made over recent years are being unraveled under a Secretary of Education, Betsy DeVos, who has spent her career supporting unregulated for-profit schools and conversion therapy.[2] Recent news about the fine line educators have to walk between job security and transparency, accompanied by reports of firings of LGBTQ educators at all levels, bear a disturbingly close resemblance to the climate Sedgwick lays out in cases from almost fifty years ago.

Alongside the rollback of protections for LGBTQ educators and students, our educational system is decades into a racial resegregation process—sixty years after *Brown v. Board of Education,* schools are central to the continued maintenance of social stratification and our contemporary capitalist formation, drawing geospatial socioeconomic boundaries around who can attend which institutions, what and how they learn, and how they are disciplined, resulting in what Jonathan Kozol (2005) calls "apartheid education."

America's public schools are historically situated, industrialized spaces that reflect and enforce the hegemony of the dominant group. As such, it is not enough to simply incorporate multicultural education practices that recognize marginalized groups, despite the call of the past few decades. Without critical education practices, bringing LGBTQ educators, resources, and spaces "out" in schools does nothing to interrogate how "unethical uses of authority and power serve to acculturate young people into consensual rituals of dominance" and hierarchical systems (Rofes, 2005, p. 18).

Until we address systemic issues that our students and their families face in the communities where schools are located, it will not be possible to "improve our schools," or the related conditions for our educators (Noguera, 2003, p. 142). However, while schools may serve as sites of reproduction, they are also sites of resistance. Counter-hegemonic principles and actions are necessary, but teachers must examine their own contexts and roles in relation to dominant forms, too. For example, aligning queer theory and critical pedagogy can open up a space for discursive and material change around multiple forms of structural oppression in places likes schools (Hickman, 2011). Regardless of sexual identity, queer pedagogy may have

[2] Also known as "reparative therapy," this pseudoscience intends to change the sexual orientation, gender identity, or gender expression of LGBT people in the context of providing health care and/or religious practice, based on the belief that being LGBT is abnormal (Mallory, Brown, & Conron, 2018).

the potential to challenge all students by calling into question the process of normalizing dominant assumptions (Winans, 2006).

Out critical educators

The eight individuals that I interviewed self-identified as lesbian, gay, bisexual, and queer educators who were "out" at school, and as teachers who strove to incorporate socially just pedagogies, which ranged from descriptions of Freirean pedagogy to Gloria Ladson-Billing's (1994) notion of culturally relevant teaching, in their classrooms. Five participants self-identified as cisgender women and the other three as cisgender men, and five self-identified as white, one as Chinese, one as Muslim-identified Afghan, and one as Black. At the time, the educators ranged in age, from twenty-seven to forty-one, and in subject matter, teaching history, social studies, language arts, sexuality/health, and art. They had all taught for at least five years, in traditional public and charter schools, from single-sex to alternative and private religious institutions.

During semi-structured interviews, I encouraged participants to tell me stories that highlighted their experiences in schools and other educational settings, trajectories toward teaching, understandings of socially just pedagogies, and experiences coming and/or being out(ed). Through their critical reflections of their intersecting identities and experiences as educators and students, co-creation of classroom norms, materials, and activities with their students, and involvement in anti-capitalist actions and movements outside of the classroom, the educators in this study work against dichotomies and the banking model of education, demonstrating the transformative potential of "bridging" beyond "coming out."

The same year these interviews were completed, sociologist Catherine Connell (2015) interviewed lesbian and gay K-12 educators about how they negotiate their identities amid tension between expectations around professionalism in the workplace, including compulsory heteronormative gender performativity, and the demands of a homonational movement to exist fully out of the closet. Connell finds that lesbian and gay teachers typically act on the tensions by becoming either "splitters, knitters, or quitters" (p. 58).

While "splitters" describe practices and discursive techniques they employ to stay closeted at school and "quitters" leave the field, "knitters" are visibly out at school, but in ways that work with their professional identities. Both resisting and assimilating, "knitters" may succeed in their goal of providing role models for LGBTQ youth, but they do so in a way that reproduces the notion of a "right" way to be out, through the policing of gender expression, which always intersects with race, class, and sexuality to produce power along intersecting axes.

In their first years of teaching, particularly pre-tenure, most of the educators I spoke to came out to colleagues when they were in monogamous relationships often involving cohabitation or engagement, reinforcing the notion of gay rights and identity as defined by marriage and similar dominant norms. A few described being outed by students during their first months in the classroom during interpersonal conflict, a developing theme that may speak to the dynamic relationship between structural and interpersonal power as it plays out in face-to-face interactions that re/produce gender, race, and class inequalities in everyday life (Schippers, 2008). When we spoke, they were all out to some degree, ranging from a queer social studies teacher in a southern city who was out with select coworkers and students, to a gay language arts educator in the northeast who came out every October 11, incorporating recent articles about LGBTQ issues and providing a personal narrative.[3]

Overall, the critical educators who I spoke with offer a different direction than those who stay closeted, leave the field, or knit their identities in a palatable homonormative display that might uphold power structures. As McLaren (2007) discusses, these educators believe that "there are many sides to a problem ... often linked to class, race, and gender issues," and self-reflect on their own intersecting identities and the ways in which they show up (p. 71). They engage in and out of the classroom: in their local anti-capitalist teacher-activist groups; on social media pages designed to allow students to ask questions they are not comfortable bringing up in class; through public speaking combating Islamophobia and homophobia; at grassroots meetings

[3] Since October 11, 1988, has been celebrated in the United States as National Coming Out Day for LGBTQ individuals and allies.

for racial, environmental, and economic justice initiatives; and by intentionally serving students who are most impacted by capitalism.

Unlike the "knitters," out critical educators strive toward intersectional approaches and do not view themselves as role models for a particular identity-based group of students, but as teacher-students actively naming and challenging dominant discourse through embodied political acts and ways of being alongside young people whose voices are often silenced in schools and society. A few educators spoke of moving between geographic and institutional spaces and its impact on their ways of being in the world.

One teacher who came into her queerness when she moved from the Midwest to a conservative community in the south said, "When you walk around and you're white [here], everyone thinks you're a Republican, so I was fascinated with finding the way I would have to live to show people that I did not agree with the things they were saying." A Muslim-identified Afghan sexuality educator identified as a feminist when she was younger, but her queer community in college brought her into activism as she recognized intersecting ways she was marginalized that her white college friends did not experience, finding that "so much of [her] resiliency came from things that [she] had been living and learning all along."

Considering the ways she engages her students through a lens of love and care rooted in black feminism, a queer black art teacher expresses, "As a person of color, you walk around and carry the legacy and the implications of race every day. You're very hyper-vigilant and aware." This embodied awareness helps her leverage her lived experiences to co-create a critical classroom community with students whose experiences "are so vast, so some of the students look like me, some don't, some might identify with me because I'm a wild teacher with purple hair, some because I'm also a New Yorker, some because, you know, I'm thick, and all the different layers of who I am."

A social studies teacher sees teaching as a core part of her identity, because she's actively an "out, queer, political, white female teacher" who engages pedagogy as a process, a "way of interacting with young people and colleagues and modeling and co-creating relationships that [she] want[s] to exist in the world." Recognizing her "tomboy privilege" she continues, "I think I get to do things in the world ... specifically because I'm a white masculine-presenting woman who is not especially butch." Although she hesitates to call it transformational, she believes this awareness and action help her engage with young men of color in a way that is productive and aspirational.

Each of these educators demonstrates the importance of praxis—critical reflection and action toward transforming structures—in their considerations of the ways they inhabit different spaces and how queerness as a set of embodied political acts might help build critical, transformative relationships across difference and against domination. Echoing Sedgwick's critique from decades earlier, they know that simply "coming out" is not enough to shift intersecting paradigms of power and that alternative paths must be forged and fortified.

From closets to bridges

Instead of speaking of being in or out of the closet, or knitting, what if we spoke of being bridges? Bridges exist to make connections, spanning obstacles without closing off that which is above or below. They allow movement in at least two directions, but also open up proliferating pathways beyond. They can be sturdy or flimsy, made more stable or precarious due to different elements and interactions. They vary in design and function, taking natural elements and context into consideration. Feminist theorists of color use the idea of "bridges" and "borderlands" to emphasize the "both/and," of identity, showing how intersecting oppressions can make it difficult to maneuver different spaces, but also lead to resistance and paradigmatic shifts (Moraga & Anzaldúa, 1983).

The educators I spoke with teach in what Mary Louise Pratt (1991) calls the *contact zones*—"social spaces where cultures meet, clash, and grapple with each other, often in contexts of highly asymmetrical relations of power" (p. 34). In his final book, published posthumously, Freire (2001) reiterates his key points and argues explicitly against the progressive liberalism often deployed to meet the call. Too often, socially just education gets implemented as multicultural affirmations for individual, rather than collective liberation.

One participant discusses how she feels she has to "live in the contradictions"—the contact zones where intersectionality can be brought to light, troubled, and acted on—which only exist as contradictions because the lens through which we think success is measured is one that does not fit our lives, identities, and backgrounds. While they each inhabit a range of identities, the out critical educators I spoke with actively reflect and act on their queerness as an asset toward bridging dichotomies, working across lines of difference and toward liberation for all. As Freire, Sedgwick, and others have, they trouble dominant narratives at the levels of language and action, naming the word and the world, interacting with the armed love that comes from studying, learning, teaching, and knowing with our entire body (Freire, 1998).

In her collection of poems bearing witness to the Truth and Reconciliation hearings post-apartheid, South African writer Ingrid de Kok (2002) reflects on the power of language in the face of great interpersonal violence, wondering, "Why still imagine whole words, whole worlds:/the flame sputter of consonants,/deep sea anemone vowels,/birth-cable syntax, rhymes that start in the heart,/and verbs, verbs that move mountains?" Following Freire's (2011) call, out critical educators know that "to exist humanly, is to *name* the world, to change it" (p. 88), acting with "armed love" as bridges in the struggle against capitalism and its oppressive structures.

References

Connell, C. (2015). *School's out: Gay and lesbian teachers in the classroom*. Oakland: University of California.

DeKok, I. (2002). *Terrestrial things: Poems*. Parts of speech (p.21). Roggebaai, South Africa: Kwela/Snailpress.

Freire, P. (1970/2011). *Pedagogy of the oppressed*. New York: Continuum.

Freire, P. (1998). *Teachers as cultural workers: Letters to those who dare to teach*. Boulder, CO: Westview.

Freire, P. (2001). *Pedagogy of freedom: Ethics, democracy, and civic courage*. Lanham, MD: Rowman & Littlefield.

Kosciw, J. G., Greytak, E. A., Zongrone, A. D., Clark, C. M., & Truong, N. L. (2018). The 2017 National School Climate Survey: The experiences of lesbian, gay, bisexual, transgender, and queer youth in our nation's schools. New York: GLSEN.

Hickman, H. (2011). Disrupting heteronormativity through critical pedagogy and queer theory. In C. S. Malott & B. J. Porfilio (Eds.), *Critical pedagogy in the twenty-first century: A new generation of scholars* (pp. 71–85). Charlotte, NC: Information Age Publishing.

Kozol, J. (2005). *The shame of the nation: The restoration of apartheid schooling in America*. New York: Crown.

Ladson-Billings, G. (1994). *The dreamkeepers: Successful teachers of African American children*. San Francisco, CA: Jossey-Bass.

Mallory, C., Brown, T. N., & Conron, K. J. (January 2018). *Conversion Therapy and LGBT Youth* (Issue brief). Retrieved May 25, 2019, from The Williams Institute on Sexual Orientation and Gender Identity Law and Public Policy website: https://williamsinstitute.law.ucla.edu/wp-content/uploads/Conversion-Therapy-LGBT-Youth-Update-Jun-2019.pdf.

McLaren, P. (2007). The future of the past: Reflections on the present state of empire and pedagogy. In P. McLaren & J. L. Kincheloe (Eds.), *Critical pedagogy: Where are we now?* (pp. 289–314). New York: Peter Lang.

Moraga, C., & Anzaldúa, G. E. (1983). *This bridge called my back: Writings by radical women of color*. New York: Kitchen Table Press.

Noguera, P. (2003). *City schools and the American Dream: Reclaiming the promise of public education*. New York: Teachers College.

Pratt, M. L. (1991). Arts of the contact zone. *Profession*, 67, 33–40.

Rofes, E. (2005). *A radical rethinking of sexuality and schooling: Status quo or status queer?* Lanham, MD: Rowman & Littlefield.

Schippers, M. (2008). Doing difference/doing power: Negotiations of race and gender in a mentoring program. *Symbolic Interaction*, 31, 77–98.

Sedgwick, E. K. (1990). Epistemology of the closet. In H. Abelove, M. A. Barale, & D. M. Halperin (Eds.), *The lesbian and gay studies reader* (pp. 33–40). New York: Routledge.

Winans, A. E. (2006). Queering pedagogy in the English classroom: Engaging with the places where thinking stops. *Pedagogy*, 6, 103–122.

19

An Eye-Witness Account of Freire's Return Back to Brazil after the Exile: Personal Reflections on Fighting Oppression

Nelio Bizzo

It was in 1979 when public pressure in Brazil reached a heightened state to return to democracy, particularly in light of the military government facing a hard time on the socioeconomic front. Moreover, worker organizations were growing, and trade unions and teacher associations were beginning to show a new kind of resistance, all of which captured the collective imagination of Brazilian society.

More radical members of student trade unions took part in clandestine meetings to better organize demonstrations and university strikes against the military government in which demanding democratic freedoms was the aim. Indeed, university students and others took to the streets to march in protest. But these resistance efforts did not come without a high price. Activists were followed by the police, working undercover to more easily apprehend protesters who were summarily imprisoned and tortured. It is estimated that as many as 20,000 people were reported tortured, with at least 434 people murdered under the auspices of the state (Comissão Nacional da Verdade, 2014).

It was within that struggle and the unfolding surge for the voice that the winds of the political climate shifted, prompting many intellectuals to return to Brazil, such as Marco Aurélio Garcia and Eder Sader, who used to welcome activist students in their own homes, holding private meetings to discuss political strategy. And, it was also during this time that the spirit of political amnesty was in the air, which paved the way for Paulo Freire to also return to Brazil, flying into Viracopos Airport in Campinas in August 1979. Many

After fifteen years away from the country, Paulo Freire was welcomed at Viracopos airport in August 1979. With his first wife, Elza, on his left, Freire was speaking to the press. Courtesy of Nelio Bizzo

people were there to greet him, including university professors, politicians, and students, from São Paulo and Campinas. Surprisingly, there was no trace of the police.

It is worth reminding that prior to Paulo's exile, he had been imprisoned for seventy-five days, was subjected to a military trial, and was forced to leave his homeland during the same year of the 1964 coup. He first went to Bolivia, then to Chile, Harvard, and spent most of his exile years working for the World Council of Churches (WCC) in Geneva, Switzerland. Working for the WCC took Freire all over the world where he was able to spread his ideas of literacy development.

It may not be easy to relate for ordinary people who live in democratic countries to understand the meaning or even the necessity of exile. For example, at the time of writing this chapter (April 2019), there is news about people leaving Brazil, after one year of the brutal murder of an elected representative of the people of Rio de Janeiro, Marielle Franco. Several people decided to flee the country after public menaces of death and organized actions against them and family members. Yet, Dilma Ferreira Silva, a workers' leader in the Amazonian region, and her husband, Claudionor Costa da Silva, refused to leave the country and were shot dead at home on March 21, 2019 (Maisonnave, 2019).

While waiting at the airport, we learned that Paulo's airplane was coming from Algeria, where a new president, from the National Liberation Front, had been recently elected. At that time, the more radical university students were naïve or ideal enough to think that the air company choice was a political option, and no one would assume that the issue was related to getting a good price for the ticket. Finally, arrival occurred earlier than planned, with no explanation for the reason. All of this contributed to creating an atmosphere of threat and fear among the young students who were there. Upon arrival, Paulo answered questions for the press but avoiding any strong statement, coupled with quickly leaving the airport.

It was years later that details about his arrival were known. For example, at the passport control, he had been stopped by two policemen. One of them asked whether he had had political problems with the Brazilian government, all the while the other one asked him to sign one of his books. He was already an idol, not only of young university students but also of those officially working for the state!

Science educational practice with adult workers

As a Brazilian and as one who has worked with adult workers who were illiterate, I certainly recognize the importance of Paulo Freire's ideas. For example, a typical case can be found when I was working in the impoverished neighborhood of Favela do Jaguaré, (SP), in the early 1980s. This night course was an initiative of the Catholic Church, coordinated by an outstanding brave nun, who is still very active in defending the rights of impoverished and indigenous people. The challenge was to teach science to a group of workers who were illiterate.

Included in the group of workers were mothers, all who were unable to write their names, bringing in histories of suffering and despair from their childhood. And though their children were attending school, most were unable to help them in their homework. An air of failure permeated, and oppression was a common feature in their narratives. The few cents they earned during the day to make a living did not compare what they were thirsting to learn in the night course. Freire's concept of "conscientização" turned to be very concrete and complex, overcoming what he called "naïve conscientiousness," and the viewing of themselves instead of objects of history to subjects of history.

Learning to read and write was an awkward dynamic for these adult learners, as they could not do what young children already did, sometimes inside their own homes. Asking adults to repeat tasks which were quickly done by children would not help them to create the desire to go further, or, to use Freire's original expression, "ser mais" ("to be more"). The idea, therefore, was to create some hands-on work, which could be taken home and seen by the student's family as something different from an ordinary child's notebook. The primary objective for these science lessons was to enable students to transmit short messages using Morse Code, developing their perception of symmetry, as the code for some letters (such as A, D, and F) has a different meaning when inverted (see figure below).

Some electricity concepts needed to be applied, and while they could not follow written instructions, some students had already worked with electric

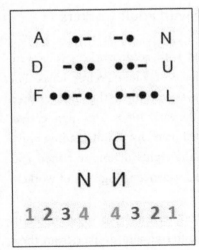
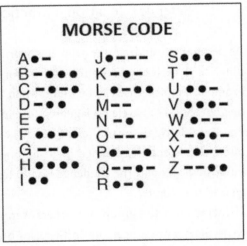

Courtesy of Nelio Bizzo

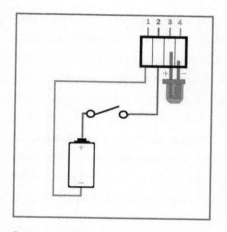 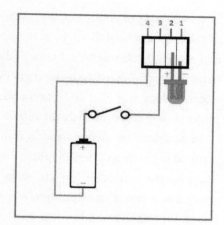

Courtesy of Nelio Bizzo

appliances. It was at this time, in the early 1980s, that the small light-emitting diodes (LEDs) were beginning to be used. They were inexpensive and could easily be found in shops around São Paulo. Thus, through a Morse Code-type pattern, we would then use short and long blinks of light, prompting students to construct words for themselves (Bizzo, 1985). Note that, because of the polarity of the LED (actually a diode), connecting the two appliances required a symmetric order (see figure above). Mirror writing has intrigued scientists for many years (Wilson & Bishop, 2018).

Within the scope of our pedagogical approach as Freirean in nature, we were always exploring to better meet the needs of our students, realizing the political nature of education, the importance of examining the theory that informed our practice, and the pedagogical approach that would best work with the adult learners who came from a variety of backgrounds and experiences (Haddad, 1985).

Advising team when Freire was secretary of education

When Paulo Freire was appointed as secretary of education of São Paulo in 1989, little did I know that years later I would be holding the same seat, albeit only for a very short stint, which is discussed later.

As secretary of education, his task loomed large with São Paulo having one of the largest school districts in the country, with almost 1,000,000 students and some 40,000 teachers. Freire looked to implement new policies for the network of schools, whereby teachers would network in such a way that would foster lifelong learning and one in which at respective schools pedagogical projects were autonomously organized.

In addition, he invited experts from different academic specialties, as he planned to create an interdisciplinary approach to organize a new curriculum. Many people, including myself, were invited to meet Paulo, taking part in group discussions that meaningfully revolved around political and pedagogical issues. We talked about how the curriculum could be changed and to include students, teachers, staff, and the community as part of that process. Yet, none of us imagined that the meetings would have such a light atmosphere. He used to amuse the group telling personal happenings, like the one at the airport passport control when he arrived back to Brazil in 1979.

The early 1990s, however, were troublesome from the socioeconomical point of view, as the country had extremely high inflation and a depressed economic level of activity which had led many people to lose their jobs, all of which had a natural impact on resourcing the schools. In other words, a limited budget and working within a system that had many who were resistant to change and wanted to hold on to authoritarian practices presented great challenges (Freire, 1993).

And yet, despite the challenges, Freire was able to accomplish a measure of success as secretary of education for the approximate two years he served in the capacity. Kirylo (2011) describes that measure:

For example, raises did occur for teachers and the democratizing of the administration clearly was evident at the Department of Education; however, the concept of school councils was not always understood among teachers, principals, and parents, creating misunderstandings regarding the role of power and decision—making and its place within a democratic environment. Buildings were repaired and some new ones constructed, in addition to the purchasing of needed equipment such as desks, televisions, videos, slide projectors, and other equipment. However, due to budget constraints, cuts in federal grants, and political party infighting, building, and repair projects were slowed down. Finally, the fostering of ongoing professional development of teachers and the reorientation of the curriculum had an overall positive impact of keeping school-aged youth from "dropping out" of school (Saul, 1993). (p. 103)

It was during that time as Paulo was ending his tenure as secretary of education that I was away completing my PhD and had heard that the bureaucratic nature of being secretary weighed heavily on him, leading him to resign and back to his writing. Soon after Paulo's resignation in 1991, I completed my doctoral studies and involved myself in many education projects, including consultancy work to the Ministry of Education.

"Wearing Freire's Shoes"

At the beginning of the year 2000, I became a member of National Council of Education (CNE) and eventually was elected vice-president of the Basic Education Chamber. However, I soon was faced with a significant challenge: Paulo Renato Souza, the late minister of education, repeatedly announced that primary teachers all over the country would lose not only their job places, but also their professional credentials if they did not get a university degree within a few years. Losing professional rights was a clear-cut issue for CNE members.

My reports at CNE defended the professional rights of teachers; they should be encouraged to go on studying to get other degrees, yet, without jeopardizing their professional rights as part of that process (Bizzo, 2003; Luce, 2005). Oppression, in this context, was related to the immense power of the new private universities' networks, which experienced extraordinary growth in recent years. One of the main targets continues to be public schools' teachers, and the argument is still the idea that a change in the school curriculum necessarily implies the loss of teacher's professional rights, an idea I have been fighting against since that time up until today (Bizzo & Andrade, 2018).

By the end of 2002, democratic elections changed the perspective of public education, and teachers began to see that their professional credentials would be respected. By this time an invitation to be secretary of education of São Paulo arrived. To be seated in the same chair that Paulo Freire occupied was a deep honor.

As soon as I took up the position, I came to realize the scope of the multiple challenges and problems that were before me, one of which was an issue of school uniforms for the one million students of the schools' network. A person, with a network of relations with agents of the federal secret service (ABIN), and a shady past, was acting as a broker and realizing the amount of money involved attempted to sell another brand of clothing, other than the brand that was originally agreed upon.

He did not accept the result of the bidding process, which I was completely unaware of. He had denounced a supposedly irregular procedure to the attorney general, who was waiting for the nomination of the new secretary of education for an official declaration, which was to be me. This ongoing attorney general investigation was a complete surprise to me, and learning that this broker was considered a highly dangerous person, I looked to surround myself with highly ethical people who, through a nomination process, would assist me in preventing any illegal transactions, in this case relative to the purchasing of school uniforms. However, the individuals I invited to work with me were not nominated, meaning I would be forced to work with an administration I did not know.

Under this completely new situation, I sent clear signs that I would not keep the new job feeling insecure to meet all the challenges, particularly when it came to corruption. Only within a few days on the job as secretary of education, I resigned. A few months later the broker was involved with other criminal activities, such as an illegal video recording of a public servant who was offered bribery. This episode triggered the so-called vote-buying "*mensalão*" scandal in 2005. It took years for the press to chronicle the school uniform incident, reporting that despite the broker's statements securing the existence of wrongdoing or illegal activity, nothing was actually found and the public prosecutor closed the investigation for lack of sound evidence.

The fight continues

In recent years, Paulo Freire's main ideas have acutely come to the forefront in Brazil. Soon after the parliamentary coup of April 2016, when the elected president Dilma Youssef was illegally impeached, many false profiles were created in social media which revealed to be part of an enormous microtargeting wave, with internet search engines. This new media regime has been increasingly influencing people, which eventually provoked a massive political disaster in Brazil, with the 2018 election of an extremely right-wing president (Jair Bolsonaro) with a very conservative parliament.

Oppression in current-day Brazil is real; many people have been murdered. In fact, among the promises of the then-candidate Bolsonaro was to literally kill left-wing people when visiting Acre, in the Amazonian region (Ribeiro, 2018), where Chico Mendes lived, before being murdered for defending the forest. Bolsonaro also used social media to encourage the "burning Paulo Freire's books" in public squares.

Oppressive forces have also dramatically reached impoverished and indigenous people, with significant cuts in health and social services. Unemployment has increased significantly, and trade unions have been attacked in many different ways. A new proposal for the rules for retirement has been presented, following the dreadful model imposed by Pinochet in Chile, critically endangering the rights of women and the most impoverished workers.

On the environmental front, the news could not be worse. Indian reserves have been invaded by mining companies, and the Amazonian forest has been suffering from huge fires. The microtargeting of social media and the fake news industry is increasingly active. In the educational field, we have seen a real disaster, with significant budget cuts and ideological persecutions, remembering the McCarthy years.

As I write these words, this extreme right-wing government is celebrating the military coup of 1964, which imposed a military dictatorship and a sociopolitical nightmare for twenty-one long years. Torturers have been praised, presented as heroes against "communism." And despite the extreme

A recent 2019 demonstration in São Paulo, Brazil, at the same police station where hundreds of people were tortured, and many died, protesting against the celebration of the 1964 coup by the ruling government. Since 2013 there has been a public appeal to transform the place into a memorial against torture. Courtesy of Nelio Bizzo

pressure from the far-right, popular organizations are encouraging people to resist oppression by all peaceful means.

In a very real way, it appears Brazil is going back in time, with many idolizing authoritarianism and not realizing how oppression works and how democratic spaces erode into a place of non-existence. There is no doubt it is time to welcome Paulo Freire again in Brazil.

References

Bizzo, N. (1985). Projeto Telégrafo: uma experiência com realfabetizandos. *Revista de Ensino de Ciências (FUNBEC)*, 14: 42–46.

Bizzo, N. (2003). *Parecer CNE/CEB 03/2003*, Consulta tendo em vista a situação formativa dos professores dos anos iniciais do ensino fundamental e da educação infantil. Brasília: CNE/MEC. Retrieved from http://portal.mec.gov.br/cne/arquivos/pdf/pceb003_03.pdf (visited March 2019).

Bizzo, N., & Andrade, C. C. (2018). Reformas Educacionais e Formação de Professores de Ciências. In D. Foguel & M. Scheuenstuhl (Eds.), *Desafios da*

Educação Técnico-Científica no Ensino Médio (pp. 77–95). Rio de Janeiro: Academia Brasileira de Ciências.

Comissão Nacional da Verdade. (2014). Relatório. Brasília: CNV. Retrieved from http://www.memoriasreveladas.gov.br/administrator/components/com_simplefilemanager/uploads/CNV/relat%C3%B3rio%20cnv%20volume_1_digital.pdf (visited March 2019).

Freire, P. (1993). *Pedagogy of the city*. New York: Continuum.

Haddad, S. (1985). *Relatório do Curso de Capacitação e Reciclagem em Metodologia de educação de Adultos para o Programa de Educação de Adultos da FABES/PMSP*. São Paulo: CEDI (mimeo). Retrieved from http://www.bibliotecadigital.abong.org.br/bitstream/handle/11465/1609/119.pdf?sequence=1&isAllowed=y (visited March 2019).

Kirylo, J. D. (2011). *Paulo Freire: The man from Recife*. New York: Peter Lang.

Luce, M. B. (2005). *Parecer CNE/CEB 09/2005*. Consulta se o curso de licenciatura (plena) em Ciências Sociais habilita para o magistério de História e Geografia nos anos finais do Ensino Fundamental e Ensino Médio. Retrieved from http://portal.mec.gov.br/cne/arquivos/pdf/pceb009_05.pdf (visited March 2019).

Maisonnave, F. (2019). *Líder de movimento social é assassinada em assentamento no Pará*. Retrieved from https://www1.folha.uol.com.br/poder/2019/03/lider-de-movimento-social-e-assassinada-em-assentamento-no-para.shtml (visited March 2019).

Ribeiro, J. (2018). "Vamos fuzilar a petralhada," diz Bolsonaro em campanha no Acre. Retrieved from https://exame.abril.com.br/brasil/vamos-fuzilar-a-petralhada-diz-bolsonaro-em-campanha-no-acre/ (visited March 2019).

Saul, A. M. (1993). São Paulo's education revisited. In P. Freire (Ed.), *Pedagogy of the city* (pp. 145–165). New York: Continuum.

Wilson, A. C., & Bishop, D. V. M. (2018). Resounding failure to replicate links between developmental language disorder and cerebral lateralisation. *PeerJ*, 6:e4217. Retrieved from https://doi.org/10.7717/peerj.4217 and https://peerj.com/articles/4217/ (visited October 2019).

Disclaimer: People's names, except when evident, were deliberately omitted.

This text is dedicated to the memory of Eder Sader (1941–88) and Marco Aurélio Garcia (1941–2017), two brave Brazilian intellectuals who fought oppression.

20

Dare to Hope: The Art of Untying the Tongue and Awakening the Resilient Spirit

Débora Barbosa Agra Junker

Art has an extraordinary ability to invite us to dialogue through all our senses: we can see or talk about it. We can touch it when allowed or feel it circulate our bodies through waves, through our pulsations. Art evokes in us responses, feelings, and estrangements. It triggers memories and provokes visceral reactions. It speaks of the present time, but it can also remind us of a past time—intentionally dormant or without any pretense of remaining static. Art, in its various possibilities, can unearth a suffocating feeling, a silenced word. It can also etch in us what has not yet been manifested, a future that we cannot yet touch, but can imagine. The work of Doris Salcedo, Colombian visual artist, has this ability to evoke these multiple reactions within us. Among her most evocative works, there is one, which translates in a visual and embodied way what this text seeks to sculpt with words in the following pages.

The politics of concealment

Shibboleth was the title of a temporary art installation constructed in 2007 by Doris Salcedo in the modern art gallery of Tate Modern, in London—the Turbine Hall. According to a critic, *Shibboleth* was the first work "to intervene directly in the fabric of the Turbine Hall," in which, instead of placing a typical sculpture within the space of the gallery, the artist "created a subterranean chasm that stretches the length of the Turbine Hall."[1] In breaking open the floor of the museum, Salcedo exposes and undresses the fissures of contemporary societies. By doing this, she encourages us to confront our past and present history constructed based on colonial exploitation and the stolen rights to the land and resources of so many peoples in colonized contexts. In Salcedo's perspective, *Shibboleth* is an invitation to reflect border and divisions, human encounters and divergences, on the life of immigrants in their experiences of segregation, racism, and displacement. The crack begins narrow and superficial. The careful observer notices, however, that the fissure takes a broader and more in-depth character, inviting viewers to follow the same trajectory of the sculpture itself—from a limited assessment of existential circumstances toward a more profound and sophisticated understanding of human contradictions.

Grounded in her social–cultural context, the Colombian artist exhibits an extraordinary sensitivity to the situation of oppressed people not only of her native land, but also everywhere. Her art is a visual display of what Boaventura de Sousa Santos (2009) calls an abyssal line that divides social reality into two sides—whatever lies on the other side of the line remains invisible or irrelevant. This line is so abysmal that it renders invisible everything that belongs or happens on the other side of the line. Further illuminating this idea, Sousa Santos argues that abyssal thinking is a feature of Western modernity, consisting of a system of visible and invisible distinctions dividing social reality into two ontologically different universes. While one side of the line corresponds to the imperial, colonial, and neocolonial north, the other side corresponds to the colonized south, which is repeatedly silenced and oppressed. In light of Santos's thinking, Salcedo's artwork is a statement about the questionable ideological foundations on which Western notions of modernity are constructed. Thus, her creation becomes, in the words of Gloria Anzaldúa (1990), a "form of political activism employing definite aesthetic strategies for resisting dominant cultural norms" (p. xxiv).

[1] The Turbine Hall has hosted some of the world's most memorable and acclaimed works of contemporary art. And the way artists have interpreted this vast industrial space has revolutionized public perceptions of contemporary art in the twenty-first century. Retrieved from https://www.tate.org.uk/whats-on/tate-modern/exhibition/unilever-series/unilever-series-doris-salcedo-shibboleth. Accessed March 2, 2019.

Furthermore, Salcedo's artwork constitutes an invitation to use all our senses to grasp the reality that engulfs us and takes away our words and our voices, helping us to acquire a consciousness of the world we inhabit and struggle. This kind of understanding—the critical reading of reality as Freire calls it—is a necessity in contemporary contexts where many are overwhelmed by the increasing deterioration of human life and natural resources. Besides, as Freire (2004) reminds, where life is denied or almost absent—as a result of the scarcity, pain, despair, and people made invisible—it is precisely in that location that we need to, stubbornly, weave the threads of the life we desire. Therefore, to break the culture of silence becomes a courageous act of resistance and defiance to challenge systemic, structural, and institutionalized forces that produce and reproduce both privilege and oppression. Because the pervasive culture of silence, as Freire (1997) articulated, negates people of their ontological condition of *"ser mais,"* this silence needs to be deliberately contested. As Freire (1997) argues:

> Human existence cannot be silent, nor can it be nourished by false words, but only by true words, with which men and women transform the world. To exist, humanly, is to name the world, to change it. Once named, the world in its turn reappears to the namers as a problem and requires of them a new naming. Human beings are not built in silence, but in word, in work, in action-reflection. (p. 69)

The culture of silence steals from people their capacity to create, to overcome the myths of inferiority, to have political clarity, and to exercise their right to participate in the transformation of their circumstances. For Freire (1985), when the right to speak is usurped, a breach, a chasm, a fissure must be created in order for this silence—imposed by the various forms of violence— to be broken. Only when people break the culture of silence and reclaim their right to speak—that is when radical structural changes take place—can society stop being oppressive. This rupture constitutes a counter-hegemonic action of making history. It means taking history in the hands and participating in the historical–cultural process of dismantling oppressive systems that destroy and nullify people. However, recognizing this fractured space does not mean immediately being released from bondage.

Nevertheless, it is the initial step toward the recognition of oneself as visible and active in the struggle for reclaiming one's word, voice, history, and one's autochthonous knowledge—fundamental elements for the social praxis that emerge from the collective effort of subalterns. It is from this place where memory is hindered, and the inflicted silence facilitates forgetfulness that an alternative disposition of mind—decolonization of the mind—must trans(ins) pire. As a result, people refusing and resisting to the imposed muteness can join in the discovery of a "collective voice" (Freire & Macedo, 2011, p. 46) which carries the potency of transformation. By expelling the internalized oppression that undermines one's autonomy initiates the process of liberation, which, according to Freire, is always communal.

The politics of intolerance

Shibboleth is a word of Hebrew origin found in the biblical book of Judges (12:1-6). It refers to the battle between the tribe of Ephraim and the Gileadites, which ended with the defeat of the former. When the surviving Ephraimites tried to cross Jordan, they found Gilead soldiers on the other side, who subjected them to a single test: to pronounce the word shibboleth. The challenge was no more than a method of quick identification of opponents. Since the Ephraimites lacked a pronunciation for the "sh" sound, they were quickly identified by their opponents. The text says 42,000 were killed at that time. It was unacceptable and dangerous not to know the tribe-identifying code.

From time to time, incidents of identification of other groups through their accent and speech have occurred. Although the greater or lesser ability to pronounce a particular word does not have such immediate and dramatic consequences as in the biblical narrative, there are subtle (and not so subtle) ways through which specific terms or accents evidence the origin of a person, and are used to separate, discriminate, immobilize, and profile people. See, for instance the book, *The Hegemony of English* (2003).[2]

---

[2] In the book, *The Hegemony of English*, Macedo, Dendrinos, and Gounari (2003) expose the neoliberal ideology of globalization and how the prominence of English should be analyzed in the context of a theory of power relations and the understanding of socio-political forces that leads to linguistic and cultural discrimination.

The potency of Salcedo's work resides in making visible this violence of discrimination and intolerance through a fissure on the grounds of a prestigious museum, thereby inviting us to reflect on the breakages in the human relationships perpetrated by a history of colonialism, patriarchalism, and capitalism; by the gap between rich and poor; by the distance between northern and southern hemispheres. Her work invites us to look at the very ground that sustains but also divides, compelling us to perceive and confront the uncomfortable truths about the foundations in which we build our world and understandings about the "other." Although her work has a direct reference to the Latin America context, her art transcends that context and speaks to global contexts and experiences of otherness and displacement.

People from the Global South know well about marks of identification and how dangerous, costly, and demanding it becomes inhabiting an inhospitable world. As a result, some have attempted to suppress their true selves by accepting an imposed knowledge and surrendering themselves to the colonization of their minds and bodies. Hence, they come to believe in the myths created by the oppressor, and instead of fighting for their liberation they internalize the image of the oppressor. In their alienation, they desire to resemble the oppressors, becoming oppressors or "sub-oppressors" themselves. To such condition, Freire (1997) declares, "It does not necessarily mean that the oppressed are unaware that they are downtrodden. However, their perception of themselves as oppressed is impaired by their submersion in the reality of oppression" (p. 27).

As a result, the oppressed marked by these deep, internal psychological characteristics need to resist, interrupt, and abandon the former stage by ejecting the oppressor within so that both personal and the systemic oppression may be counteracted. This resistance and ejecting dynamic can be a complicated psychological, even spiritual, process. For the oppressed, the liberation of this state of alienation will only be possible to the extent that there is a critical understanding of these contradictions, not only in theory and practice, but also in the praxis that integrates action and reflection as two complementary movements in permanent tension, which Freire calls a process of *conscientização*. Practices and theories from an ahistorical reading of reality will inevitably succumb to a "liberating fatalism" widely denounced by Freire.

According to him, liberation pedagogy always implies a process of critical reading of reality and an effort to transform oppressive systems. Moreover, Freire conceives his pedagogy from "the other" and "with the other"—the wretched of the earth—who from his or her position can dare to think a world different from the one that exists.

The politics of hope

Contemporary societies have experienced a tremendous social, political, economic, and migratory crisis that has been conducive to the rise of racist rhetoric, violent actions, police brutality, xenophobic attacks, and religious intolerance. The threats to people's lives and the planet have deteriorated the vital harmony of human existence and have produced countless personal and collective traumas. As a result of these everyday realities, skepticism, disengagement, and hopelessness have settled in the minds and hearts of many, eliciting a feeling of disenchantment and indifference. In this context of existential angst, one wonders if it is still worthy of continuing fighting for changes increasingly unrealizable and elusive. The challenges facing societies today are not so different from the conflictive circumstances Freire lived through in the 1960s. His critical pedagogy—which radically believed in the educability of human beings despite their shortcomings—continues necessary today to contest the banalization of misery and violence, and to declare the right to dream for a world that is yet to come.

In the first pages of the *Pedagogy of Hope* (2007), Freire declares his conviction about the need to educate our hope. He advises, however, that to ascribe to hope simply for hope's sake can lead to despair. He states, "Hope, as an ontological need, demands an anchoring in practice. As ontological need, hope needs practice to become historical concreteness" (p. 2). Likewise, he insists that the emblematic dehumanization of our contexts is not cause for hopelessness but for hope that leads us to the incessant search for the humanization of all in solidarity with those who are made invisible in our societies.

Freire's pedagogy of hope speaks of a different way of seeing that does not bend to the neoliberal, supremacist, sexist whims, and intentions. It is an insistent, persistent, and resilient pedagogy. It blows the wind of the new, the rebelliousness, the non-acceptance of determinism, inevitability, destiny, or fatality of present conditions of injustice and inequity. It is a hope that is not shy, not submissive, nor foolish. It is a subversive hope that rebels and reveals itself in solidarity with the poor, dispossessed, and unprotected—those who are called surplus.

Although many are led to believe that a colossal hope is necessary in order to contain the immense problems that afflict society today, perhaps hope should be sought and nurtured through little gestures and little things. Therefore, cultivating tiny hopes—through small expressions of love and kindness—can become a persistent way of confronting hopelessness; small pockets of resistance; delicate seeds to bother a world full of great projects and grandiose ideas. Freire (2004) confirms this when he says:

> But precisely because we find ourselves subjected to an endless number of constraints—obstacles challenging to overcome, dominant influences of fatalistic conceptions of history, the power of neoliberal ideology, whose perverse ethics is based on the logic of the market—never, perhaps, we have had more need to stress through the educational practices, the sense of hope needed today. Hence, among several fundamental practices of educators, whether liberal or conservative, it notes the following: change is difficult but possible. (p. 100)

In addition, Freire challenges progressive educators to reveal the possibilities for hope, no matter the obstacles they might face. As a fundamental construct, hope is indispensable to a liberating education and becomes the dynamic force to generate structural, personal, and collective changes.

Final thoughts

As we reflect on Freire's legacy, we might find ourselves perplexed at how his thinking remains urgent and relevant in the present times. Although we have celebrated the fiftieth anniversary of the *Pedagogy of the Oppressed*, we sadly recognize countless worldwide attempts to suppress critical thinking, of silencing policies propositions, of weakening of democratic processes, of the violence against women and minoritized people, to mention but a few examples.

The collection of essays in this text is a vivid reminder of how Freire's work has traversed distinct contexts and time. Like a work of art, his pedagogy crosses our bodies, pierces our senses, and impregnates our lives with a patiently impatient hope. It is a pedagogy that emerges between the breaches of selfishness and the hunger for power. It is a pedagogy that cracks in as a resilient, life-propelling force that pulsates beneath the hard, barren surface of the concrete walls we try to build to separate "them" from "us." It constitutes simultaneously a pedagogy of hope and indignation (Freire, 2004). Ultimately, it is a pedagogy that believes in the "transformative and emancipatory power of love" (Darder, 2015, p. 47).

The social–political commitment and genuine love for human beings that Freire exhibits throughout his writings and interactions is a concrete example of what Sousa Santos (2018) describes as the act of "corazonar." According to him, *corazonar*—an Andean cultural concept—means "to experience the misfortune or unjust suffering of others as one's own and to be willing to join in the struggle against it" (p. 100). Thus, *corazonar* means the warming up of the heart; that is, the heart guiding the reason and the emotion. It implies vital energy compelling toward solidarity, coexistence, and resistance. This is precisely what Freire compels us to embrace through our educational endeavor—an enduring capacity for wonder and indignation, that is nonconformist and destabilizing, but always ethical and compassionate.

In some respects, Salcedo's artwork provokes this destabilization and rebellious awareness. Her art–political statement carved not only her message in the museum and its history denouncing past and current efforts to prevent people to "be more," but her ability to speak metaphorically about these life conditions altered the structure of the museum forever. After the exhibition concluded, the mark caused by the crack she introduced on the hall's floor remains. Although cement was poured over to "close the gap" the scars are still visible on the floor—a memory of what happened to the terrain of the museum remains. Her quiet but assertive statement denounces the abyssal lines while at the same time encourages, as Santos does, a paradigmatic transition that includes new relationships between epistemologies and politics, new cartographies, new participants.

The art of Salcedo—as well as other works of art invested in reflecting the political urgencies of our times—makes us see our limitations, our contradictions, and what we lack. In addition, it has the potential to complete us by returning what was silenced, usurped, and muffled. So, in art, as it is in life, the emergence of the new possibilities can save us from our cracks, from the cords that try to immobilize and control us, and from the circumstances that try to freeze our imagination and creativity. The elements that separated and mutilated us in the past must be present in our memory so that we do not fall into the same breaches. They are places we do not want to go back to because they make us less human. Thus, instead of abysms we should have signpost-memories where our desire to create new paths can mobilize all our senses.

Emerging epistemologies of the South—which Freire is one of the most relevant proponents—have multiple glances, new accents, new languages, and new expressions. They trust on the political commitment of educators and students who, conscious of their place in the world, can mobilize, resist, and denounce the injustices and abuses of those who try to colonize them and steal their rights "to be more." The epistemologies of the South, like Freire, challenge us to rescue and strengthen the liberating, loving, and ethical aspects of education. Inspired by these emergent epistemologies, people are invited to create a less barbaric, less predatory, and less unjust world where instead of abysms that accentuate distances, new horizons are open to other alternative ways of coexistence.

Perhaps this is the time to hear the voices of those who come from the suffering corners of the earth because they bring ancestral wisdom imprinted on their bodies. Although we may not be able to speak their language, we may be able to embody their wisdom as found in the ancient Peruvian Quechua word, *Qonakuy*. This exceptional concept captures the essence of Freire's legacy. The term means offering the best of oneself in mutuality and reciprocity with affection. May we dare to hope walking on this earth offering the best of ourselves in reciprocity and with affection.

References

Anzaldúa, G. (1990). *Making face, making soul. Haciendo Caras. Creative and critical perspectives by feminists of color.* San Francisco, CA: Aunt Lute Books.

Darder, A. (2015). *Freire and education.* New York: Routledge.

Freire, P. (1985). *The politics of education: Culture, power, and liberation.* South Hadley, MA: Bergin & Garvey.

Freire, P. (1997). *Pedagogy of the oppressed.* New York: Continuum.

Freire, P. (2004). *Pedagogy of indignation.* Boulder, CO: Paradigm Publishers.

Freire, P. (2007). *Pedagogy of hope: Reliving pedagogy of the oppressed.* New York: Continuum.

Freire, P., & Macedo, D. (2011). *Alfabetização: Leitura do Mundo, Leitura da Palavra.* Rio de Janeiro, RJ: Paz e Terra.

Macedo, D., Dendrinos, B., & Gounari, P. (2003). *The hegemony of English.* New York: Paradigm Publishers.

Santos, B. de S. (2009). *Una Epistemologia del Sur.* Buenos Aires, AR: CLACSO: Coediciones.

Santos, B. de S. (2018). *The end of the cognitive empire.* Durham, NC: Duke University Press.

Paulo Freire Fifty Years Later: An Afterword

Antonia Darder

More than fifty years after *Pedagogy of the Oppressed* was first released in English, the inequalities and injustices that Paulo Freire was addressing then continue to persist in the United States and around the world today. In many instances these conditions have worsened in the last three decades, with the infusion of neoliberal imperatives into policies and practices of education. It is important then to begin a discussion about Paulo's legacy here, in that often, it has been precisely Freire's revolutionary critique of capitalism and the link of schooling to class struggle, that have been stripped away, resulting in watered down and diluted versions of his ideas.

As a woman of color born in Puerto Rico and a colonized subject who lived in abject poverty into my late twenties, I have always been convinced that the center of gravity of oppression for those of us deemed as "other" is not simply the psychological aberration of white people toward people of color. Rather, the racialization processes experienced by the oppressed are intractably connected to the manner in which the colonial matrix of power persists in the domination and exploitation of our communities by the wealthy and powerful elite—and enacted, for the most part, by those who are not themselves affluent, but who still chase the false myth of the American Dream in these neoliberal times.

With this in mind, I want to argue that, although seldom acknowledged by mainstream discourses of Freire's work, there are clear distinct ways in which radical Black, Latino, Native American, and Asian American working-class activists of the 1960s and '70s embraced Paulo Freire's ideas. For many of us,

This text draws from a keynote address delivered at the Freire50 Conference at the University of South Carolina in October 2018.

Freire was one of the few philosophical educational theorists of our time to speak directly to our grounded understanding of racialized oppression as powerfully linked to the larger international imperialist project. In other words, if we were to counter the impact of the historical and contemporary wounds of genocide, slavery, and colonialism upon our lives, we had to contend with the manner in which racism has always been inextricably tied to the imperatives of social class formation and economic exclusion and domination of the majority of the world's population.

For activists of color, the struggle was not foremost about "celebrating diversity," cultural identity, or the acknowledgment of our cultural legitimacy, but rather a larger struggle for our humanity and our survival, given that we had suffered, in the flesh, the violence of oppression at every level of our existence. Hence, we recognized that our local political struggles for self-determination—then as today—have to also be anchored to a larger international class struggle against the ravages of advanced capitalism, racism, and patriarchy. As such, we critically understood our struggles as tied to the historical violence of colonialism. As such, an underlying purpose of our engagement with Paulo Freire's work was as much about unveiling the deep structures of domination, as it was about the decolonization of our minds, hearts, bodies, and spirits (Darder, 2018).

In this sense, Freire's articulation of the Oppressor–Oppressed contradiction echoed the ideas of political activists and writers of color of the twentieth century, such as Frantz Fanon, Aime Cesaire, and others who spoke to this phenomenon in their political articulations about the struggles of oppressed populations. As such, they sought to unveil the deep asymmetrical relations of powers that led to our subordination and the erasure of our historical knowledge and social understanding as an oppressed collectivity, within the context of US hegemony. Restoring the integrity of our voices and centering our cultural and historical knowledge of survival became an essential political quest for us, in an era where our voices and participation remained relatively absent, ignored, or silenced, within the spheres of power and decision-making across the nation.

The genesis of *Pedagogy of the Oppressed* must be understood as rooted in a tremendously contentious moment in the world's history, when the oppressed were fighting back. At the time of the book's writing, Freire was living in Chile, exiled from Brazil for his emancipatory literacy efforts with poor communities from the countryside. Yet, he attributed his ideas in *Pedagogy of the Oppressed* to what he learned in his relationship with those who were most dispossessed and to his comrades in Chile, who further enlivened his revolutionary spirit (Darder, 2018). As such, Paulo inspired in activists and educators around the world with a political clarity and commitment that reinforced the significance of theory, but only within its connection to everyday life.

Hence, Paulo challenged us to embody our commitment to political consciousness and social transformation, within the relationships we forged with those within and outside our cultural communities. More importantly, what we understood was that the pedagogy of the oppressed was not only for the classroom, but rather it was a living pedagogy that has to be infused into all aspects of our lives—within both the personal and the political. This to say, *teaching to transgress* constitutes a moral stance, often belittled and diminished by the mainstream. So much so that it caused bell hooks (1994) to write, "It always astounds me when progressive people act as though it is somehow a naive moral position to believe that our lives must be a living example of our politics" (p. 48).

Hence, for those betrayed by our schooling, Paulo offered the possibility of a local educational project for our children tied to a larger democratic vision—one that resonated with our anti-colonial struggles for self-determination and our desire to control our own destinies. Hence, Freire's pedagogy is truly one of transgression—transgression of oppressive ideas, attitudes, structures, and practices within education and a global political economy that has sought to rob us of our humanity.

Love as a political force

In a footnote in chapter 3 of *Pedagogy of the Oppressed*, Paulo (1970) wrote:

I am more and more convinced that true revolutionaries must perceive the revolution, because of its creative and liberating nature, as an act of love. For me, the revolution ... is not irreconcilable with love. On the contrary: the revolution is made by [people] to achieve their humanization. What, indeed, is the deeper motive which moves [individuals] to become revolutionaries, but the dehumanization of [people]? The distortion imposed on the word "love" by the capitalist world cannot prevent the revolution from being essentially loving in character, nor can it prevent revolutionaries from affirming their love of life. (pp. 77–78)

Paulo's view on the significance of love to both our pedagogical and personal lives remained steadfast and resoundingly embodied across the landscape of his writings and his everyday life. Freire believed deeply—from the personal to the pedagogical to the political—in the emancipatory and transformative power of love. His radical articulation of love spoke to both a personal and political Eros, grounded in an unwavering faith in the oppressed to generate the political will necessary to transform our lives and the world. In Freire's eyes, to attempt daily engagement with the societal forces that dehumanize and undermine our existence, without the power of love on our side, is to be like lost travelers in a vast desert, without water to complete the crossing.

It' s not surprising then that Paulo (1970) often came back to the notion of an "armed loved—the fighting love of those convinced of the right and the duty to fight, to denounce, and to announce" (p. 42). His is a concept of love meant not only to comfort or relieve the suffering of the oppressed, but also to awaken within us the historical thirst for justice and the political wherewithal to reinvent out world. Paulo's love permeated his existence as a man and an educator. He could be gentle, tender, and inspiring, while at the same time, critical and challenging—strategically unveiling individual or collective follies. Freire's pedagogy of love challenged deeply the *false generosity* of those whose ideologies and practices work to sustain a system of education that transgresses at its very core every emancipatory principle of social justice and democratic life. It was this lucid recognition of love as an untapped political force of consciousness that most drew me to his work and continues to fuel my commitment to the emancipatory political project he championed throughout his life.

In my academic preparation, never had another educational theorist so fearlessly given the question of love such primacy in his philosophy, pedagogy, or politics. Moreover, Paulo did this wholeheartedly without concern for the consequences of mean-spirited critiques that cast him as unsystematic, unscientific, or irrelevant. For an impoverished student whose life was mired by the lovelessness of oppression, Paulo's (2005) commitment to "the creation of a world in which it will be easier to love" (p. 40) spoke to the suffering in my heart, the weariness of my spirit, and the yearning of my soul. So, it is not surprising to speak of his pedagogy of love as a political force for our times—a pedagogy that deeply inspired my political and intellectual formation as a critical scholar and, thus, my praxis in the classroom and in the world.

For Freire (2000), *love as a political force* was essential to his revolutionary vision of consciousness and transformation. There was, moreover, an inseparability in how he viewed love and his motivation to struggle, insisting, "I have a right to love and to express my love to the world and to use it as a motivational foundation for struggle" (p. 71). Paulo did not see love as a mere sentimental exchange between people, but rather love constitutes an intentional and communal act of consciousness that emerges and matures through our social and material practices, as we live, learn, and labor together as educators and activists. Across his writing is found this critical view of love, often glossed over by the very people who most need to comprehend deeply his humanizing intent. Sometimes more directly and other times more subtly, Freire reminded us that a politics of love must serve as the underlying force of any political project that requires us to contend daily with structural and relational forms of oppression, as we simultaneously seek new radical possibilities for social and economic justice.

Paulo wrote of the politics of love by engaging with the personal and communal exchanges he considered important to the relationship between teachers and students. In particular, he spoke to the importance of cultivating greater intimacy between self, others, and the world, in the process of our teaching and learning. In this way, living with democracy and deepening it, so it has concrete meaning in students' everyday lives (Carnoy, 1987), becomes a central political concern of the classroom. Here, democracy and the solidarity of difference, necessary for its evolution, are made possible through a pedagogy fortified by a universal regard for the dignity and equality of all people, no matter their cultural differences or economic circumstances. And, as such, unity does not require uniformity or assimilation, but rather a shared political vision for a more just world.

Paulo's view of love as a dialectical force that simultaneously unites and respects difference must be imagined as a radical and interdependent sense of lived kinship, if we are to effectively challenge the material inequalities and disaffiliation that are the hallmark of capitalism. Freire speaks to a love generated from political grace and born of collective consciousness, which emerges from our shared suffering, creativity, and imagination, giving meaning to both our political resistance and our struggle for liberation (Darder, 2015). Through a commitment to love, learn, labor, and dream together for a more just world, he sincerely believed that relationships of solidarity could be nurtured and political dreams of freedom regenerated. He often asserted the notion that we, as human beings, must unite ourselves with the world and others in the process of social and political co-creation, so that our collective participation in the labor of struggle could also impel us toward a deeper understanding of ourselves and our communities. This also entails a force that propels us beyond spiritual transcendence, personal-abnegation, or political negation of the inextricable relationship between consciousness and the material. Instead, Paulo asserted a love that is born and emerges directly out of our social participation and unwavering political commitment to the transformation of the historical moment in which we exist as grounded subjects of history.

Keeping all this in mind, we can better appreciate Paulo's concern with the colonizing forces so prevalent in the banking model of schooling. He was adamant about the political necessity to unveil hegemonic practices of authoritarian pedagogies that obstructs the pleasure of life and the principle of love, generating alienation between teachers and students and a deep sense of our human estrangement from nature. This, in turn, arouses deep anxieties and insecurities that interfere with cultivating and nurturing the political imagination, epistemological curiosity, and joy of learning necessary to our practice. He worked to counter this colonizing disregard for the respect and dignity of students mired in the debilitating dynamics of assimilative schooling, asserting that oppression is best served by keeping the oppressed confused and estranged from one another, steeped in sentiments of a fatalism and inferiority that blames students for their academic failure and workers for their material misfortunes.

In his conceptualization of love as a motivational force for struggle, Paulo linked his pedagogy of love to political values that nurture emancipatory relationships. Some of these include faith and dignity in our relationships with others, social responsibility for our world, participation in the co-construction of knowledge, and solidarity across our differences. Directly and indirectly, Freire engaged the essence of love as inseparable to our labor as educators and democratic citizens of the world. Similar to Erich Fromm's (1964) vision, Freire embraced the idea that "one loves that for which one labors, and one labors for that which one loves" (p. 26).

Although there have been a few feminist critiques of Freire's ideas and language, it is nearly impossible—true to feminist sensibilities—to separate the political and the personal when engaging Freire's work. Throughout his life, he resisted the tyranny of binaries in his own philosophical ideas, political interpretations, and pedagogical praxis. Grounded in an enormous sense of responsibility to use his privilege in the interest of the oppressed, Paulo stressed the importance of practicing respect, patience, and faith, if we are to dismantle structures of domination that alienate and exploit those who exist, overwhelmingly, as slaves of capital.

Freire's own capacity for love was an exercise in precisely the humanizing relational dynamic he espoused—a personal and political dynamic that seeks to empathize with the core of another, beyond simply kneejerk responses or stereotypical distortions. For example, often working-class students or activists of color are perceived as being angry. But, rather than to see us beyond preconceptions of anger, or to acknowledge that all human beings who are anxious, worried, isolated, fearful, repressed, or suffering will exhibit symptoms of anger, most teachers stay at the surface and, from there, issue racialized characterizations, devoid of insight into the oppressive conditions or suffering that generate our anger or frustration.

Paulo, however, noted that the right to be angry, just as the right to love, can serve as a legitimate motivational foundation for our decolonizing struggles; for just anger reminds us that we are not meant to live as objects of exploitation, persecution, or domination. In the same light, he (2000) asserted, "My right to be angry presupposes that the historical experience in which I participate tomorrow is not a given, but a challenge" (p. 71). And, as such, our just anger is grounded in our indignation over the inhumanity that persists in the world. Therefore, one of the most important tasks of a pedagogy of love is to create the conditions for students to "engage in the experience of assuming themselves as social, historical, thinking, communicating, transformative, creative persons; dreamers of possible utopias, capable of being angry because of [their] capacity to love" (p. 45).

This is particularly so, given that many educators are so disconnected from the conditions of "the other" and frightened by their racialized misconceptions to allow themselves to genuinely know our children as vital human beings. Instead, students remain objects to be managed, manipulated, and controlled, in ways that may eventually draw out of them the prescribed answers. However, neither students nor communities are objects to be manipulated or tweaked here and there. Freire knew that learning, like loving, is an act that students must choose freely to practice, through the exercise of their social agency and personal empowerment. With this at the core of our pedagogical sensibilities, we can avert fixed notions or prescriptions of "the other"; for given the ever-changing and evolving nature of our humanity, seldom can we know our students or even ourselves fully. At best, we can know one another only in context and only in relation to our shared labor or lived experiences.

Paulo's pedagogy of love also sought to shatter preconditioned or patterns of hegemonic schooling in how we name the world, by demythologizing the context in which we, as teachers, student, and activists, labor. This to say, we are encouraged to move away from fixed or prescribed views of life and toward a relational and contextual emancipatory understanding of knowledge, history, community, and society. This is particularly relevant to a critical literacy, informed by Freire's (1993) understanding of literacy as a decolonizing practice, which is "above all, a social and political commitment" (p. 114). In the process of *reading of the word and the world*, Paulo (2002) also sought to explore the relationship between political purpose and pedagogy as vital to building consciousness, mobilization, and organization for our liberation. Hence, Paulo's reading of the word and the world is connected to a larger political struggle against cultural and linguistic genocide, which entails a critical literacy that prepares students to harness their cultural knowledge, in order to create a more just future.

This implies an evolutionary process of consciousness, by which individuals become critically aware that their active involvement in the historical process is directly linked to their commitment to denounce injustice. Resistance, in this sense, is anchored to a dialectical process of consciousness, from which we collectively name, challenge, and act to counter the consequences of values, policies, and practices that threaten our dignity and right to be. Hence, resistance is understood as an important precursor to becoming critically conscious, in that it is a response rooted in love.

Conscientização: Conscientization

For almost five decades, Paulo's work has invited us to embrace the struggle for critical consciousness and social transformation as a road yet to be made; which, because it is unknown, must be traced out, step by step, in our organic relationship with the world and in the process of our labor as educators, activist, and revolutionary leaders. For Freire (1983), conscientization "does not take place in abstract beings in the air but in real men and women and in social structures ... it cannot remain on the level of the individual" (p. 130). The struggle for change begins, then, at the moment when we become both critically aware and intolerant of the oppressive conditions in which we exist and push toward new ways of knowing and being.

This process signals that moment of consciousness when we in communities experience a breakthrough and decide to take another path, despite risk or an uncertain future. Conscientization as an essential principle of his critical pedagogy opens the epistemological field for the expression of curiosity and imagination. Emancipatory consciousness is then one of the roads we must follow, if we are to deepen our awareness of the conditions that defy and betray our revolutionary dreams. Similarly, Paulo's notion of human consciousness as *unfinished* can be linked to a critical evolutionary process, whose openness enlivens our dialectical relationship with the world and beckons us toward a new humanizing paradigm, where the connection between matter and consciousness is inextricably tied to our interdependent existence with all life.

This evolution of social consciousness is well echoed, as Freire himself reminded us, in the Spanish poet Antonio Machado's words, *se hace el camino al andar* or *we make the road by walking*. This again signals social consciousness as a tied to a dialectical process, which develops and evolves through our social agency and self-determination, as we contend collectively with the concrete conditions that perpetuate our personal and collective suffering. Rather than adhere to prescribed roles and structures that repress our humanity, Paulo (1998) urged for the development of emancipatory consciousness, through a critical pedagogy of love that requires our ongoing participation and co-creation as cultural citizens, who know that we are in the world to change the world.

In this way, knowledge and breakthroughs of consciousness reflect the evolving social experience of people involved in collective struggle. And so, breakthroughs of emancipatory awareness are not the privilege of any one person. In fact, experiences that facilitate breakthroughs of social consciousness are fundamentally born of communal relationships of loving solidarity that expand our vision about what is possible. Critical consciousness, then, does not occur automatically or individually. Instead, emancipatory consciousness arises through an organic human engagement, which requires interactions that nurture relationship of love and respect with ourselves, with one another, and with the world.

Paulo expressed a grounded appreciation for the dialectical tension that exists, between the empowerment of the individual and the democratic well-being of the community; for neither can be sacrificed in a pedagogy of love. This idea nurtures the forging of critical consciousness, in that neither dialogue nor social consciousness can arise in the absence of others. Of this, he argued, "We cannot liberate others, people cannot liberate themselves alone, because people liberate themselves in communion, mediated by the reality which they must transform" (Davis, 1981, p. 62). Similarly, critical dialogue constitutes an existential necessity of a pedagogy of love, in that it is the means by which we forge coherence, intentionality, and solidarity. Thus, we seek to act, think, and speak about our reality in ways that are coherent with *both* subjective experiences and objective principles of life. As a politically dynamic process, critical dialogue serves as an important pedagogical and political means for self-vigilance, by which we make connections between our thoughts and our actions as co-participants and co-creators in our history.

True to his own understanding of knowledge as historical, there was a deepening in Paulo's articulation of consciousness over the years, as he gave far greater salience to the role of feelings, sensations, and especially the idea that we co-create through our bodies and it is our embodied collective consciousness that makes the world. Merleau-Ponty (2002) argued, "The body is our general medium for having a world. We know not through our intellect but through our experience" (p. 169). In other words, we cannot transform the world alone or in our head. Yet, so often we speak of teaching and learning as if they happen somewhere outside the body.

Teaching in the flesh

The process of teaching and learning must then be acknowledged as a process of human labor that happens in the flesh. For racialized subjects, this embodied labor also emerges from our efforts to make sense of the repressive material conditions and social relations of violence that shape our histories of survival. This understanding of schooling can assist teachers to construct a revolutionary practice of education, where students are not asked to deny the wisdom of their bodies, nor to estrange themselves from one another, in the name of debilitating competition or deadening meritocracy. In direct contrast, a pedagogy of love begins with acknowledging students as fully embodied subjects, from the moment they enter our classrooms. To do so, educators must be prepared to contend, in the flesh, with the embodied histories of the oppressed *and* the social and material forces that impact our labor as teachers committed to democratic life. Paulo (1993) argued for the indisputability of the body in teaching and learning, focusing on the sensualism of the body—a sensualism inseparable to rigorous acts of knowing the world. His perspective undoubtedly echoes Marcuse's (1955) thesis in *Eros and Civilization*, where he boldly argues for widening our experience of the body by embracing a *polymorphous sensuality*—a sensuality more in line with our human need to exist as freely empowered subjects of our lives.

Yet, it is precisely this passionate sensual freedom, from which we produce revolutionary thought and action, that is held hostage by hegemonic schooling. In the process, conscious, sensual bodies that could potentially defy the perversities of Bourgeois capitalism are systematically conditioned to normalize the depravities of globalized greed and impunity. It is this, colonizing Western logic, with its mind–body split, that still shapes hegemonic schooling today. And despite classroom efforts to control the body's desires, pleasures, and mobility, students seldom surrender their bodies completely or readily acquiesce to authoritarian practices—practices that often provoke resistance in students whose lived histories are excluded within mainstream education (Shapiro, 2015). Instead, many of them engage in the construction of their own cultural forms of resistance.

More often than not, expressions of student resistance are enacted through counterculture alterations of the body—be they clothing, hairstyle, posturing, manner of walking, way of speaking, the piercing and tattooing of the body. These are not only acts of resistance but alternative ways of experiencing and knowing the world, often perceived by officials as transgressive to the social order. Such perceptions are exacerbated by what Henry Giroux (1998) calls a "new form of representational politics [that] has emerged in media culture, fueled by degrading visual depictions of youth as criminal, sexually decadent, drug crazed, and illiterate. In short, youth are viewed as a growing threat to the public order" (p. 28).

Accordingly, many teachers, consciously or unconsciously, reproduce a variety of authoritarian classroom practices—in the name of classroom management—in efforts to maintain physical control of their students. Teachers who struggle in this repressive climate to implement liberating strategies are often forced to wear masks of deception—saying what the principal or district office wishes to hear, while they try to do, behind closed doors, what they believe students need. Unfortunately, having to shoulder the hidden physical stress of this duplicity can drive some of the most effective teachers away from the class—leaving so they can remain in integrity with their liberatory commitment. While others, who begin to sense defeat, in frustration adopt more authoritarian approaches to manipulate and coerce *cooperation*, while justifying their actions, in the name of helping students succeed academically.

What cannot be overlooked here is the manner in which authoritarian practices are designed not only to "blindfold students and lead them to a domesticated future" (Freire, 1970, p. 79), but also to alienate and estrange teachers from their labor. Concerned with the need to restore greater freedom, joy, and creativity in their classrooms, Paulo (1998) urged teachers to reject this domesticating role within their classrooms by demythologizing authoritarianism and working with students to create new possibilities for teaching and learning in the intimacy of their shared world. Instead, Paulo (2000) insisted, "What is important in teaching is not the mechanical repetition of this or that gesture but a comprehension of the value of sentiments, emotions, and desires ... and sensibility, affectivity, and intuition" (p. 48). This powerful assertion of our human sensibilities, beyond cognition, is indeed a hallmark of his painstaking efforts to challenge the necrophilic grip of hegemonic schooling, while calling forth a decolonizing view of cognitive justice in our contemporary struggle for liberation.

The contemporary moment

As noted earlier, in the last three decades, neoliberal policies and practices have deeply transformed the landscape of education in the United States and abroad. This has resulted in staggering changes to state and national educational policy debates about the curriculum, assessment and accountability, teacher preparation, educational leadership, and conditions under which research is carried out. Simultaneously, material conditions have become increasingly grim within subaltern communities, where economic conditions of urban life, widespread gentrification, and ecological destruction have appallingly become the norm. The debilitating global consequences must then be understood as part of a structural and epistemic political economic project that overwhelmingly configures power relations both domestically and internationally in the interest of the wealthy and powerful. And, although technological advances have been made over the last three decades, humanity still remains deeply divided between the haves and have-nots. Moreover, the tendency to overlook or ignore poverty as a necessary prerequisite of the international capitalist economy conserves deceptive myths and deficit views of the oppressed—myths that function to preserve institutional structures of what Freire (1970) called "cultural invasion," associated with colonizing forms of social and material control.

Hence, shameless domination and sweeping control over the internationalization of capital, the movement of people, and knowledge production have resulted in the concentration of power, wealth, and resources among a very small percentage of the world's population. And, although there is much talk internationally about social justice in education, mainstream notions of equity are incapable of leading us toward a just future. One of the reasons for this is that mainstream views of equity are predicated on the myth that we all are playing on a level field and that it is just a matter of tweaking the individual a bit here and there. Nothing could be farther from the truth, in that what we are contending with are long-standing inequalities that not only persist but in some instances are widening, as the wealthy and powerful celebrate drones, Artificial Intelligence, increasing automation, mobile supercomputing, intelligent robots, self-driving cars, neuro-technological brain enhancements, and genetic editing in their pronouncements of the Fourth Industrial Revolution—reminiscent of the alarmist rhetoric of the early days of the globalization era.

Meanwhile, worldwide poverty continues to take a devastating toll on the lives of more than 600 million people, who live in extreme poverty. Closer to home, there are 95 million people in the United States living in poverty, including 1 child in every 5. Income inequality is increasing, and the toxic combination of tax breaks for the rich, growing unemployment, increasing indebtedness, and devastating cuts to the social safety net belies any well-intentioned rhetoric of global education.

An ethics of liberation

In light of an unrelenting consumer-driven international economic agenda, those committed to liberation must grapple seriously with the role and purpose of higher education and the kind of world we want to create. Inherent to such reflection, as Paulo often reminded us, the struggle of liberation must be grounded on democratic principles tied to an ethics of liberation, as articulated by the Latin American philosopher Enrique Dussel. For, in the face of the contemporary hegemonic forces we are facing, all aspects of our lives are being colonized and commodified technologically, from birth to death, leaving the majority of people deeply dissatisfied, estranged, and disempowered. With this in mind, the ethics that underlie Freire's pedagogy moves us away from mere reformism, calling for a fundamental critique of the capitalist system as the *root of domination*, while embracing a life-affirming ethos that places the needs of the oppressed at the center of the pedagogical and political discourse. Essential here is the understanding that educational equity or social justice cannot exist within a political economic state that absolutely requires the material impoverishment and political oppression of the majority of the world's population.

Paulo insisted that our liberatory work in schools and communities requires us to re-imagine a world not governed by the law of profit and greed or a social order predicated on the economic anarchy of money gods. Inherent in this vision is the need to confront immoral justifications that perpetuate economic apartheid around the world. For example, the often-repeated cliché, "the poor will always be with us" conveniently serves to obscure and deflect responsibility from those most responsible for global poverty and human suffering. In the United States, for example, we are governed by a tyrannical administration of wealthy economic anarchists who perpetuate and justify human suffering and destabilize democratic dissent, while they glorify the unsustainable economic delusions of the free market. This is accompanied by oligarchic pursuits of an authoritarian regime that toys with the fears of the powerless and fuels the flames of reactionary populism and racializing discontent.

In such a world, democratic critiques are often belittled, while those involved in social protests or acts of civil disobedience are demonized and criminalized, while the perpetrators of capitalist exploitation garner the nation's resources for their exclusive wealth building; leaving the majority of the world's populations in an economic borderland of impoverishment where efforts toward democratic wealth distribution are thwarted, while the poor are blamed for their own poverty. In this context, a populist ethos serves as political manipulation, promising all without any real intent to deliver beyond superficial benefits. In contrast, an ethics of liberation disrupts the perversion of this colonizing capitalist logic, in order to ask new questions, to consider new solutions, and seek anticolonial forms of cultural, political, and economic life.

In these times, there is a need for an embodied consciousness of liberation, shaped by a liberatory ethics of transformation that can move us toward holistic, multidimensional, and interdependent ways of knowing; where the inseparability of consciousness and matter nurtures grounded and collective forms of leadership and decision-making to reshape and reconstruct the concrete conditions of inequalities in our world. Such a way of knowing and being supports the belief that we are one humanity, while also respecting the cultural differences and particularities that exist between communities, given our histories of struggle and survival. From such an ethics of liberation, the suffering of one is always the suffering of all.

A pedagogy of love emerges then from a communal way of knowing that embraces in solidarity the needs of the suffering, as historical subjects and necessary co-creators in the struggle for our liberation. And, as such, through our ethics and our actions, we confront the brutal alienation of racism, patriarchy, and poverty, which strips away our dignity and freedom to be; usurping our humanity, in the interests of the rich and powerful. Assata Shakur (2001) argued that "nobody in the world, nobody in history, has ever gotten their freedom by appealing to the moral sense of the people who were oppressing them" (p. 139). I believe that Paulo (1970) was telling us this when he penned *Pedagogy of the Oppressed*. For, ultimately, the purpose of a pedagogy of love is to uncompromisingly disrupt the logic of oppression, by posing new questions and solutions generated from the cultural worldviews and lived histories of the excluded, exploited, and oppressed. For it is through such an ethics of liberation that we break our dependence on the logic of conquest and work collectively to create an emancipatory praxis, as educators, cultural workers, and movement activists, uncompromisingly committed to the revolutionary belief that another world is possible—not as "pie in the sky" but as concrete social and material conditions of revolution within and across nations—conditions that affirm the dignity of our humanity and the preciousness of all life on this planet.

Lastly, I want to express my great appreciation for Paulo's love. What I most recall was his capacity for tenderness. In so many ways, it was his tenderness that opened him to intimacy with others and the world—despite the pain he experienced over his life, including his exile from Brazil. I was recently reminded of this quality in Paulo, when reading Zenju Earthlyn Manuel's (2015) *The Way of Tenderness*. So, it seems this is a fitting way to close this Afterword: "Oppression is a distortion of our true nature. It disconnects us from the earth and from each other. Awakening from the distortion of oppression begins with tenderness: we recognize our own wounded tenderness, which develops unto the tenderness that comes with heartfelt and authentic liberation" (p. 4)—both personal and collective. May we find in ourselves and with one another the courage to embrace such tenderness, as we labor together for a more just and loving world.

References

Carnoy, M. (1987). Foreword to *Pedagogy of the heart* by P. Freire (pp. 7–19). New York: Continuum.

Darder, A. (2015). *Freire and education*. New York: Routledge.

Darder, A. (2018). *The student guide to pedagogy of the oppressed*. London: Bloomsbury.

Davis, R. (1981). *Education for awareness: A talk with Paulo Freire*. In R. Mackie (Ed.), *Literacy & revolution* (pp. 57–69). New York: Continuum.

Freire, P. (1970). *Pedagogy of the oppressed*. New York: Seabury Press.

Freire, P. (1983). *Education for critical consciousness*. New York: Seabury Press.

Freire, P. (1993). *Pedagogy of the city*. New York: Continuum.

Freire, P. (1998). *Teachers and cultural workers: Letters to those who dare to teach*. Boulder, CO: Westview Press.

Freire, P. (2000). *Pedagogy of freedom*. Lanham, MD: Rowman & Littlefield.

Freire, P. (2002). *Pedagogy of hope*. New York: Continuum.

Freire, P. (2005). *Pedagogy of the oppressed* (30th Anniversary Edition). New York: Continuum.

Fromm, E. (1964). *The heart of man*. New York, NY: Harper & Row.

Giroux, H. (1998). Teenage sexuality, body politics and the pedagogy of display. In J. Epstein (Ed.), *Youth culture: Identity in a postmodern world* (pp. 24–55). Malden,

MA: Wiley-Blackwell. Retrieved from www.henryagiroux.com/online_articles/teenage_sexuality.htm.

Hooks, b. (1994). *Teaching to transgress*. New York: Routledge.

Manuel, Z. E. (2015). *The way of tenderness*. Summerville, MA: Wisdom Publications.

Marcuse, H. (1955). *Eros and civilization*. Boston, MA: Beacon Press.

Merleau-Ponty, M. (2002). *The phenomenology of perception*. New York: Routledge.

Shakur, A. (2001). *Assata: An autobiography*. Chicago, IL: Lawrence Hill Books.

Shapiro, P. (2015). *Pedagogy and the politics of the body*. New York: Routledge.

Index